T0265475

The Foresighted
AMBEDKAR

'The book takes readers on a captivating journey through key moments in Dr Ambedkar's life, examining how his ideas challenged the status quo and shaped the constitutional discourse for a newly independent India. It not only pays homage to Dr Ambedkar's intellectual legacy but also prompts readers to reflect on the contemporary relevance of his ideas. Anurag Bhaskar explores Dr Ambedkar's groundbreaking contributions by delving into his writings, speeches, constitutional debates and archival sources. The book is an indispensable resource for scholars, policymakers and anyone interested in understanding the intellectual roots of the Indian Constitution and the enduring impact of Dr Ambedkar's visionary contributions'—Justice B.R. Gavai, judge, Supreme Court of India

'*The Foresighted Ambedkar* illuminates Indian constitutional history with vignettes from Dr Ambedkar's transformative professional journey. It admirably situates Dr Ambedkar's role in the Constitution-drafting process within the long history of negotiations and deliberations on the founding values of our *grundnorm*. This painstakingly researched book sheds light on not just his four-decade-long engagement with constitutional values as a distinguished lawyer, scholar and politician but also how his erudite interventions led to the evolution of our vibrant constitutional culture. This is what makes it a must-read for all students and practitioners of Indian constitutional law, politics and history. This is a valuable contribution by Anurag Bhaskar as a young legal scholar to Indian constitutionalism'—Justice B.V. Nagarathna, judge, Supreme Court of India

'It gives me immense pleasure to learn that Anurag Bhaskar has authored a book titled *The Foresighted Ambedkar: Ideas That Shaped Indian Constitutional Discourse*, showcasing the contribution, thoughtfulness and spirit of Dr B.R. Ambedkar in the noble cause of nation-building. From the initial sparks of constitutional discourse to the final strokes of the drafting pen, Dr Ambedkar's foresight, intellect and commitment to justice stand as a beacon that continues to guide the nation. The reasoned advocacy of patriotic Dr Ambedkar has transcended the boundaries of time and his contribution to nation-building continues to inspire generations. As the sole individual involved in all stages of drafting the Indian constitutional document since 1919, Dr Ambedkar's influence resonates through every chapter of this book, thus making it an indispensable exploration of the intellectual foundations that underpin contemporary Indian constitutional thought. The nation owes a lot to Dr Ambedkar, for immensely contributing to the development of modern institutions, inspiring us to build a just society based on the vibrant democratic spirit and meticulous and strong fundamentals of the Indian Constitution. This book goes beyond a mere historical account; it is a scholarly odyssey that deals with Dr Ambedkar's ideas and vision, offering readers a nuanced understanding of the profound impact he had on shaping the constitutional ethos of India'—Arjun Ram Meghwal, minister of state for law and justice, and parliamentary affairs and culture

'In this engrossing, inspiring account of Dr Ambedkar's life and work, Anurag Bhaskar confirms Dr Ambedkar's status as the "father of India's Constitution". He shows how this towering, learned figure from the Dalit community called for a moral revolution, still unfinished, against caste oppression and inequality. Bhaskar, himself an heir of that revolution, shows the relevance of Dr Ambedkar's vision for present-day debates about equality, democracy and human dignity'—Michael J. Sandel, author of *The Tyranny of Merit: What's Become of the Common Good?*

'Anurag Bhaskar has written what might be called "the long intellectual history" (from the 1910s to the 1950s) of the man who has justly been called "the father of the Indian Constitution". Dr B.R. Ambedkar was an early exponent of the "annihilation of caste" and became an important voice for including protections in the Indian Constitution for traditionally disadvantaged castes, including "reservations" (i.e., affirmative action) in political representation, education and other spheres. Often invoking Dr Ambedkar's own words, Bhaskar has written a lively, broadly accessible and deeply informed history that should be of interest not only to students of Indian constitutional law but also to ordinary Indian citizens committed to social justice, and indeed to people all around the world interested in issues at the intersection of race, democracy and constitutionalism'—Michael J. Klarman, Charles Warren Professor of Legal History, Harvard Law School

'Anurag Bhaskar powerfully documents the intellectual and constitutional history to focus on Dr B.R. Ambedkar's vision and significant contributions to the Constitution of India. Drawing on many archival sources, he argues for a more careful understanding of the politics of participatory democracy and citizenship in modern India and successfully illuminates why Ambedkar is rightly considered the Father of India's Constitution. Bhaskar's work is a valuable contribution, which adds a new and different voice to the history of Indian Constitution-making'—Shailaja Paik, Charles P. Taft Distinguished Professor of History, University of Cincinnati

'Deeply researched and written with forensic insight, Bhaskar reconstructs the constitutional thought of Dr Ambedkar over four decades of his career to underscore how central his vision and imagination was to the underlying promises that the Indian Constitution made to its people. Demolishing myths with original insight, *The Foresighted Ambedkar* is a resource and inspiration for our times'—Rohit De, associate professor of history, Yale University

'No understanding of the Indian Constitution is complete without a deep appreciation of the ideas of Dr Ambedkar. This book offers a compelling and accessible account of those ideas, set against his foundational constitutional, political and social contributions to the Republic'—Farrah Ahmed, professor, Melbourne Law School

The Foresighted
AMBEDKAR

Ideas That Shaped Indian Constitutional Discourse

Foreword by
the Chief Justice of India

ANURAG BHASKAR

PENGUIN
VIKING

An imprint of Penguin Random House

VIKING

Viking is an imprint of the Penguin Random House group of companies
whose addresses can be found at global.penguinrandomhouse.com

Published by Penguin Random House India Pvt. Ltd
4th Floor, Capital Tower 1, MG Road,
Gurugram 122 002, Haryana, India

First published in Viking by Penguin Random House India 2024

Copyright © Anurag Bhaskar 2024

All rights reserved

10 9 8 7 6 5 4 3 2

The views and opinions expressed in this book are the author's own and the
facts are as reported by him which have been verified to the extent possible,
and the publishers are not in any way liable for the same.

ISBN 9780670097401

Typeset in Requiem Text by MAP Systems, Bengaluru, India
Printed at Thomson Press India Ltd, New Delhi

www.penguin.co.in

To all those who preserved the memory of Dr Ambedkar

Contents

Dr Justice D Y Chandrachud
Chief Justice of India

Foreword

I am delighted to write the foreword for this book, which is undoubtedly a work of academic brilliance. More significantly, Anurag's work represents the labour of his love and reverence for Babasaheb Dr Bhimrao Ambedkar. I have interacted with Anurag in various capacities-as an intern during my tenure as a judge at the Allahabad High Court; as a judicial law clerk in my chambers at the Supreme Court; as a promising young academic at the Harvard Law School; as the deputy registrar (research) of the Supreme Court's Centre for Research and Planning and now as a scholar in his own right. As he navigates each of these roles, his work ethic, interactions, and worldview undoubtedly embody the ideals of Babasaheb Dr Bhimrao Ambedkar.

In the second chapter, the book refers to Dr Ambedkar being a voracious reader for whom books were "an all-absorbing passion". During Anurag's tenure as an intern and law clerk in my chambers, I would often see him buried under a pile of books-reading far, wide, and deep-his quest to learn never satiated. As a part of his role at the Centre for Research and Planning at the Supreme Court, Anurag has played a vital role in spearheading research initiatives that have benefited the Court immensely. Recently, on Constitution Day, the Supreme Court installed a statue of Dr Ambedkar to celebrate a hundred years of his legal practice.

5 Krishna Menon Marg, New Delhi 110 011
+91-11-2379 3733 I 2379 3515   justice.dychandrachud@sci.nic.in

Anurag's contribution to the ideation and installation of the statue cannot be adequately underscored.

Significantly, akin to Dr Ambedkar, Anurag does not view the privilege of his premier education as a mere individual achievement, but as an enhanced responsibility to his own community and other marginalized communities. He is one of the founders of CEDE (Community for the Eradication of Discrimination in Education and Employment), an organization that works towards increasing representation in the legal profession and the judiciary in India. As a part of this endeavour, he mentors, trains, and supports students from marginalized communities, ensuring that the obstacles due to unequal access to power and resources do not hamper their ability to realize their potential. To chronicle the ideas that shaped Dr Ambedkar and his contribution to our Constitution is no easy task, requiring someone who has not just studied Babasaheb academically but also emulated and understood his values at every stage of life. Indeed, no one is better placed than Anurag to undertake this mammoth task.

There is a plethora of literature on Dr Ambedkar and his vision for the Constitution. Most of the work in this regard can be slotted into two categories-biographical works and scholarly examination of his ideas. Anurag, however, takes a distinctive approach in this book. The book goes far beyond a mere documentation of events in the life of Dr Ambedkar or a limited focus on his writings and speeches. Instead, Anurag artfully combines scholarly insights into Dr Ambedkar's ideas with his personal experiences at appropriate junctures . Indeed, the book recognizes that Dr Ambedkar's life-his childhood, education, political life, and social activism-contained a multitude of experiences, each of which were

5 Krishna Menon Marg, New Delhi 110 011
+91-11-2379 3733 I 2379 3515   justice.dychandrachud@sci.nic.in

reflected in his life in different ways. Dr Ambedkar's views of education cannot be divorced from the influence of Jyotiba Phule on his life. Similarly, his views on discrimination and marginalization, cannot understood in isolation from the experiences of untouchability that he faced throughout his life. For Dr Ambedkar, the political was also the personal. Anurag does justice to that interconnection. Dr Ambedkar's life and work are thoroughly examined in the book. Commonly repeated claims are responded to, and addressed with meticulous research.

As I extend my best wishes to Anurag for the success of this book, I want to emphasize a sentiment I shared during the Constitution Day celebrations at the Supreme Court. Dr Ambedkar belongs to all of us. We have moved beyond the era where we could perceive him through the narrow lens of being only a 'leader of Dalits.' He stands as a representative of the nation's voice, and his endeavours for social reform were aimed at transforming Indian society as a whole. I applaud Anurag for this exceptional book and offer him strength, blessings, and support as he continues to ardently advocate not only for Dr Ambedkar but also for the enduring essence of the Indian Constitution.

Dhananjaya Y Chandrachud

Disclaimer: This foreword has been replicated verbatim as provided by the author and there has been no editorial intervention on the part of Penguin Random House India.

I

Introduction

Dr B.R. Ambedkar was a powerful twentieth-century figure who shaped the course of history. He not only played an impactful role in deciding India's future as the world's largest democracy but also provided us with a broader understanding of the ideas of humanity, fraternity and justice, which resonate in global discourse. Dr Ambedkar knew about the importance of visionary ideas. As he once remarked, 'Men are mortal. So are ideas . . . An idea needs propagation as much as a plant needs watering. Both will otherwise wither and die.'[1] It is for this reason that Dr Ambedkar spent a lot of time writing down his thoughts and reflections, even while he was leading social movements, negotiating with the British and with other nationalist leaders, and even in his last days before his death.

Dr Ram Manohar Lohia, the prominent socialist leader, once described Dr Ambedkar as 'a great man in Indian politics', 'learned, a man of integrity, courage and independence', who could be shown to the outside world as a 'symbol of upright India'.[2] The legacy of Dr Ambedkar invites us to look at the missing parts of Indian history or, in other words, the histories of social justice that have been ignored and erased. This was highlighted in a judgment of the Supreme Court of India thus: 'Reading Dr Ambedkar compels us to look at the other side of the independence movement. Besides the struggle for independence from British rule, there was another struggle going on for centuries, which still continues. That struggle has been for social emancipation.'[3]

The world must turn to Dr Ambedkar not only because of the game-changing contributions he made but also to gain a better perspective on contemporary challenges. This is because several scenarios that Dr Ambedkar argued have indeed turned out to be prophetic.[4] Furthermore, Dr Ambedkar was a predecessor of many theoretical approaches that emerged over time. For instance, he theorized that in ancient Indian history, the 'revolution' or movement towards equality met with a 'counter-revolution' of caste inequalities,[5] which finds its parallel in the critical race theory that the history of civil rights in the US is not linear; that every progress of civil rights was succeeded with new forms of racial entrenchment.[6] Dr Ambedkar stated that the 'growth of personality is the highest aim of society',[7] similar to the modern 'capability approach' in human development.[8] Scholarly works now made in defence of affirmative action find a resemblance to arguments made by Dr Ambedkar from the 1920s. The points that Dr Ambedkar wrote and spoke of did not emerge from his imagination. Rather, they arose from his vast reading, lived experiences, his lifelong struggles and his relentless efforts to find comprehensive solutions to prevailing problems.

The amount of literature that Dr Ambedkar read and wrote validates his position as a scholar and philosopher of the highest standard. Dr Ambedkar wrote on many issues, bearing a common theme: how to change the nature of how we think of society. His wide reading of global history and politics enabled him to present novel solutions to contemporary challenges. To critically engage with the problems of his time, he would often cite a wide list of philosophers of different times.[9] Dr Ambedkar's clarity of thought can be understood from his writings on the ideas of democracy, constitutionalism, majoritarianism, nationalism, hero worship, representation and inclusion, political conscience among oppressed castes, minority protection, constitutional morality, equal citizenship, etc. His visionary thoughts are the reason his views have such significance today, as compared to any other leader of his time. The voluminous collected writings and speeches of Dr Ambedkar (often cited academically as BAWS [Dr Babasaheb Ambedkar: Writings and Speeches]) open a door into the ideal world of his vision.

This book deals with the vision of Dr Ambedkar and his influence on Indian constitutional discourse. It shows Dr Ambedkar as one of the dominant figures to shape the nature of constitutional discourse in India over four decades between 1919 and 1956. It highlights the unique contribution made by him, based on which contemporary Indian constitutional discourse rests. In doing so, the book argues that India's Constitution was drafted not just between 1947 and 1950, but over the course of four decades. Dr Ambedkar was the only person who was involved in all the stages related to the drafting of the Indian constitutional document since 1919. These stages bear the imprint of his contribution and role. When Dr Ambedkar arrived on the public scene, the constitutional discourse was in its initial phases. He positioned himself uniquely to negotiate with the British government as well as with nationalist leaders at the same time. The book covers different constitutional moments as and when they happened, and highlights Dr Ambedkar's role in those moments.

This book is not about constitutional doctrines. It is a book on intellectual and constitutional history, and an effort to demonstrate how Dr Ambedkar is rightly called the father of the Indian Constitution.

The chapterization of this book is as per the sequence of historical events as they occurred and the role played by Dr Ambedkar in them. Chapter 2 of the book deals with the rise of Dr Ambedkar on the Indian public scene, and his development as an influential person in Indian public affairs. Chapter 3 highlights the constitutional discourse prior to the appearance of Dr Ambedkar in the public sphere. Chapter 4 covers Dr Ambedkar's engagement with the Southborough Committee in 1919 and demonstrates how Dr Ambedkar's conception of citizenship transcended the paradigm of franchise, and conceptualized it in terms of universal rights. Chapter 5 is an exploration of how Dr Ambedkar began shaping the language of rights through his public engagement with initiatives such as *Mooknayak* ('the leader of the voiceless'), a newspaper he founded in 1920, and through a deep analysis of social, economic and political inequality. Consequently, Chapter 6 narrates the history of the Mahad Satyagraha, and describes it as a *striking moment* in Indian constitutional discourse, which foregrounded the conception of Dr Ambedkar's constitutional project. This chapter argues that the provision of non-discrimination under the Indian Constitution finds its social origins in the struggle led by Dr Ambedkar.

Following this, Chapter 7 deals with Dr Ambedkar's position before the Simon Commission, and elucidates his vision of equal voting rights by explaining how, to him, the issue of universal franchise was intrinsically tied with adequate representation of oppressed groups and other civil liberties such as the right to education. Chapter 8 covers the arguments made by Dr Ambedkar in response to those who were opposed to his demand for constitutional reservations (affirmative action) for Backward Classes, and highlights his contention that it was, in fact, the oppressor castes that had historically enjoyed reservations in their favour, and had wrested social and political power. In Chapter 9, there is a detailed account of Dr Ambedkar's negotiations at the Round Table Conferences in the early 1930s and the framing of the Government of India (GOI) Act 1935. It clearly shows that Dr Ambedkar had a significant role to play even in the framing of this Act, and underlines his conception of an ideal government. Consequently, Chapter 10 offers a constitutional perspective on Dr Ambedkar's classic, *Annihilation of Caste*, published in 1936, and indicates how his conception of democracy could not be separated from his ultimate pursuit to annihilate caste.

Chapter 11 deals with Dr Ambedkar's proposal to deal with the communal problem, and reflects on his envisaged division of political power in a manner that preserved institutional autonomy and prevented the rise of authoritarianism. Chapter 12 throws light on the range of sources from which Dr Ambedkar drew inspiration to formulate a truly global imagination of participative democracy. Chapter 13 gives an account of Dr Ambedkar's statesmanship during the initial days of the establishment of the Constituent Assembly. Chapter 14 discusses Dr Ambedkar's original draft Constitution which he prepared as a document called 'States and Minorities', and points to how his idea of civil political rights could not be separated from the struggle for the socio-economic rights of citizens. Chapter 15 details how Dr Ambedkar took up the responsibility of building an inclusive, democratic practice by trying to institute a truly participative form of rights and government in the Constitution. This chapter discusses his direct role in framing several provisions of the Constitution.

Chapter 16 discusses how Dr Ambedkar's qualifications and experience made him an appropriate candidate for the position of chairman. Chapter 17 is a compilation of how Dr Ambedkar's colleagues from the Drafting Committee considered his contributions towards the Constitution

indispensable and praiseworthy. Chapter 18 goes over the
meaning and purpose of Dr Ambedkar's vision of democracy.
Following this, Chapter 19 foregrounds how Dr Ambedkar
envisaged the Constitution as the means towards an anti-
caste and democratic politics. Chapter 20 contextualizes
Dr Ambedkar's comments on 'burning the Constitution'
by refocusing historical truths surrounding his statement. It
rejects the claim that he wanted to 'burn the Constitution'
in a literal sense or as a matter of principle. Finally, Chapter
21 debunks the myth that he intended reservations to be
protected for ten years, and proves that Dr Ambedkar was
not in favour of any time limit on reservations. The Epilogue
concludes by positing—with a sense of gratitude—the true
breadth of Dr Ambedkar's contributions.

(Note: In this book, the terms 'Untouchables', 'Depressed Classes',
'Scheduled Castes' and 'Dalits' have been used interchangeably.)

2

The Rise of Dr Ambedkar

In order to understand the decisive role and the foresight of Dr Ambedkar, it is necessary to reflect on the processes and experiences by which he acquired his thoughts and ideas. Dr Ambedkar did not evolve in a vacuum. The thoughts he had did not emerge suddenly. Rather, they were the result of hundreds of years of accumulated thoughts—his own and the thoughts of those who influenced him. It is thus necessary to understand, as Prof. Christophe Jaffrelot says, 'how Ambedkar *became* Ambedkar'.[1]

There have been some efforts to situate Dr Ambedkar in the sociopolitical circumstances of his time.[2] As Chief Justice of India Dr D.Y. Chandrachud once noted: 'Dr Ambedkar brought with himself ideas, values and scholarship, which were derived from the experiences and struggles which singularly were his own. He drew as well from other social reformers in their movements against social injustice.'[3] In particular, Jaffrelot tries to understand Dr Ambedkar's thinking 'by situating him in the context of Maharashtra and in his family as well as social environment'.[4]

Jaffrelot analyses the factors that contributed to the creation of a conducive environment that facilitated the personal growth of Dr Ambedkar. He begins by examining

the sociocultural developments of the nineteenth century.
This was when British schools and religious missions offered
a critique of the caste system.[5] These discourses introduced
the egalitarian values of the West, which generated a feeling
of support among the oppressed castes and formed the basis
of the anti-Brahmin movement in Maharashtra.[6] This social
reform movement questioned the social order existing in the
nineteenth century.

Jyotiba Phule, the prominent social reformer, played a crucial
role in leading these reforms. Hailing from an oppressed lower
caste (he was a *mali* or gardener), he was influenced by the values
of the West, as he received an English education. He dedicated
his—now famous—book *Gulamgiri* (Slavery) to 'the good people
of the United States as a token of admiration for their sublime
disinterested and self-sacrificing devotion in the cause of Negro
Slavery; and with an earnest desire, that my countrymen may
take their noble example as their guide in the emancipation
of their Shudra Brethren from the trammels of Brahmin
thraldom'.[7] Jaffrelot narrates how Phule believed in providing
education for the development of the oppressed castes. It was
Phule's desire to set up the kind of schools established by the
missionaries, who used to welcome oppressed castes to their
institutions. Therefore in 1853, he set up schools for the purpose
of educating the Mahar and Mang castes. Additionally, Phule
wrote a number of political pamphlets on education, portraying
Brahmins as the oppressors who used their authority to further
ignorance and superstition, and exploit the most marginalized
groups in society. Phule also founded the Satyashodhak Samaj in
1873 to unite the lower castes and the Untouchables. The social
reform movements, such as those led by Phule, prepared the
ground for the 'emergence of a social and political consciousness
among some of the lower castes',[8] at a time when Dr Ambedkar
was ready to start his public career. As historian Shailaja Paik

notes: 'Ambedkar, however, deepened Phule's programme by making the development of svaabhimaan (self-respect), dignity, and modern citizenship (naagarikatva) the core of education and pedagogy.'[9]

The family background of Dr Ambedkar also played an important role in shaping his thoughts and ideas.[10] Dr Ambedkar belonged to the Mahar caste in Maharashtra; many of the members of this caste were a part of the British Army. This position gave them social mobility and enabled their migration to cities. Military service also exposed them to British institutions and to the imagination of a new political order and opportunities. This social advancement in urban settings also encouraged them to get educated. The Mahars were also influenced by the bhakti movements in Maharashtra, which believed in the rejection of caste distinctions. Thus, both social mobility and education engendered an egalitarian conscience within the community. Jaffrelot notes that Dr Ambedkar inherited all these legacies and invented his own vision.[11]

Dr Ambedkar's father was a part of the British Army. As education was mandatory for the children of military personnel, everyone in the Ambedkar family, including the women, was literate. Dr Ambedkar went to a cantonment primary school and later completed his graduation in Bombay.

The support of two individuals proved to be influential for Dr Ambedkar. The first was the Maharaja of Baroda, Sayajirao Gaekwad III. After graduation, Dr Ambedkar initially joined as a lieutenant in the army of the state of Baroda in 1913, but later decided to pursue higher studies in the US with financial support from Maharaja Gaekwad. The young man received a scholarship on the strength of his intelligence and hard work, and on condition that after completing his studies, he would return and serve the state of Baroda for ten years. The other individual was the Maharaja of Kolhapur, Chhatrapati Shahuji, who, impressed with Dr Ambedkar's capability and potential, supported his further studies in London and his efforts towards launching the newspaper, *Mooknayak*. Without the financial support given by these two maharajas, Dr Ambedkar would not have been able to pursue his higher education abroad. Foreign education exposed him to a wealth of ideas, a number of scholars and a sense of pragmatism. Jaffrelot notes:

> [T]he decisive factor in shaping his revolt against the caste system was his education overseas, which exposed him to egalitarian values and allowed him to interrogate the mechanisms of caste. On returning to India, he further refined his tools of sociological analysis to better contest the social system of which untouchables were the prime victims.[12]

This influence on Dr Ambedkar has also been documented by other leading scholars such as Eleanor Zelliot. She wrote:

> The three years Ambedkar spent at Columbia, 1913-1916, awakened, in his own words, his potential. Columbia was in its golden age, and a list of Ambedkar's professors reads like a catalogue of early twentieth-century American educators. The transcript of Ambedkar's work at Columbia reveals that he audited many classes, more than he could have taken for grades, including such subjects as 'railroad economics'.[13]

Furthermore, historian Anupama Rao notes: 'Ambedkar was in the [New York] city at a fertile time: the modern social science disciplines were just beginning to take on clear definition . . . Attention to associational dynamics on the [Columbia] University campus reveals key connections between public activism, a diversifying student body and the politics of the classroom'.[14] Some professors at Columbia had a great influence on his thoughts on democracy and society.[15] As scholar Scott Stroud notes: 'Later in life, Ambedkar would see philosophical tools such as John Dewey's notion of democratic community as an ideal or hope that loneliness could be erased and bridges with dignity be built between agreeing and disagreeing community members.'[16]

In an article written for the Columbia alumni magazine in 1930, Dr Ambedkar made a nostalgic note of his time in the US, 'The best friends I have had in my life were some of my classmates at Columbia and my great professors, John Dewey, James Shotwell, Edwin Seligman and James Harvey Robinson.'[17] Dr Ambedkar also examined the problems of African Americans in the US. Later on, he would use these experiences and learnings as a comparative perspective during the drafting of India's Constitution. Zelliot noted, 'It is more likely that in those early years in America his own natural proclivities and interests found a healthy soil for growth, and the experience served chiefly to strengthen him in his life-long battle for dignity and equality for his people.'[18] Dr Ambedkar maintained his intellectual ties with Columbia University, even after graduation. The University also kept in touch with him; in 1930, the Alumni Bulletin reported his address at the Round Table Conference in London.[19]

Dr Ambedkar's time at the London School of Economics (LSE) was documented in the archive files released during an online exhibition held by LSE in June 2021. The online exhibition made 'available for the first time the entirety of Ambedkar's LSE student file'.[20] Dr Ambedkar first became a part of LSE in 1916 when he was twenty-five years old. He is believed to be the first Indian to receive a doctorate from the LSE.[21] In 1920, Prof. Seligman of Columbia University wrote to Prof. Herbert Foxwell of LSE, recommending Dr Ambedkar and requesting Foxwell to help him in his research.[22] Since Dr Ambedkar already had a doctorate, Prof. Foxwell wrote to the school secretary, Ms Mair, that 'there are no more worlds here for him to conquer'.[23] But Dr Ambedkar wanted to study further. He acquired his second master's and a PhD from LSE.[24] His professors at LSE included influential intellectuals like Leonard Hobhouse and Halford Mackinder, among others.

In London, Dr Ambedkar also pursued law from Gray's Inn to become a barrister-at-law. He studied law, as it provided him with the tools that would help him assert the rights of marginalized social groups.[25] Dr Ambedkar wanted to equip himself with the knowledge of legal systems, as he often referred to principles of law to question acts of injustice in India. He recognized that legal practice was also a means for resistance and contestation.[26] He once mentioned that the law gave him 'liberty and free time to perform social work'.[27] He also recounted later that 'legal practice and public service are thus the alternating currents in my life'.[28]

LSE records also indicate that while he was in London to attend the Round Table Conferences, Dr Ambedkar met some of his former classmates and professors at LSE. In 1932, his former supervisor Edwin Cannan wrote a letter to William Beveridge (then director of the LSE) to ask him to engage with Dr Ambedkar during his stay, and described him as: 'I always said he was by far the ablest Indian we ever had in my time.'[29] Dr Ambedkar also 'maintained a relationship with LSE, and there is evidence that he was heavily involved in financing students from Dalit communities to be able to study abroad, including at LSE, in the 1950s'.[30]

However, it was not just Western education that exposed Dr Ambedkar to egalitarian ideas. It was his own experiences as a child and as an adult that made him choose the course of education and the choice of subjects he studied. Anti-caste activists and writers Urmila Pawar and Meenakshi Moon state that Dr Ambedkar held progressive views even before he finished his education in the West. When Dr Ambedkar was a student in the US, he wrote a letter to Jamadar Jadhav, his neighbour from Satara (Maharashtra), congratulating him for sending his daughter to school. Later on, when Dr Ambedkar opened a co-educational college, he also arranged for a bus service from the college, so that girls could attend in large numbers.[31]

In his own biographical account, Dr Ambedkar shared a few personal experiences of discrimination, which shaped his thought process and world view. Dr Ambedkar's account of his childhood is so deeply personal that it needs to be reproduced here. Dr Ambedkar narrated,

> . . . in the school I could not sit in the midst of my classmates according to my rank [in class performance], but that I was to sit in a corner by myself. I knew that in the school I was to have a separate piece of gunny cloth for me to squat on in the classroom, and the servant employed to clean the school would not touch the gunny cloth used by me. I was required to carry the gunny cloth home in the evening, and bring it back the next day.[32]

As a child, Dr Ambedkar could not even drink water on his own in school. He shared,

> While in the school I knew that children of the touchable classes, when they felt thirsty, could go out to the water tap, open it, and quench their thirst. All that was necessary was the permission of the teacher. But my position was separate. I could not touch the tap; and unless it was opened for it by a touchable person, it was not possible for me to quench my thirst. In my case the permission of the teacher was not enough. The presence of the school peon was necessary,

for he was the only person whom the class teacher could use for such a purpose. If the peon was not available, I had to go without water. The situation can be summed up in the statement—no peon, no water.[33]

Dr Ambedkar narrated a traumatic incident, a 'nightmare', which he faced at the age of nine, which left a deep impact on his mind about untouchability and the caste system. Dr Ambedkar wrote:

The . . . incident . . . occurred in about 1901, when we were at Satara. My mother was then dead. My father was away on service as a cashier at a place called Koregaon in Khatav Taluka in the Satara District, where the Government of Bombay had started the work of excavating a Tank so as to give employment to famine-stricken people, who were dying by thousands (sic).

As Dr Ambedkar's father's job prevented him from leaving his station to come to Satara, he asked his kids to come to Koregaon and spend the summer vacation with him. As per the plan, his father's peon was supposed to receive young Bhimrao and his brothers at the railway station. But when they reached, the peon had not come. When the kids tried hiring a bullock cart, 'not one of [the cartmen] was prepared to suffer being polluted, and to demean himself carrying passengers of the untouchable classes'. One cartman finally agreed, but on two conditions: that the kids would drive the cart themselves and that they would pay double the fare. On the way, the kids could not even get water. When their cart halted for the night at the toll collector's place, Dr Ambedkar lied to the toll collector (a Hindu) that he was a Muslim, in order to get water. But even then, they were refused water.

When Dr Ambedkar and his brothers reached Koregaon, they found that their father could not come to receive them because his servant had forgotten to tell him about their travel plans. Dr Ambedkar noted later,

> This incident has a very important place in my life. I was a boy of nine when it happened. But it has left an indelible impression on my mind. Before this incident occurred, I knew that I was an untouchable, and that untouchables were subjected to certain indignities and discriminations . . . But this incident gave me a shock such as I had never received before, and it made me think about untouchability—which, before this incident happened, was with me a matter of course, as it is with many touchables as well as the untouchables.[34]

Dr Ambedkar also narrated an incident which took place after he returned to India in 1916 from the US. He wrote: 'My five years of staying in Europe and America had completely wiped out of my mind any consciousness that I was an untouchable, and that an untouchable wherever he went in India was a problem to himself and to others.'[35] As Dr Ambedkar's studies in the US were financially supported by the erstwhile Baroda State, he was supposed to work for the State. But he could not find a single place to stay. He was able to stay in a small room in a Parsi inn, only after convincing the Parsi manager that he would impersonate a Parsi.

The allotted room was not in good condition. He shared,

> The inn on the first floor had a small bed-room, and adjoining it was one small bath room with a water tap in it. The rest was one big hall. At the time of my stay the big hall was filled up with all sorts of rubbish—planks, benches, broken chairs, etc. In the midst of these surroundings I lived, a single solitary individual.

He further shared,

> I was appointed as a probationer in the Accountant General's
> Office by the Maharaja of Baroda. I used to leave the inn at
> about ten a.m. for the office, and return late at about eight
> in the evening, contriving to while away outside the inn
> as much time in [the] company of friends as I could. The
> idea of returning to the inn to spend the night therein was
> most terrifying to me, and I used to return to the inn only
> because I had no other place under the sky to go for rest. In
> this big hall on the first floor of the inn there were no fellow
> human beings to talk to. I was quite alone. The whole hall
> was enveloped in complete darkness. There were no electric
> lights, nor even oil lamps to relieve the darkness . . . I felt that
> I was in a dungeon, and I longed for the company of some
> human being to talk to. But there was no one.

All this made Dr Ambedkar angry. But he said, 'I subdued
my grief and my anger through the feeling that though it was
a dungeon, it was a shelter, and that some shelter was better
than no shelter.' After some days, the local Parsis found out
that Dr Ambedkar was impersonating a Parsi. A 'dozen angry-
looking, tall, sturdy Parsis, each armed with a stick' came to his
room, and questioned him about his identity. As Dr Ambedkar
feared being assaulted, he stayed silent. When the Parsis
asked him to vacate the room, it was a feeling of doom for
Dr Ambedkar. He said:

> At that time my shelter I prized more than my life. The
> threat implied in this question was a grave one. I therefore
> broke my silence and implored them to let me stay for a
> week at least, thinking that my application to the Minister
> for a bungalow would be decided upon favourably in
> the meantime. But the Parsis were in no mood to listen.

They issued an ultimatum. They must not find me in the inn in the evening. I must pack off. They held out dire consequences, and left. I was bewildered. My heart sank within me. I cursed all, and wept bitterly. After all, I was deprived of my precious possession—namely, my shelter. It was no better than a prisoner's cell. But to me it was very precious.

Fearing an attack, he spent the entire afternoon in a public garden and left the place by the night train. The trauma stayed with him though,

This scene of a dozen Parsis armed with sticks lined [up] before me in a menacing mood, and myself standing before them with a terrified look imploring for mercy, is a scene which so long a period as eighteen years has not succeeded in fading away. I can even now vividly recall it—and never recall it without tears in my eyes. It was then for the first time that I learnt that a person who is an untouchable to a Hindu is also an untouchable to a Parsi.[36]

Another such experience took place in the year 1929. The Bombay government had appointed a committee to investigate the grievances of the Untouchables. Dr Ambedkar was appointed a member of the committee, which was mandated to 'investigate the allegations of injustice, oppression and tyranny'. At Chalisgaon, the Untouchables came to the railway station and requested Dr Ambedkar to rest there for the night. The horse carriage that was carrying Dr Ambedkar met with an accident of such force that he fell out of the carriage and received several injuries, including a leg fracture. When Dr Ambedkar inquired how the carriage went out of control, he was told that the carriage men had refused to drive an Untouchable passenger. As the Untouchables could not tolerate this violation of Dr Ambedkar's dignity, they hired the horse carriage and got one of their own people to drive. The person who took the reins could not control the carriage, as he was inexperienced. Dr Ambedkar noted,

> To save my dignity, the Mahars of Chalisgaon had put my very life in jeopardy. It is then I learnt that a Hindu tongawalla, no better than a menial, has a dignity by which he can look upon himself as a person who is superior to any untouchable, even though he may be a Barrister-at-law.[37]

Dr Ambedkar also benefited tremendously from the presence of two women in his life—Ramabai Ambedkar (his first wife, who passed away in 1935) and Dr Sharda Kabir (his second wife, who is known by the name of Dr Savita Ambedkar). Both these women were equal partners of Dr Ambedkar during different phases of his life. No study of Dr Ambedkar's life can be complete and accurate without acknowledging them.

The expanse of Dr Ambedkar's knowledge and vision also resulted from his wide reading. The personal accounts of several individuals who were associated with him, as well as his own voluminous writings and speeches, clearly show that he was widely read and presented novel analyses for each of the problems he grappled with. D.G. Jadhav, a close associate, noted that Dr Ambedkar used to tell everyone to invest at least 10 per cent of their income in purchasing books.[38] Another associate, Kartar Singh 'Polonius', stated that books were 'an all-absorbing passion' of Dr Ambedkar.[39] His collection of books was probably the richest and most diverse in the country at that time. Polonius noted,

> His devotion to books is so great that he studies well into the early hours of the morning, every night. In the art of

writing, he is the master of a very forceful and original style. He marshals his facts very ingeniously and his logic is masterly and disarming. He does not believe in mincing words and likes to call a spade a spade.'[40]

In his work on the intellectual history of Dr Ambedkar's ideas, Stroud states: 'His library at the time of his death in December 1956 was reputed to be around 50,000 volumes. Significant portions of this library were donated to the colleges he started, Siddharth College in Mumbai and Milind College in Aurangabad, for their general collections.'[41] Several books bore Dr Ambedkar's annotations.[42] Scholar V. Geetha notes: 'As his priceless collection of books shows us, his was both a restless and practical imagination, at once utopian and pragmatic, ethical and historical.'[43]

In his writing, Dr Ambedkar also referred to the histories of different countries to make a point about learning from one's past mistakes. He would often quote various philosophers and statesmen to emphasize a point. For instance, he quoted Edmund Burke during the Round Table Conference, mentioned American constitutional history in *What Congress and Gandhi Have Done for the Untouchables,* and would refer to a plethora of writers such as historian George Grote on Greek history, Thomas Jefferson on American constitutionalism, and Abraham Lincoln on statesmanship while drafting India's Constitution. Interestingly, he once noted:

In fact no author is my hero. I am very selective. I choose what is worth choosing from any author worthy of perusal— and assimilate into myself and build my own personality which if you will allow one to say is not an imitation of anybody howsoever high. It is my original self.[44]

Dr Ambedkar's vision was also shaped by the many social movements and community involvement initiatives that he undertook. Public movements such as the Mahad Satyagraha, Kalaram Temple Entry Movement, etc., were learning experiences for him. These movements further impacted his drive to increase the public and political participation of marginalized castes. He emphasized the need to enshrine access to public resources such as water and places of public worship as an enforceable egalitarian value. This view would later be adopted into the Indian Constitution, whose drafting process he chaired. These movements show the efforts of Dr Ambedkar to build a public discourse on the notion of rights and justice in a democratic framework that he envisaged for the country. Ashok Gopal, author of a recent biography on Dr Ambedkar, notes: 'As Gail Omvedt, a scholar of Dalit movements in India, explained in *Dalits and the Democratic Revolution,* Ambedkar was as much "the creation of the movement he led as its creator". The spark that ignited the dual processes was, like the breaking down of the gates of Bastille on 14 July 1789, the culmination of several actions that were not part of a preconceived plan.'[45]

The various court battles he fought against social evils also taught him when to engage in judicial processes, and when to adopt public engagement and street protests as a process to negotiate the acceptance of demands.[46] His ability and 'skills as a lawyer led to successful legal action, which led to political action, which led to the achievement of his aim of securing an improvement in the position of the Dalits'.[47] The details of the cases argued by Dr Ambedkar can be found on a webpage launched by the Supreme Court of India in November 2023 to celebrate the centenary of his enrolment as a lawyer.[48]

Dr Ambedkar was a person made by collective struggles towards emancipation, yet unique in his convictions.

3

Constitutional Discourse before Dr Ambedkar and in Subsequent Years

It is generally accepted that the Indian Constitution was drafted between December 1946 and January 1950. Another belief asserts that a group of leaders worked on the finalization of the Constitution of India. However, such an understanding doesn't capture the enormity and depth of the specific circumstances amid which the Constitution of India came into being. The process of how the Constitution was finalized needs to be understood by analysing various developments in history related to the enactment of various laws by the British. This is because the framework and the values that were finally adopted into the Indian Constitution did not suddenly emerge in 1946; they became part of the national discourse due to the developments that took place in the previous three decades.

Dr Ambedkar played a significant role in the adoption of these values into mainstream discourse. To understand his influence, one needs to analyse history before and after Dr Ambedkar came on to the public scene. Dr Ambedkar's views can be witnessed from 1915, when he presented his writings at Columbia University. Therefore, one needs to look at the constitutional discourse pre- and post-1915. Very often, the initial constitutional reforms are credited to the revolts

against the British. Accordingly, let us take the nineteenth
century as the starting point.

Constitutional discourse in the nineteenth century

Like the US, India also had a system of legalized slavery.
Several oppressed castes were enslaved in the princely State
of Travancore and other states.[1] Historian P. Sanal Mohan
notes: 'Exercise of hegemonic power in society leads to the
internalization of dominant ideas, which make possible
structures of dominance and subordination.'[2] This slavery was
only abolished in 1855, due to the growing consciousness of the
slave castes.[3]

Similarly, the initial revolts against British rule in India
were led by the indigenous Adivasi communities. There were
close to forty major tribal revolts across the country.[4] As far
back as 1774–79, the Halba tribe had revolted against the East
India Company in what is today Bastar, Chhattisgarh.[5] This
was followed by other major incidences such as the Bhil revolt
of 1818, and the Kol uprising of 1831.[6] A major uprising, known as
the Santal Hul (revolution), against the British happened during
1855–56, when thousands of Santal community members,
supported by oppressed caste peasants, revolted against the
forces of the East India Company and against landlords and
moneylenders.[7] The British suppressed the movement with
the utmost brutality.[8] However, these revolts have been erased
from what is considered mainstream history. Rather, the focus
has been mainly on the Sepoy Mutiny of 1857, also sometimes
cast as the First War of Indian Independence, which was also
suppressed by the British East India Company.

In response to these revolts, the British government, in
November 1858, took control of Indian territory, bringing it
within the direct purview of the Crown. Queen Victoria was

then proclaimed the empress of India. The proclamation assured the princely states that the treaties that the East India Company had signed with them would be maintained. The proclamation also aimed to restrict interference in the social and religious practices of Indian society.[9] This maintained the social hierarchies and power relations of pre-colonial society. After the proclamation, a series of legal reforms were initiated, focusing on establishing institutions such as high courts and civil services.[10] Historian Rohit De termed this period as 'The Viceregal Age [of] Petitioning and Representation'.[11] Indians filed petitions before the viceroy.

Around the same time, the established democracy of the US was going through a historical change, influencing the manner in which equality and rights were to be imagined by anti-caste thinkers in India. The Civil War in the US had been fought in the 1860s on the issue of the legalized slavery of the Black community, a system that the Southern states wanted to continue reinforcing. Harvard Professor Michael Klarman, an authority on American constitutional history, has documented how the lengthy history of racial oppression contains the complicity of the law, which largely viewed slaves as property.[12] This established a culture of slavery and White supremacy and helped to preserve existing social relations.[13] The Civil War symbolized an important rupture during which democratic developments started to take place. This was an important moment in which the contest between freedom and slavery became very pronounced.[14] Abraham Lincoln played a significant role in championing the battle against slavery. He said, 'Slavery is founded in the selfishness of man's nature— opposition to it is in his love of justice.'[15] After the War, the Thirteenth Amendment to the US Constitution was passed to abolish slavery. The Amendment was the first recognition of the rights of African Americans in the US.

Ideally, Indian nationalist leaders who had received an English education, and were observing global developments, should have initiated a similar discourse for ending the oppression of marginalized communities in India. Nothing of the kind happened. Interestingly, most leaders were from oppressor castes. However, the American struggle against the treatment of human beings as property offered new ammunition to the anti-caste struggle. In a sharp critique of the discourse of 'mainstream' Indian leaders and caste oppression, Jyotiba Phule wrote *Gulamgiri* in 1873. As previously mentioned, he dedicated the book to the people of the US. This appears to be the first aspiration emphasizing the principle of equality in Indian constitutional discourse. Phule's appeal was, however, ignored by the nationalist discourse.

A discourse on fundamental rights was missing from the prevalent anti-colonial discourse. Franchise and the right to contest elections were not given to Indians at that time; later, these rights were extended only to those who were educated.[16] As the right to education was not extended to everyone, the Depressed Classes were largely disenfranchised; the practice of untouchability denied the Depressed Classes access to any education within the religious set-up. In any case, the British were 'for a long time silent on the question of promoting education among the native population'.[17] Therefore, the denial of the basic civil rights of marginalized sections of the population resulted in the political suppression of their voices.

Around the same time, the British passed the Criminal Tribes Act (CTA), 1871, which led to the criminalization of the marginalized communities. The Act empowered the governor general to declare 'any tribe, gang or class of persons' as a 'criminal tribe'.[18] A few scholars have noted that the declaration of certain communities as criminals was not just a British experiment but reflected the deep-rooted discrimination within Indian society.[19] Historian Ramnarayan S. Rawat notes: 'Colonial practices not only drew from existing Brahminical frameworks but also played an important role in reifying and perpetuating them.'[20] That is to say, the caste philosophy already considered several communities as criminals.[21] Furthermore, as historian Stewart N. Gordon notes:

> The development of the idea of the 'criminal tribe' was the merging of two intellectual traditions, both with deep roots. First, there was the tradition of the Brahmin subordinates of the new British rule. Theirs was the plainsmen's fear of the forest, the cultivators' fear of hunting-and-gathering peoples, the high-castes' fear of people without caste, the Hindus' fear of non-Hindus and the bureaucrats' fear of an uncontrollable population. To this was added the strangely parallel British tradition; it included a long legal association of migrating with 'vagabondage' and the association of forests with crime and outlaws. To this mix were added the more recent ideas of criminals as a race apart, and finally, in line with nineteenth-century ideas of progress, the idea of redeemability. This entire heritage became crystallized and 'institutionalized' in the criminal tribe laws of nineteenth-century India.[22]

Besides, under CTA, the term 'tribe' was not limited to indigenous communities, as we understand it now. It also included 'caste' within the meaning of 'tribe'. As a result, apart from the criminalization of several indigenous communities, some marginalized castes such as Chamars were characterized by the British as having 'criminal tendencies'.[23] In addition, the CTA categorized 'eunuchs' as 'reasonably suspected of kidnapping or castrating children'. The British also exploited the labour of the oppressed castes in their domestic lives in violent ways.[24] Such colonial oppression and stereotyping of the already marginalized was not a concern for the nationalist leaders, as it adhered to the social values of the oppressor castes.

For a long time, the nationalist leaders were only concerned with constitutional reforms that would improve the representation of Indians in the British system and with the idea of self-governance. According to historian Rohit De, following direct control by the British Crown, elite Indians began to claim for themselves the rights of a citizen equivalent to those received by British citizens, rather than opposing British rule. However, the British did not recognize such rights.[25] In 1892, a few Indians were nominated, with limited roles, to the Governor's Council.[26] In 1895, Gopal Krishna Gokhale emphasized the inclusion of Indians in the administrative machinery of the British, while making his submissions before the Welby Commission.[27] The commission was appointed in 1895 by the British government to inquire into the administration and management of the military and civil expenditure incurred under the authority of the secretary of state for India-in-council.[28] Gokhale had submitted:

> A kind of dwarfing or stunting of the Indian race is going on under the present system. We must live all the days of our life in an atmosphere of inferiority and tallest of us must bend in order that the exigencies of the existing system may be satisfied. The upward impulse, if I may use such an expression, which every schoolboy at Eton or Harrow may feel that he may one day be a Gladstone, a Nelson, or a Wellington, and which may draw forth the best efforts of which he is capable, is denied to us. The full height to which our manhood is capable of rising can never be reached by us under the present system.[29]

Since only a few communities—such as Brahmins who had power and privilege—could get access to English education, the demand for the 'Indianization of services'[30] ended up being limited to the inclusion of oppressor castes into the services.

In 1895, the Constitution of India Bill was prepared under the supervision of Bal Gangadhar Tilak. It provided a 'small list of broadly worded rights that included right to free speech and expression, property, personal liberty, inviolability of one's home, equality before law, equality to admission to public and the offices, right to petition for redress of grievances'.[31] The Bill provided that 'the political rights of an Indian citizen' would be 'lost by . . . physical or moral incapacity' and also stated that 'the Sovereign of Great Britain and Ireland shall reign and rule over the Empire of India.'[32] Furthermore, the Bill neither provided for the rights of the marginalized communities nor prohibited caste discrimination or untouchability. This was not surprising, as Tilak held questionable views on such matters. He was opposed to the Indian National Congress taking up questions of social reforms.[33] In 1891, he opposed the Age of Consent Bill, which raised the age of consent for consummation from ten to twelve years.[34]

While Tilak has been largely referred to as a leading figure in Indian political history, he was opposed to the views of important radical thinkers and movements, that advocated a removal of caste. One of the leaders whom he opposed was Phule. Tilak criticized Phule as he believed that the latter's work dispelled 'reverence' towards Brahmins, a foundational aspect of caste structure.[35] He was of the belief that the time-honoured customs and institutions of the Brahmins had to be continued and preserved.[36] Tilak was in favour of carrying on with Varna occupations; he wrote,

You take away a farmer's boy from the plough, the blacksmith's boy from the bellows and the cobbler's boy

from his awl with the object of giving him liberal education
. . . and the boy learns to condemn the profession of his
father, not to speak of the loss to which the latter is put by
being deprived of the son's assistance at the old trade.[37]

He was also opposed to a proposal that recommended a
co-educational set-up for women and men in college classes.[38]
Tilak further argued, 'What is urgently wanted is primary
schools for girls that would give them such knowledge as is
useful in domestic life . . . teaching English would prove to turn
out girls to be a dead weight on their husbands.'[39] He opposed
the compulsory education of oppressed caste children, often
advocating that it would result in harm.[40] In 1881, he opposed
the compulsory enrolment of children from the 'Kunbi'
community.[41] He also was critical of separate supportive hostels
for backward communities.[42]

Later, Tilak was reported to have said in Sholapur (now
Solapur) that he did not understand 'why the oil pressers,
tobacco shopkeepers, washermen, etc.'—referring to the non-
Brahmins and the Backward Classes—'should want to go into
the Legislature'.[43] In his opinion, they should just obey the laws
and not aspire for the power to make laws.[44] (Dr Ambedkar
would note in 1945: 'The late Mr. Tilak could never forget that
he was a Brahmin and belonged to the governing class.' By
'governing class', Dr Ambedkar meant oppressor castes, who
were ruling over the oppressed castes.)[45] Therefore, Tilak's
understanding of 'home rule' was not egalitarian.

Contrary to this, a few princely rulers who believed in social
justice were initiating policies to promote the inclusion of the
oppressed castes into the mainstream. Several princely states
and provinces initiated similar reservations for the Backward
Classes.[46] For instance, on 26 July 1902, Shahuji Maharaj issued

an order to ensure a 50 per cent quota for the Backward Classes in the Kolhapur State services.[47] As Bhagwan Das notes:

> Some of these princely states were progressive and eager to modernise through the promotion of education and industry; and by maintaining unity among their own people. Mysore in south India and Baroda and Kolhapur in western India took considerable interest in the awakening and advancement of the minorities and deprived sections of society. It should not surprise us then that the very first records of implementing reservations policies are from these princely states.[48]

Later, due to negotiations by the Congress and the Muslim delegation, the Morley–Minto Reforms were brought in to provide limited electoral representation. The Indian Councils Act of 1909, brought under the Morley–Minto Reforms, created electoral systems to elect some Indians to the provincial and central legislature.[49] However, the British bureaucrats retained a majority in the central legislature. The executive also remained under British control and exercised a veto on any decision. Special electorates were created to represent provincial landowners, tea plantations, regional merchants, landlords and Muslims.[50] However, voting rights were not extended to everyone. Electoral roles were limited to property holders and certain educational requirements were imposed as well.[51]

It needs to be highlighted that the discourse in law did not touch the system of social inequalities in India; rather, it retained the caste system. The British courts were administering law in matters of social conduct, as they were told to by the priests.[52] The judicial and legal system created by the colonial state followed a dual policy of non-interference and codification of customs—which effectively enabled the power of the Brahmins. Caste Hindu groups enjoyed the active support of colonial courts that relied on the scriptural interpretations of Brahmin priests. American scholar Marc Galanter highlights how the understanding of the colonial policy, to not interfere in religious law and property rights, further solidified caste oppression. Caste hierarchical practices were either tacitly or directly supported by colonial law.[53]

For example, by looking at temple entry cases, it is clear that the working of the British judicial system further enabled caste hierarchies. In some cases, injunctions were granted by colonial courts to prevent members of oppressed castes from entering temples.[54] Additionally, dominant caste communities derived open support from the courts in getting compensation for the violation of their caste-based customs.[55] Parallelly, the courts did not intervene to enable all castes to be able to use tanks and wells. Instead, the Untouchable castes were actively prevented from accessing public resources equally, through the logic of private property.[56] Therefore, British courts relied on conceptions of temples as arenas of personal ownership and property, in order to repeatedly pronounce judgments favourable to caste Hindus.[57] Furthermore, the police and the courts did not help oppressed caste communities to take advantage of the law.[58] Caste control was made more pronounced through colonial protections of religious practice. Another scholar Bernard Cohn points out how economic power and grasp of court procedures and knowledge enabled oppressor castes to out-manoeuvre the oppressed castes in the course of litigation.[59]

The British courts did not implement criminal law, even in cases where the oppressed castes were assaulted.[60] Celebrated scholars and activists Bharat Patankar and Gail Omvedt noted that attempts to resist caste hierarchy by accessing temples and tanks and wearing the sacred thread were not protected by the British system of rights.[61] They noted:

> Religious and ritual restrictions (e.g., the exclusion of oppressed castes from temples) were enforced by the courts, defilement of religious restrictions was treated as a criminal offence and so punished, and courts refused to take action against upper castes who acted on their own to 'discipline'— i.e., terrorize and punish—low castes who tried to rebel.

Patankar and Omvedt stated that 'the position of non-interference taken by the British officials and the law amounted in practice to upholding caste hierarchy.'[62] Colonial law was thus neither neutral nor fair. Within its language, it espoused discriminatory undertones.

British criminal law therefore mingled with the pre-colonial understanding of who should be disciplined and punished. Disha Wadekar, scholar and lawyer, theorizes that the criminalization of marginalized castes is a result of their continued resistance to social oppression.[63] The creation of *deviant* communities through the CTA—that criminalized peasant, nomadic and forest-dwelling communities and treated them as inherently delinquent—and the lack of the assurance of justice to the caste-oppressed communities by the British courts must be located within the fact that these communities regularly resisted the humiliation imposed by caste society and, therefore, were consequently silenced by law.[64] In this way, the British *re-criminalized* a significant population of various castes and tribes as 'criminals', thereby declaring them criminal by birth and erasing their rights and identity in all ways.

It is thus clear that in the initial decades after 1857, the constitutional discourse was extremely limited, and the focus was on improving the representation of Indians in the British system. The issues of social reform and untouchability were not raised by nationalist leaders.

Constitutional Discourse: 1915-50[65]

The seeds of a serious and constant constitutional discourse were sown in the mid-1910s. The British had promised constitutional reforms, in return for Indian support to them during the First World War.[66] In 1917, Edwin Samuel Montagu, then secretary of state for India (1917–22) held deliberations with Lord Chelmsford, viceroy of India (1916–21) on the issue of constitutional advancement. Montagu said that the policy of the British government towards India would focus on 'increasing association of Indians in every branch of the administration, with a view to the progressive realization of responsible government in India as an integral part of the empire'.[67] Under the directions of the secretary of state, the Southborough Committee on Franchise was constituted to 'advise on franchises and constituencies in each province with the object of securing as broad a franchise and as representative a council as present circumstances in each province permit' and on how to secure adequate and effective representation 'of minorities of special interests or of backward classes'.[68] At the same time, Congress recognized the problem of untouchability only in 1917. The 1917 resolution to abolish untouchability was termed as a 'strange event' by Dr Ambedkar because the erstwhile Congress 'had never done such a thing before although it had functioned for thirty-two years'.[69] He later had this to say:

> The passing of the Resolution was a heartless transaction. It was a formal fulfilment of a condition which the Depressed Classes had made for giving their support to the Congress-League scheme. Congressmen did not appear to be charged

with any qualms of conscience or with any sense of righteous indignation against man's inhumanity to man which is what untouchability is. They forgot the Resolution the very day on which it was passed. The Resolution was a dead letter.[70]

Historian Chinnaiah Jangam notes: 'B.R. Ambedkar never ceased to point out the failure of the caste Hindu-led anti-colonial struggle to address issues of social inequality and the denial of basic humanity to the oppressed majority.'[71]

Dr Ambedkar was invited to present his submissions before the Southborough Committee (discussed in a subsequent chapter). The report of the Southborough Committee and the larger Montagu–Chelmsford Report[72] led to the enactment of the GOI Act 1919. The Act provided for bicameral legislation. It authorized the division between central and provincial subjects, and the ability to have statutory and administrative divisions between the two. When elections were held subsequently in 1921, they were conducted at both central and provincial levels.[73] The report of the Southborough Committee and the consequent 1919 Act were criticized by Dr Ambedkar, who later described the Southborough Committee as '[s]o grossly indifferent . . . to the problem of making adequate provision for safeguarding the interests of the Depressed Classes'.[74]

The Act also contained a provision, which had imposed an obligation on the British government, to appoint a Commission at the end of ten years 'to investigate into the working of the Constitution and report upon such changes as may be found necessary'. Consequently, in 1928, a Royal Commission was appointed under the chairmanship of Sir John Simon. However, the Commission did not include any Indian as a member, for which the Indian National Congress boycotted the Commission.[75]

The Simon Commission came on its first visit to India in February 1928 to start its work on reviewing the GOI Act 1919.

The Congress organized its own all-party conference in May 1928 and appointed a committee headed by Motilal Nehru to draft a 'Swaraj Constitution' for India.[76] The Nehru Committee engaged in deliberations with various parties and representatives during June–August 1928 and prepared a draft Constitution. However, the Committee neither invited nor included the Bahishkrit Hitakarini Sabha (Society for the Welfare of the Excluded), founded in 1924 by Dr Ambedkar, in its process. Dr Ambedkar criticized the Report for its inaction towards including any provision for the cause of the Depressed Classes.[77]

On behalf of the Bahishkrit Hitakarini Sabha, Dr Ambedkar submitted a memorandum to the Simon Commission, demanding a joint electorate with reservation of seats for the Depressed Classes.[78] Eighteen other Depressed Class Associations submitted their memoranda to the Commission. Sixteen associations demanded separate electorates for the Depressed Classes.

As the Commission was facing opposition, the British government also announced that after the Commission finished its work and deliberations, an assembly of Indians would be taken to discuss the formation of a new constitution for India. The Round Table Conference (RTC) was initiated in 1930 to bring Indian representatives and the British government together to hold further discussions. Invitations were sent to various Indian leaders, including Dr Ambedkar.[79] The first RTC was boycotted by the Congress. Dr Ambedkar travelled to London to place his powerful submissions on constitutionalism and statesmanship, which earned him appreciation from all quarters.[80] Later, Dr Ambedkar participated in two subsequent RTCs, while the Congress and M.K. Gandhi participated only in the second RTC. The Conferences saw the first articulation of several key ideas in the Indian constitutional discourse.[81] Dr Ambedkar demanded separate electorates for the Depressed Classes, which was a change in his position since the Simon Commission deliberations. (These will be discussed in the chapter on RTCs.) Furthermore, due to opposition by Gandhi to the idea of separate electorates for the Depressed Classes after the second RTC, Dr Ambedkar had to negotiate his demands with him. This led to the Poona Pact, which accepted the system of joint electorates with reserved seats for the Depressed Classes.

The Conferences and the Poona Pact were significant, as they led to the enactment of the GOI Act 1935. According to historian Rohit De:

> The Act reflected many of the recommendations of the Simon Commission, including the idea that the Constitution should contain within itself a provision for its own development, and should not be rigid. Implicit in the notion of constitutional progress was the idea that representative government could only evolve in India through stages. While the Constitution was a statute, the preamble acknowledged that the convention within the British empire was that the details of the Constitution would not be exhaustively drafted but would develop naturally through conventions or terms of instruction issued from London.[82]

The Act was, however, criticized for extensively expanding the powers of the governor-general, conferring independent powers of legislation on him.[83] The Act did not contain a list of fundamental rights for Indians.

A radical imagination of constitutionalism was done by Dr Ambedkar in his speech titled 'Annihilation of Caste', which he was supposed to deliver at a public event organized by Jat-Pat Todak Mandal in 1936. As the content of the speech was very radical, Dr Ambedkar's event was cancelled. Later, he published the undelivered address in the form of a book, where he highlighted the importance of the constitutional ideas of liberty, equality and fraternity in any society. In the social justice discourse, Dr Ambedkar's undelivered address was the highlight of the decade. He defined the meaning of 'liberty, equality, and fraternity' in the Indian context, and linked it with the idea of democracy. This shall be discussed in detail in the subsequent chapter.

In the 1940s, as the Second World War took place, the negotiations between the Congress leaders, the Muslim League, the British and the Depressed Classes sharpened. The Cripps Proposal of 1942 promised to recognize India as a dominion. However, the proposal was not accepted by any stakeholder. As India was going through a time of conflict, Dr Ambedkar volunteered to draft a constitutional framework to solve the problem of representation of all social groups. In his work 'Communal Deadlock and How to Solve It', written in 1945, he proposed the idea of 'balanced representation' which would prevent the communal majority from becoming a political majority.[84] It also provided safeguards to the minorities in the form of guaranteed representation in the legislature and the executive. The proposal was made before the Cabinet Mission Plan was announced in 1946. Dr Ambedkar's suggestions were not considered in the Plan or by any leaders of the Congress or Muslim League.

It was due to the lack of consensus over the Cabinet Plan that a Constituent Assembly was set up in December 1946. Dr Ambedkar prepared a draft Constitution called 'States and Minorities' in March 1947. The draft was a far-reaching articulation of socio-economic rights. Several provisions of this document were considered for discussion during the initial days of the Constituent Assembly. The task of shaping the drafting process fell on the Drafting Committee and the Advisory Committee, created by the Constituent Assembly. In August 1947, the Constituent Assembly selected Dr Ambedkar as the chairman of the Drafting Committee, which was assigned the task of preparing a draft Constitution and managing its passage for independent India. Dr Ambedkar was one of the most active members of the Advisory Committee. Several of his foresighted ideas, though not accepted, remain relevant to contemporary discourse. Eventually, the Constitution was adopted on 26 January 1950.

The period of 1915–50 saw several constitutional milestones, which shaped India's sociopolitical discourse. Dr Ambedkar was involved in all of these milestones and played a role in setting the discourse. Dr Ambedkar's original constitutional ideas continue to influence the discourse even after the adoption of the Constitution.

4

Ideas on Popular Government
and Citizenship

As mentioned previously, the Untouchables were not considered for any constitutional right in the Indian Councils Act of 1909. The Indian National Congress did not consider the issue of social reforms or untouchability until 1917[1] when, at a conference, it was decided to take up social reforms against untouchability. However, Dr Ambedkar did not consider the efforts made by the nationalist leaders serious enough. Though he had returned to India in 1917, he did not participate in events organized by the Congress or any other organization. After a humiliating stint at Baroda where he faced several acts of discrimination, Dr Ambedkar joined Sydenham College, Bombay, as a professor.[2]

It was a period when the British were reconsidering the demand for franchise (right to vote) made by the Indians. Franchise rights were extremely limited at that time, as they were only available if someone had a specific level of education and owned property.[3] As several communities such as the Untouchables could not get educated or own property due to exclusionary caste-based social customs and untouchability, they were by default denied any right to vote or be a part of the legislature.[4]

Under the Morley–Minto reforms, the Southborough Committee on franchise was set up to deal with the issue. There was a view among the British that India was not suited for a democracy.[5] So, in a way, the issue being deliberated was not just that of franchise, but also the larger issues of democracy and the composition of the popular government. Several leading individuals from different communities were invited to make submissions before the Committee.[6] Dr Ambedkar too was invited because of his expertise.

As the deliberations of the Committee were going to lead to the enactment of a new legislation by the British government, Dr Ambedkar used the opportunity to put forward not just 'a systemic articulation of arguments in favour of remedies against caste discrimination'[7] and untouchability, but also to reflect on what the larger conceptions of *popular government* and *citizenship* ought to mean.

In his submissions, Dr Ambedkar made a clear distinction between 'government for the people' and 'government by the people'. A 'government for the people' claims to work for the people, while not involving them in the decision-making process. In common language, there are 'saviour' tendencies involved in such an imagination.[8] At that time, this could have been a reference to the British government, which wanted to rule Indians without involving them in governance. Dr Ambedkar rejected such a conception of the government. He argued that *popular government* does not mean 'government for the people' but 'government by the people'. In his view, it is only when the government consists of members of various communities that it can be considered as representing different opinions and different communities. He noted that the conception of 'government for the people' tends to treat people not as citizens but as subjects who need to be governed. A *popular government* cannot be based on a master–subject relationship but should involve equal participation.

Dr Ambedkar argued that in a democracy, a popular government should benefit everyone equally. As he noted:

A Government for the people, but not by the people, is sure to educate some into masters and others into subjects; because it is by the reflex effects of association that one can feel and measure the growth of personality. The growth of personality is the highest aim of society. Social arrangement must secure free initiative and opportunity for every individual to assume any role he is capable of assuming provided it is socially desirable. A new rule is a renewal and growth of personality. But when an association—and a Government is after all an association—is such that in it every role cannot be assumed by all, it tends to develop the personality of the few at the cost of the many—a result scrupulously to be avoided in the interest of Democracy. To be specific, it is not enough to be electors only. It is necessary to be lawmakers; otherwise who can be lawmakers will be masters of those who can only be electors.'[9]

Dr Ambedkar's conception of democracy and government was based on the welfare of the people.

In order to make the government truly representative, Dr Ambedkar questioned the conditions and standards existing for someone to be a part of the government and administration or even a participating voter. As stated previously, the conditions of education and property, for having franchise rights, led to the exclusion of several marginalized communities from the electoral process. Dr Ambedkar submitted that if the conditions of franchise do not allow members of a community to join the government or be eligible to become a part of the government, then it is against the concept of popular government. He noted, 'Any scheme of franchise and constituency that fails to bring this about fails to create a popular Government.'[10]

Dr Ambedkar then questioned the British argument that 'India is unfit for representative Government because of the division of her population into castes and creeds.' Even though Dr Ambedkar was speaking on behalf of the Untouchables, he ensured that his stand was not used by the British to deny the demand for democracy in India. Dr Ambedkar argued that India is fit for popular government in the same way as any European country or the United States of America, where democracy exists despite social divisions in their respective societies.[11] Rejecting the British invocation of caste as grounds to deny the demand for popular government, Dr Ambedkar pointed out that the real issue to be addressed is that of untouchability, which creates isolation among different communities in India.[12]

The prevalence of caste relations posed a serious problem for the formation of a truly participatory government. Dr Ambedkar's biographer, Dhananjay Keer, believed that during the time of the Southborough Committee, Dr Ambedkar foresaw the importance of *home rule* for all caste communities. However, he also knew that self-determination would be meaningful only when there were no disparities between different social groupings. Writing in newspapers, Dr Ambedkar noted that the responsibility for dismantling caste oppression was upon dominant castes too. Therefore, Dr Ambedkar advocated that because they possessed a privileged position in society, powerful castes had to advance the position of the oppressed castes through their education.

By creating distinctions between the pure and Untouchable castes, the existence of untouchability also acted as a significant obstacle to the free interaction of social groups. Dr Ambedkar also highlighted how social divisions and practices such as untouchability 'operate to the prejudice of the political life of some communities'. Consequently, the oppressor castes, who had access to education and property, gained extra political rights in British India. Dr Ambedkar pointed out how Brahmins, despite being fewer in numbers, were over-represented as voters in proportion to their population. He therefore demanded a relaxation in the conditions of eligibility to become a voter, so that the proportion of non-Brahmin voters could increase. This would equalize the undue position that one community held. As he noted,

> It is in the interest of all that the Brahmin should not play such a preponderant part in politics as he has been doing hitherto. He has exerted a pernicious influence on the social life of the country and it is in the interest of all that his pernicious influence should be kept at a minimum in politics. As he is the most exclusive, he is the most anti-social.[13]

Dr Ambedkar further demanded the lowering of eligibility standards of franchise for the Untouchables, since otherwise there were no more than ten individuals from the community in Bombay state who could get franchise rights. He proposed,

> To this I should like to add that we should differentiate the qualifications for a vote not merely between provinces or parts thereof but between communities of the same province. Without this differentiation some communities with a small but wealthy or educated population will secure more votes than a large community consisting of poor and uneducated members. Uniformity in franchise should be dispensed with.[14]

Dr Ambedkar submitted that the political rights of the Untouchables were most important not just because their political demands were not being considered but because their very existence was at stake. Since caste oppression denied the oppressed their basic humanity, basic civil rights were a question of the survival of the community. He noted,

The untouchables are usually regarded as objects of pity but they are ignored in any political scheme on the score that they have no interests to protect. And yet their interests are the greatest. Not that they have large property to protect from confiscation. But they have their very *persona* confiscated. The socio-religious disabilities have dehumanized the untouchables and their interests at stake are therefore the interests of humanity. The interests of property are nothing before such primary interests.[15]

Dr Ambedkar highlighted how the Untouchables were treated as slaves in Indian society, and were denied even the basic rights of citizenship. They were denied the dignity that everyone deserved. The discrimination forced on them was such that they lost their ability to resist. He summarized their situation in the following words:

If one agrees with the definition of slave as given by Plato, who defines him as one who accepts from another the purposes which control his conduct, the untouchables are really slaves. The untouchables are so socialized as never to complain of their low estate. Still less do they ever dream of trying to improve their lot, by forcing the other classes to treat them with that common respect which one man owes to another. The idea that they have been born to their lot is so ingrained in their mind that it never occurs to them to think that their fate is anything but irrevocable.[16]

Dr Ambedkar also submitted that untouchability denied basic civil rights to the Untouchables. He gave an example from the Konkan area:

Not only has untouchability arrested the growth of their personality but also it comes in the way of their material

well-being . . . For instance, in Konkan, the untouchables are
prohibited from using the public road. If some high caste
man happens to cross him, he has to be out of the way and
stand at such a distance that his shadow will not fall on the
high caste man.

Such denial of civil rights violates the idea of citizenship. For
Dr Ambedkar, the conception of civil rights was interlinked
with the idea of citizenship. In that sense, he noted, 'The
untouchable is not even a citizen.'[17]

He explained that citizenship cannot be understood
in abstraction, but needs to be conceptualized in terms of
universal rights. He submitted,

> Citizenship is a bundle of rights such as (1) personal liberty,
> (2) personal security, (3) rights to hold private property,
> (4) equality before law, (5) liberty of conscience, (6) freedom
> of opinion and speech, (7) right of assembly, (8) right of
> representation in a country's Government and (9) right to
> hold office under the State . . . The right of representation
> and the right to hold office under the State are the two most
> important rights that make up citizenship.'[18]

The citizenship framework proposed by Dr Ambedkar was
broader, as it allowed everyone not just civil and political rights
but also the right to be a part of the government. This was in
line with his imagination of a popular government which meant
'government by the people'. This broader idea of citizenship
opened the gates for the marginalized castes and communities
to argue for their inclusion in a government system.
Dr Ambedkar argued that the interests of the Untouchables
cannot be voiced by Brahmins, Muslims or the Marathas, but
by the Untouchables themselves. Therefore, he submitted, 'we
must find the untouchables to represent their grievances which

are their interests and, secondly, we must find them in such numbers as will constitute a force sufficient to claim redress'.[19]

The inclusion of the Untouchables could not have happened by merely extending franchise to them as it would have been difficult for an Untouchable to get elected to a seat/constituency comprising oppressor communities, who would not vote for them. He demanded special provisions for ensuring their adequate representation, i.e., a provision to ensure that a specific minimum number of candidates from the Untouchable community would enter the legislature.

There was another argument against extending franchise to the Untouchables. Some believed that 'franchise should be given to those only who can be expected to make an intelligent use of it'.[20] Dr Ambedkar rejected this and argued passionately that franchise would promote the political awakening of the marginalized communities who were kept out of politics and the mainstream of society. He quoted sociologist and political theorist L.T. Hobhouse who said,

> The exercise of popular Government is itself all education . . . enfranchisement itself may precisely be the stimulus needed to awaken interest. The ballot alone effectively liberates the quiet citizen from the tyranny of the shouter and the wirepuller. An impression of existing inertness alone is not a sufficient reason for withholding responsible Government or restricting the area of suffrage.'[21]

Dr Ambedkar added that the 'chief import of a political right' is that it is 'educative'. He emphasized, 'The chief significance of suffrage or a political right consists in a chance for active and direct participation in the regulation of the terms upon which associated life shall be sustained.' That is to say that the Untouchables will have a deciding power on issues that affect them.

Dr Ambedkar stated that if the Untouchables did not have as many voters as other communities, it was not their fault. Rather, society and oppressor castes are to be blamed, for subjugating them in exclusion and indignity. Dr Ambedkar argued, 'The very untouchability attached to their person is a bar to their moral and material progress. The principal modes of acquiring wealth are trade, industry or service. The untouchables can engage in none of these because of their untouchability.'[22]

Dr Ambedkar gave several examples of the unjust treatment meted out to the Untouchables by the oppressor castes:

From an untouchable trader no Hindu will buy. An untouchable cannot be engaged in lucrative service. Military service had been the monopoly of the untouchables since the days of the East India Company. They had joined the Army in such large numbers . . . But after the mutiny when the British were able to secure soldiers from the ranks of the Marathas, the position of the low-caste men who had been the prop of the Bombay Army became precarious, not because the Marathas were better soldiers but because their theological bias prevented them from serving under low-caste officers. The prejudice was so strong that even the non-caste British had to stop recruitment from the untouchable classes. In like manner, the untouchables are refused service in the Police Force. In a great many of the Government offices it is impossible for an untouchable to get a place. Even in the mills a distinction is observed. The untouchables are not admitted in Weaving Departments of the Cotton Mills though many of them are professional weavers. An instance at hand may be cited from the school system of the Bombay Municipality. This most cosmopolitan city ruled by a Corporation with a greater freedom than any other Corporation in India has two different sets of schools . . . one for the children of touchables and the other for those of the untouchables. This in itself is a point worthy of note. But there is something yet more noteworthy. Following the division of schools it has divided its teaching staff into untouchables and touchables. As the untouchable teachers are short of the demand, some of the untouchable schools are manned by teachers from the touchable class. The heart-killing fun of it is that if there is a higher grade open in untouchable school service, as there is bound to be because of a few untouchable trained teachers, a touchable teacher can be thrust into the grade. But if a higher grade is open in the touchable school service, no untouchable teacher can be thrust into that grade. He must wait till a vacancy occurs in the untouchable service! Such is the ethics of the Hindu social life.[23]

Dr Ambedkar hoped that the Southborough Committee would not deny representation to the Untouchables 'because of their small electoral roll but will see its way to grant them adequate representation to enable the untouchables to remove the evil conditions that bring about their poverty'. He appealed, 'At present when all the avenues of acquiring wealth are closed, it is unwise to require from the untouchables a high property qualification. *To deny them the opportunities of acquiring wealth and then to ask from them a property qualification is to add insult to injury.*'

According to Dr Ambedkar, the marginalized Untouchables did not need token appointments, but actual representation. It was a view of the moderates that 'one or two representatives of the untouchables in the Legislative Council would suffice'. Dr Ambedkar opposed this. He argued that having one or two representatives was as good as having none. He was sceptical about whether the caste Hindus would work for the rights of the Untouchables if the presence of adequate numbers of the Untouchables was not ensured. He noted,

> A Legislative Council is not an old curiosity shop. It will be a Council with powers to make or mar the fortunes of society. How can one or two untouchables carry a legislative measure to improve their condition or prevent a legislative measure worsening their state? To be frank, the untouchables cannot expect much good from the political power to be given over to the high caste Hindus. Though the power may not be used against the untouchables and one cannot be altogether sure of this, it may not be used for their betterment.

Furthermore, in order to bring the Untouchables on a level playing field, it was necessary that they be provided with capacities and 'power to fix the social conditions'.

Dr Ambedkar therefore sought a revision of the existing legal framework to allow the presence of Untouchables in the legislature according to their proportion in the total population, and not token appointments. To cite Dr Ambedkar:

> If the conditions are too obdurate, it is in the interest of the untouchables as well as of the touchables that the conditions should be revised. The untouchables must be in a position to influence the revision. Looking at the gravity of their interests, they should get their representation as proposed in proportion to their population. One or two is only kind but neither just nor sufficient. As Lord Morley says in an earlier quotation, needs, not numbers, should govern the extent of representations.[24]

Even at that time, the demands of representation by the Untouchables were responded to by caste Hindus to suggest that 'it will perpetuate social divisions'. The moral hollowness of such arguments led Dr Ambedkar to state that, 'The fun of it is that those who uphold the social divisions are the loudest in their expression of this adverse argument.' He argued that the 'chief effect' of special representation would be that it would bring together people from 'diverse castes who would not otherwise mix together into the Legislative Council'. In that way, 'The Legislative Council will thus become a new cycle of participation in which the representatives of various castes who were erstwhile isolated and therefore anti-social will be thrown into an associated life.' Dr Ambedkar also believed that active participation in an associated life would be better than each caste or group remaining isolated, and held the potential to dilute caste barriers.

Lastly, Dr Ambedkar highlighted that the 'trend of nationalism in India does not warrant us to believe that the few who are sympathetic [to social justice] will grow in volume'.[25] He argued that if the accumulation of power and education is confined to only one class of citizens (the oppressor castes), then it 'may lead to the justification and conservation of class interest; and instead of creating the liberators of the downtrodden, it may create champions of the past and the supporters of the *status quo*'.[26] Dr Ambedkar's final submission was, 'Therefore, instead of leaving the untouchables to the mercy of the higher castes, the wiser policy would be to give power to the untouchables themselves who are anxious, not like others to usurp power, but only to assert their natural place in society.'[27]

After the submissions of Dr Ambedkar, one member of the Committee, W.M. Hailey, noted,

Untouchables were persons to whom certain rights of citizenship had been denied. For instance, it was the right of every citizen to walk down the street, and if a man were prevented from doing so, even temporarily, it was an infringement of his right. Whether a man was prevented from exercising his rights by law or social custom, made very little difference to him'.[28]

He further acknowledged that as the British government had recognized custom (which excluded and discriminated against the Untouchables), 'persons belonging to the untouchable classes were not employed in Government service'.[29]

The Southborough Committee, and the Morley–Minto Reforms, led to the enactment of the GOI Act, 1919. However, the concerns of the Untouchable community were not recognized in the Act. Only one nominated seat was provided to the Untouchables in Bombay.[30] The legislation provided for the review of the conditions after a period of ten years. Dr Ambedkar successfully highlighted the larger issues of popular government, citizenship and civil rights as interlinkages. He established that the imagination of the popular government and citizenship could not take place without providing civil rights equally to everyone. This idea would consistently emerge through the next three decades between 1920 and 1950 in different constitutional moments, agreements and social movements. Dr Ambedkar was a powerful force who compelled others to deal with this issue in those decades.

The stand of Dr Ambedkar on the extension of franchise to everyone would influence later developments on the issue. He would bring up the issue of equal voting rights in the Constituent Assembly in 1946–47. But the seeds were sown by him in 1919 itself. History suggests that Dr Ambedkar proved foresighted about the political conscience which franchise would generate among the oppressed castes. The participation of the oppressed castes in the democratic electoral process after independence made them assertive in making their demands. The emergence of Dalit rights-based political parties led to the evolution of a politics of dignity. The rise of the influence of oppressed castes in the politics of the country has been rightly termed as 'India's silent revolution'.[31]

5

Shaping the Language of Rights

Since submissions before the Southborough Committee did not lead to the desired results, Dr Ambedkar spent the next few years shaping the sociopolitical discourse through public engagement and mass action. At the same time in 1920, he decided to finish his studies at the London School of Economics to highlight the situation of public finance in British India.[1] Through his efforts, Dr Ambedkar was trying to achieve two aims: first, to awaken the conscience of the Depressed Classes, and second, to place their concerns before the British authorities and within the national discourse.

Dr Ambedkar used the language of rights to situate the concerns of the Depressed Classes. This approach was significantly different from that of the other leaders, who saw the situation of the Depressed Classes as an issue of social reform, which they distinguished from political demands. For instance, no Congress president had discussed the issue of social reforms for around two decades.[2] It must be noted that by the 1920s, Gandhi was handed over the command of the Indian National Congress, and was advocating against untouchability as a reform measure within Hindu society. However, Dr Ambedkar's approach was different owing to his rights-based approach. Eventually, by the end of the 1930s, we can observe a conflict in the ideas and approaches of Dr Ambedkar and Gandhi.

In the meantime, Dr Ambedkar received tremendous support from the Maharaja of Kolhapur, Shahuji Maharaj. He was a Maratha ruler, who was inspired by Jyotiba Phule. Shahuji Maharaj was dedicated to the advancement of the Depressed Classes. He tried to help the members of the Untouchable community in whatever way he could. His key focus was on providing Untouchable students with free education and representation in jobs.[3] In 1919, Dr Ambedkar, through a common contact, came in touch with Shahuji Maharaj. Dr Ambedkar convinced him to provide financial support for starting a fortnightly publication, which would highlight the concerns of the Depressed Classes. The publication was titled *Mooknayak*. The first issue of *Mooknayak* came out on 31 January 1920. The title of the publication seems to be inspired by Bhakti poet, Tukaram. The following quatrain (translated into English here) was printed below the title:

> 'What would I do by harbouring wishes?
> Why should I needlessly blow my trumpet?
> The world does not hear the voice of the dumb (voiceless).
> There is no respect for them; their interests are of no importance.'[4]

It must be noted that the Bhakti saints of medieval history, who challenged the caste-based hierarchy of Hindu society, can be considered some of the historical proponents of equality. For instance, another Bhakti saint, Ravidas, envisaged a place called 'Begumpura', where there would not be any sorrow.[5] Ravidas wrote:

> 'The regal realm with the sorrowless name
> they call it Begumpura city, a place with no pain,

no taxes or cares, none owns property there,
no wrongdoing, worry, terror, or torture.
Oh my brother, I've come to take it as my own,
my distant home, where everything is right . . .
They do this or that, they walk where they wish,
they stroll through fabled palaces unchallenged.
Oh, says Ravidas, a tanner now set free,
those who walk beside me are my friends.'

As Ravidas said, those who walk beside me in Begumpura are my friends. This was contrary to the caste system, which did not allow the Untouchables to even walk near the oppressor castes.

Dr Ambedkar's vision behind launching *Mooknayak* was to give voice to the 'voiceless' Untouchables. In the first issue of *Mooknayak,* Dr Ambedkar wrote:

> There is no better source than the newspaper to suggest remedies against the injustice that is being done to our people at present and will be done in future, and also to discuss the ways and means for our progress in future. If we throw even a cursory glance at the newspapers that are published in Bombay Presidency it will be found that many among these papers take care in protecting the interest only of some (oppressor) castes. And these have no interest in caring for the interest of other castes.[6]

One incident that occurred at the time of the launch of *Mooknayak* shows how the voice of the Depressed Classes was neglected by the nationalist leaders. It was a tradition that established newspapers would share an announcement about the launch of a new publication. However, *Kesari* newspaper, which was founded and edited by Bal Gangadhar Tilak, refused to publish a simple announcement about the launch of

Mooknayak. Even when a fee was offered, *Kesari* did not agree. Tilak was alive at that time.[7]

The publication 'laid the foundations of a mass churning that aspired for democratic values'.[8] If one reads the editorials published in *Mooknayak,* it can be seen that Dr Ambedkar was trying to chart a course for the work that he intended to do. In the first editorial, he highlighted the 'glaring inequality' of Indian society.[9] He stated,

> Hindu society is just like a tower which has several storeys without a ladder or entrance. The man who is born in the lower storey cannot enter the upper storey however worthy he may be and the man who is born in the upper storey cannot be driven out into the lower storey however unworthy he may be.

Dr Ambedkar highlighted how historical and systemic privileges benefit the oppressor castes and increase inequalities. He noted,

> ... the feelings of inequality among the castes are not based on the merit or demerit of individuals. The man born in a high caste, however unmeritorious he may be, is always regarded as high whereas the man born in a low caste, however meritorious he may be, must always remain low ... Some castes are regarded as untouchables which means that their touch pollutes other castes. Because of this notion of pollution the untouchables rarely come in contact with other castes ... Brahmins who are the highest in social grade feel that they are gods on earth. Therefore, this inequality is advantageous to these gods on earth who think that all other castes are born only to serve them. Therefore, by their self-created privileges they are enjoying the fruits of their social position exacting the services of all other castes.

Dr Ambedkar also highlighted how the oppressor castes 'taking advantage of their easy access to the British Government in India misrepresent the case of the untouchables to the Government'.

He used the platform of *Mooknayak* to challenge the notion of Swaraj (self-rule) advanced by Tilak and Gandhi and reconceptualized it in terms of a broader rights-based framework. In one editorial, he argued that if the concept of Swaraj did not have fundamental rights for the Depressed Classes, it would not mean Swaraj to them. For the Depressed Classes, it would be 'a new slavery'.[10] Dr Ambedkar posed pertinent questions to the proponents of Swaraj. These questions have been summarized as follows: 'Swaraj for whom? Would Swaraj also be for the ostracized and the Untouchables? Would it usher in freedom for them, too? Or would Swaraj only mean freedom for the oppressor castes who had been committing atrocities against the Untouchables for ages?'[11] He asked a direct question to the nationalist leaders: 'What have you done for paving the way for the development of the personalities of the six crore ostracized people (population of Untouchables at that time)?'

He thus argued that 'for the realization of genuine Swaraj (self-rule) the untouchables must have a share in the country's political power through their independently (separately) chosen representatives'. He highlighted the demands of the Untouchables:

> Therefore, the Untouchables have complained to the government over the stand taken by the upper caste Hindus who in their stand have opposed the demand made by the untouchable communities. The untouchables have now understood the tactics of caste Hindus who by gaining political power, it is likely, would use that power

to perpetuate the social inequality. This agitation of the untouchables against the design of the caste Hindus is a sign of growing awakening among the untouchables.'

In another editorial, Dr Ambedkar stated that it was not enough for India to be an independent country. Rather, it must be a good state, guaranteeing equal status in all matters—religious, social, economic and political—to all classes. It must offer every person 'an opportunity to rise in the scale of life and creating conditions favourable to his advancement'.[12] Dr Ambedkar further argued that if the Brahmins were justified in their opposition to the unjust power of the British government, then the Depressed Classes were justified a hundred times more so in their opposition to the rule of the Brahmins, who had historically ruled for thousands of years.

It is important to highlight that none of the editorials written by Dr Ambedkar on the issue of Swaraj opposed the demand for freedom from British rule. Rather, he focused on imagining a broader conception of Swaraj, which not only meant freedom from colonial rule, but also freedom from the rule of the social oppressor communities over the marginalized communities.

Mooknayak was published in Marathi, but it became a platform for Untouchables across India to directly share their concerns and experiences. The newspaper included a regular section of open letters, sent by individuals from the Untouchable community, drawing attention to their cases of caste oppression and violence.[13] These letters shaped the collective emotions of the Untouchable community. It was probably the first time that common Untouchables could even share and complain about their grievances. At the same time, it documented everyday caste violence and discrimination perpetrated by the oppressor castes. Furthermore, the popularity of the newspaper could be understood from the fact that those who could not read would ask others to read it aloud to them.[14]

As Dr Ambedkar was a professor in a government college, he did not hold an official position at *Mooknayak*. But all the management, editing and selection of articles for publication was managed by him for the first six months. Pandhurang Nandram Bhatkar—an activist based in Bombay—was the first official editor of *Mooknayak*. In July 1920, D.D. Gholap replaced Bhatkar as the editor. Gholap was the first nominated member from the Untouchable community to find a place in the Bombay Legislative Council during 1920–23.

From 1920, Dr Ambedkar also started participating in public meetings and conferences. *Mooknayak* documented the proceedings of two conferences of the Depressed Classes which happened in Mangao and Nagpur in 1920.[15] Dr Ambedkar presided over the first conference organized on 21 March 1920 at Mangao in Kolhapur state. In his speech, he highlighted how the caste system and untouchability excluded the Untouchables and deprived them of even basic rights. He stated:

> [People] considered lower and impure by virtue of birth are known as depressed classes. According to the Hindu religion, we are not entitled to any rights in social life. We cannot go to schools. We cannot draw water from the common wells. We cannot walk on roads. We cannot use vehicles. Thus, we are prohibited from exercising our human rights.[16]

Dr Ambedkar then explained how the deprival of rights led to material losses for the Untouchables, by stating that:

> On account of the incapacity and impurity by birth, we have faced tremendous losses economically. Business, services and agriculture, which are three prime sources of earning, are not open to us. The curse of untouchability takes away all the

customers and thus running a business is almost impossible. Being untouchables, we do not get jobs and sometimes, in spite of being highly talented, people do not work under us because of our caste. Such feelings have resulted in a decrease in our numbers in the military service. Same goes with agriculture. We simply do not possess pieces of fertile land. A society with such defects would never progress.[17]

Dr Ambedkar linked the issue of exclusion with the need to have strong political representation. He argued:

Natural abilities and favourable environment are the two primary reasons for progress . . . There is indeed no shortage of talent in the depressed classes. The sole reason causing a hindrance in their progress is the unhealthy social environment. Numerous solutions for improving our state are offered time and again. But in order to progress, we must empower ourselves politically and for that we need a political representation based on caste. The principle 'truth alone prevails' is a hollow one. For the truth to win, we must continue to agitate.[18]

Dr Ambedkar also attended the first All India Conference convened by Untouchables in Nagpur in May 1920. Here, he publicly opposed the statement submitted by an organization called the Depressed Classes Mission, which was founded and headed by Vithal Ramji Shinde, a leader from the Maratha community working in the area of social reform. The Depressed Classes Mission had submitted to the then Government of Bombay Province that the representatives of the Untouchables should not be selected from the Depressed Classes, but must be selected from the members of the existing Legislative Council (which did not have members from Depressed Classes).[19] It was Dr Ambedkar's core belief that the Untouchables should represent themselves by having a share in the legislature. The Conference extended its unanimous support to Dr Ambedkar.

In July 1920, Dr Ambedkar left for London to resume his studies at both the London School of Economics and at Gray's Inn. While he was focusing on his studies, he would regret not being able to contribute directly to *Mooknayak*. In one of the letters he sent home, he shared (as his biographer Dhananjay Keer noted) that 'it is very painful for the foundation of a newspaper to break away from it'.[20]

On 28 June 1922, Dr Ambedkar was called to the Bar.[21] As Steven Gasztowicz KC, a lawyer based in the UK and a contributor to an edited book on Dr Ambedkar's time in London, notes: 'This would have been a moment of great pride for Ambedkar . . . this achievement should also be seen in the context of other social barriers to legal training at [that] time.'[22] Gasztowicz also speaks about the importance of Dr Ambedkar's law degree, as he states:

> What was different about Ambedkar, however, was that unlike most of his Indian lawyer-politician contemporaries, or British equivalents, he came from a low-caste family unexperienced in legal or governmental matters, with no capital behind him. This was in sharp contrast to others— most famously, Gandhi, Jinnah and Nehru . . . In contrast, Ambedkar, with no contacts, took a brave decision to train as a lawyer, obtaining his own funding and employment to finally achieve this, with it being speculative as to whether he would actually succeed in a legal or similar career.[23]

Regarding Dr Ambedkar's doctorate at LSE, the critical analysis of the British regime in his thesis 'The Problem of the Rupee' had offended the imperialist examiners.[24] The file on Dr Ambedkar at LSE notes that '[the thesis] was revolutionary in character for that period of time', and he was asked to rewrite it.[25] As Dr Ambedkar was short of funds, he returned to Bombay in April 1923, and spent the next few months revising his thesis. At the same time, he registered at the Bar to start his legal practice in Bombay. In June 1923, he borrowed money from his close friend, Naval Bhatena, to apply for a *sanad* (license provided by the Bar Council.)[26] Law practice was difficult for him in the early years. As Dr Savita Ambedkar noted: 'Doctor Saheb began practising in July 1923 as a lawyer at the Bombay High Court. But even there, the stigma of being an untouchable prevented him from getting sufficient response. Touchable solicitors would not allow him to come close to them as he was a Mahar barrister; nor would he get touchable clients. As a result, Barrister Ambedkar was compelled to accept whatever cases he could manage to get in the suburban and/or district courts.'[27]

Unfortunately, before Dr Ambedkar arrived back in India, *Mooknayak* was shut down in his absence. The newspaper faced several challenges in the areas of funding and management, after Dr Ambedkar's departure for London.[28] Though he tried to restart the newspaper with a new name *Abhinav Mooknayak*, it could not be sustained due to the lack of finance.[29]

Interestingly, Gholap, as a member of the Bombay Legislative Council, moved a resolution recommending that the Bombay government make primary education compulsory so that the Depressed Classes might be able to avail of it.[30] An important resolution (4 August 1923), touching upon the rights of the Untouchables, was moved by S.K. Bole, a social reformer from the Bhandari community and a member of the non-Brahmin party in Maharashtra.[31] Bole later became a key associate of Dr Ambedkar.[32] Bole resolution's noted: 'We resent the segregation policy of the South African colonies and therefore we must set our house in order. It is in our interests and in the interests of the country that the Depressed Classes

should be given better treatment.'[33] The resolution provided
that 'the council recommends that the untouchable classes be
allowed to use all public watering places, in dharamshalas which
are built and maintained out of public funds administered by
parties appointed by government or created by statute, as well
as public schools, courts, offices and dispensaries'.[34] Following
the resolution, the Bombay government issued a direction to
the heads of all the departments on 11 September 1923 to give
effect to the resolution so far as it related to public places and
editions, belonging to and maintained by the government.[35]

The developments in the Bombay Legislative Council
were not in isolation. Anti-caste movements were emerging
in different parts of the country in the 1920s. Some of these
were influenced by previous social movements such as the
Satyashodhak Samaj started by Jyotiba Phule in 1873.[36] Bharat
Patankar and Gail Omvedt, activists and scholars of the Dalit
movement, note:

> The most important of the early Dalit movements were the
> Ad-Dharm movement in the Punjab (organized 1926); . . .
> the Namashudra movement in Bengal; the Adi-Dravida
> movement in Tamil Nadu; the Adi-Andhra movement
> in Andhra which had its first conference in 1917; the Adi-
> Karnataka movement; the Adi-Hindu movement mainly
> centred around Kanpur in UP; and the organizing of the
> Pulayas and Cherumans in Kerala.[37]

The Justice Party, which emerged out of non-Brahmin
politics and formed the government in the Madras Presidency
(1920–23), passed a government order, providing for fixed
quotas for all castes and communities in educational institutions
and public employment. (As noted in the last chapter, quotas
or job reservations for the Backward Classes were previously

started by Shahuji Maharaj in Kolhapur in 1902.) Dr Ambedkar was a keen observer of these developments.[38]

By the end of 1923, Dr Ambedkar had finished all his academic engagements. After sending back his revised thesis, he was awarded a doctorate in economics from LSE, thereby becoming the first Indian to do so.[39] In December 1923, he published his thesis as a book. At that time, Dr Ambedkar was the only Indian with so many foreign degrees. This brought him generous offers. For instance, he was offered the position of district judge in 1923 with a promise of promotion to the High Court in three years.[40] However, he refused the offer saying:

> I was living in a single room in [a] chawl built for very poor people. Still, I refused this offer only because acceptance of that job, though very highly paid and which would have ensured my financial well-being during my lifetime, would have naturally obstructed me in the fulfilment of my life's aim to work for the well-being and uplift of my fellow brethren.[41]

He was now focused on strategizing for his plan of social action. In March 1924, Dr Ambedkar worked to launch a social movement for the Untouchables.[42] A meeting on 9 March 1924 was convened by him in Bombay to delve into the need for establishing an organization for the advancement of the Untouchables and placing their grievances before the government.[43] Thus, the foundations of the 'Bahishkrit Hitkarini Sabha' were laid down. It must be noted that Dr Ambedkar had spent a good amount of time in New York, where a similar organization called the National Association for the Advancement of Colored People (NAACP) was founded in 1909 to advance the cause of justice for African Americans. His professors at Columbia, Seligman and Dewey, were co-founders of NAACP.[44] Dr Ambedkar would often make references to American slavery to highlight the grave impact of untouchability. For instance, in a speech on 24 May 1924, he stated:[45]

> Untouchability is in fact worse than slavery. History is replete with examples wherein slaves were liberated and then became independent citizens of the State. But there is not a single example in India, where Untouchables became Touchable.[46]

In the same speech, Dr Ambedkar also emphasized the need for Indian independence. He criticized the British government's complicity in maintaining caste-based customs to the disadvantage of the oppressed castes (as mentioned in Chapter 2). He stated:

> [Independence] will be the historic day when all these transformations will really take place. But the big question is how to make this transition actually happen. Sometimes amelioration of social injustice takes place only under the initiative of the governments. The British government had decided not to interfere in the caste system and customs. In this context, a welcome development is the possibility of attaining independence for our country.[47]

He explained to his people that Indian independence would not mean the return of Peshwa rule. The reference to Peshwa rule was to highlight the injustices done to the Untouchables under the Peshwa rule before the British East India Company took over. He later explained these injustices as:

> Under the rule of the Peshwas in the Maratha country, the untouchable was not allowed to use the public streets if a Hindu was coming along, lest he should pollute the Hindu

by his shadow. The untouchable was required to have a black thread either on his wrist or around his neck, as a sign or a mark to prevent the Hindus from getting themselves polluted by his touch by mistake. In Poona, the capital of the Peshwas, the untouchable was required to carry, strung from his waist, a broom to sweep away from behind himself the dust he trod on, lest a Hindu walking on the same dust should be polluted. In Poona, the untouchable was required to carry an earthen pot hung around his neck wherever he went—for holding his spit, lest his spit falling on the earth should pollute a Hindu who might unknowingly happen to tread on it.[48]

To build the confidence of the oppressed castes in the goal of Indian independence, he noted:

> Our people are somehow afraid of independence, and they feel Peshwa rule will return after independence. It must be remembered that there is a big difference. Peshwas did not rule with the consent of the people, they ruled by hereditary regimes. It wasn't people's rule. In future, no State will rule without the consent of the people. Swaraj with the consent of people at large is the best possible political system. I am rather surprised that our people are apprehensive about such a rule. We must clearly understand what Swaraj, that is, independence, portends.

He, however, added a rider—that independence ought to recognize equal rights for everyone. Interestingly, his emphasis was on the right to vote—a right he had highlighted before the Southborough Committee, and would consistently demand in the future as well. He said:

> We must pursue this issue. If independence is attained, then we must get equal rights as everyone else, and to achieve that we must secure the right to vote. Today, the right to vote is

so limited that only two per cent of people are qualified to vote. Securing the right to vote will help us in two ways. One, the Legislative Council will no longer ignore our plight. Those people who get elected because of our votes, will not be able to overlook our interests. Moreover, it will no longer be possible to maintain the Varnashram Dharma. If a Brahmin has to beg for votes from Untouchables, what would remain of the Varnashram Dharma? It will also be a great assault on the caste system. We must accept this course to begin with.[49]

This speech shows that Dr Ambedkar's agenda was clear— to reimagine the meaning of independence in terms of social equality. This was his attempt to shape the nationalist discourse in terms of equal rights for everyone.

Bahishkrit Hitakarini Sabha was officially registered on 20 July 1924. Dr Ambedkar became the chairman of its Managing Committee. The motto of the organization was empowering: 'Educate, Organise, and Agitate'.[50] The organization aimed to promote the spread of education among the Depressed Classes by opening hostels, to spread the culture of education among them by opening libraries, social centres, classes and study circles, to advance the material conditions of the Depressed Classes, and to highlight their grievances before the government. The organization started gaining mass support by organizing various meetings and conferences under its banner. Dr Ambedkar would address these meetings, where he focused on the self-respect and political awareness needed among the Depressed Classes.[51]

Dr Ambedkar was also trying to shape the language of rights through his legal practice. One such instance was in 1926. Dr Ambedkar defended a writer from the Maratha community, Keshav Jedhe, who had written a book in Marathi titled *Deshache Dushman* (Country's Enemies). In the book, Jedhe criticized Brahminism and described Bal Gangadhar Tilak and Vishnushastri Chiplunkar as the 'enemies of the nation' for their defence of Brahmin privileges. The book was banned, and a local Brahmin leader filed defamation charges against Jedhe.[52] As the colonial courts respected caste-based customs, there was a certainty that they would not rule in favour of the defendant. Dr Ambedkar devised a strategy to deal with the issue by highlighting two points: first, since the two defamed persons were dead, the complainant had no basis for filing, and second, the book was not an attack on individuals but on the Brahmin community.[53] Thus, he advanced the discourse on the democratization of cultural ideas, while questioning the legal standing of the colonial judiciary rooted in caste-based customs.[54]

In 1927, Dr Ambedkar was nominated to the Bombay Legislative Council. He used the platform to promote issues of social welfare, civil rights and social security. This will be elaborated upon in a subsequent chapter.

6

The Mahad Satyagraha—
First Walk to Freedom

Dr Ambedkar's focus on equal access to public facilities such as water bodies was seen in the Mahad struggle. This movement can be termed as the 'first walk to freedom',[1] as thousands of oppressed Untouchables walked several kilometres, under the leadership of Dr Ambedkar, to demand their basic right: access to water. Dr Ambedkar led the Mahad struggle to broaden the constitutional imagination of rights.

As mentioned in the previous chapter, the segregation of oppressed castes was manifold. Dr Ambedkar had once described the segregations as follows:

> In every village the Touchables have a code which the Untouchables are required to follow. This code lays down the acts of omissions and commissions which the Touchables treat as offences. The following is the list of such offences:
> 1. The Untouchables must live in separate quarters away from the habitation of the Hindus. It is an offence for the Untouchables to break or evade the rule of segregation.
> 2. The quarters of the Untouchables must be located towards the South, since the South is the most inauspicious of the four directions. A breach of this rule shall be deemed

to be an offence. 3. The Untouchable must observe the rule of distance pollution or shadow of pollution as the case may be. It is an offence to break the rule . . . [and many similar exclusionary conditions].'[2]

The Untouchables were also prohibited from drawing water from any source that was used by oppressor castes. Such practices continue in some places even to this day.[3]

The Mahad Municipality passed a resolution to open the Chavdar tank for the Untouchables, following a direction from the Bombay government consequent to the Bole resolution.[4] The hypocrisy of the oppressor castes could be understood from the fact that the use of the tank was permitted for people of other religions such as Muslims and Christians, but not for the Untouchables. The Municipality's resolution remained on paper, as the Untouchables could not draw water from the Chavdar tank due to aggressive opposition from the oppressor castes in the area.

Dr Ambedkar deemed access to public places and water resources a civil right. Initially, when he was approached by Sambhaji Tukaram Gaikwad and R.B. More, organizing leaders of the Depressed Classes of the region, about organizing a conference in Mahad to implement the Bole resolution, Dr Ambedkar sent his colleagues to 'assess the readiness of the people for action'.[5] Thereafter, the Kolaba District Depressed Classes, in coordination with Dr Ambedkar and Bahishkrit Hitakarini Sabha, decided to hold a conference in Mahad on 19–20 March 1927.[6] The call given by the leaders led to a gathering of ten thousand delegates, workers and leaders of the Depressed Classes from different districts of present-day Maharashtra and Gujarat who attended the conference. The crowd, ranging in age from fifteen to seventy, had travelled hundreds of kilometres to reach Mahad. The marchers constituted men, women and children. Women carried their babies in their arms and men carried children on their backs as they marched to their destination.[7]

On the first day, Dr Ambedkar explained how British rule had been detrimental to the Untouchables. Besides the colonial courts that followed caste-based customs in matters of social conduct, the British had also banned Untouchables from the military following pressure from the oppressor castes, who were unwilling to serve under senior officers from the Untouchable community. Dr Ambedkar pointed out how this was an act of discrimination: 'It is greatly unjust to ban any member of public from getting [a] government job. It is unjust politically, morally and also economically. Banning Untouchables from army recruitments is not only discriminatory, it is also a breach of trust and unfriendly.'[8]

Dr Ambedkar then emphasized why the Untouchables had to oppose the British government. The principle of resistance underlined by him remains relevant for any government operation. He stated:

Gentlemen, it is my opinion that the Government always neglects us because we are cooperative. We accept whatever Government offers; we do whatever we are told to do; we live in whatever conditions we are kept. This very nature of servitude is a cause of our neglect by the Government. We meekly tolerate all kinds of injustice. If somebody slaps us on one cheek, we offer another instead of raising our hand in defence. We blame our fate for all kinds of problems. Sooner we discard this suicidal attitude, the better. We must try to the best of our ability to remove the ban on our recruitment in the army.[9]

Dr Ambedkar appealed to the Untouchables to 'not let this fire of awakening douse'.[10]

On the first day (i.e., 19 March), several important resolutions were passed by the conference. These were:

> By one resolution the Conference appealed to the Caste Hindus to help the Untouchables secure their civic rights, to employ them in services, offer food to Untouchable students, and bury their dead animals themselves. Lastly, it appealed to [the] Government to prohibit the Untouchables by special laws from eating carrion, enforce prohibition, provide them with free and compulsory primary education, give aid to the Depressed Classes hostels and make the Bole Resolution a living reality by enjoining upon the local bodies, if necessary, to proclaim section 144 of [the] Indian Criminal Procedure Code at their places, for its enforcement.[11]

On the next day (20 March 1927), it was decided at the conference to march towards the Chavdar tank and draw water. Dr Ambedkar led the peaceful procession. As he bent forward and drew water from the tank, the crowd of thousands followed him to exercise their right.

The procession walked back peacefully to the place of their gathering. However, a couple of hours later, the peaceful gathering was attacked by a large crowd of people from the oppressor castes, who came with sticks and stones to hit the protestors. Dr Ambedkar controlled the group of protestors, who clearly outnumbered the attackers. As Dr Ambedkar's biographer Keer noted:

> A word of provocation from Dr. Ambedkar would have turned Mahad into a pool of blood and destruction. The number of delegates still lingering in the town, in the pandal and in the Bungalow together could have easily outnumbered the hooligans and battered down their skulls. Hundreds among the Untouchables were men who had

seen, fought and moved actively in the theatres and battles of the First World War. But discipline was wonderfully maintained at the behest of their leader. They set their faces against the aggressors. Their struggle was non-violent and constitutional. They did not dream of breaking the law. Thus, a more serious riot was averted. At nightfall all the delegates left for their respective villages.[12]

The incident of the attack showed that the Depressed Classes maintained self-restraint, despite violent provocation from the oppressor castes. It also demonstrated that the oppressor castes were not willing to allow the Depressed Classes to enjoy such basic civic rights as taking water from public water bodies.[13]

The Mahad Satyagraha was not a simple act of protest. It was the first collective attempt to demonstrate their right to equal access and equality, which had been denied to them for thousands of years. It was also one of the earliest non-violent movements for equality led by oppressed groups in any part of the world. As Gail Omvedt noted: 'The Mahad Satyagraha was in many ways the determinate and founding event of the Dalit liberation struggle. It began as a struggle for rights, the legally endorsed right to use public facilities.'[14] The historic attention that should have been given to the Mahad Satyagraha has largely been lacking. While history books are full of the Mahatma Gandhi-led Dandi March against the British Salt Tax, the same has not happened for the Mahad Satyagraha. The act of resilience in Mahad was deeper and more impactful. It ought to be counted on the same lines as the Montgomery bus boycott in 1955 in the US, which was a sociopolitical protest against the policy of racial segregation on the public transit system. In Montgomery, Alabama, Rosa Parks, an African American woman, was arrested for refusing to vacate her seat for a White person. The consequent litigation led to a

US Supreme Court decision declaring segregation on public buses as unconstitutional.[15]

However, the newspapers run by the oppressor castes criticized Dr Ambedkar's movement and dismissed the incidents of violence at Mahad. One newspaper reported that the news about the incidence of violence against the Depressed Classes was untrue.[16] To counter these claims, Dr Ambedkar started a new mouthpiece on 3 April 1927 in Marathi and called it *Bahishkrit Bharat* (Ostracized India). As biographer Ashok Gopal notes: 'The inaugural issue of *Bahishkrit Bharat* was mainly about the first Mahad conference held on 19–20 March 1927, and work on the issue commenced immediately after the event.'[17]

The Mahad Satyagraha had a tremendous impact on the psyche of the Untouchables. As Dhananjay Keer puts it,

> The struggle inaugurated by their educated leaders gripped their minds and enkindled the flame of self-respect and self-elevation. They now smarted under the insults and humiliations inflicted upon them at Mahad. They applied their minds to self-improvement and self-culture as never before. As a result of this Conference, the Untouchables gave up eating carrion, skinning carcasses, and stopped begging for crumbs.[18]

Anand Teltumbde, contemporary writer and activist says,

> The Mahad conference created a wave of awakening among the Untouchables and lent them strength and confidence to work for their emancipation. The notions of inferiority instilled in them by the Hindu religious scriptures, which had shackled their existence for millennia suddenly began cracking, freeing their self-confidence. [Dr Ambedkar] was

extremely happy. He felt that the Untouchables, if they won the war against the decadent custom of caste, could claim veritable credit for freeing all Hindus from the bondage of irrationality of their religion. In order to reach this goal he felt that the Untouchables should keep the torch of struggle for their civil rights burning.[19]

To plan the future course of action, Dr Ambedkar wrote three articles in *Bahishkrit Bharat*. These articles were 'Crusade of Mahad and the Responsibilities of the Touchables' (22 April 1927), 'Crusade of Mahad and the Responsibilities of the Government' (6 May 1927), and 'Crusade of Mahad and the Responsibilities of the Untouchables' (20 May 1927).[20]

In the first article addressed to the oppressor castes, he gave the examples of Western countries, to explain how they had violated the principle of equality. He said:

In Western countries, social equality is a well-entrenched principle. By instituting rights to vote, they have even established political equality, which has abolished the notion that someone is ruling over us without our consent . . . Following social and political equality, they have rather began to discuss why there should be inequality in the economic sphere . . . In light of this, the question naturally arises what the elite have done in Mahad. We feel that the elite should have made efforts to remove accusations of hypocrisy levelled against Hindus on account of their mouthing that all humans are forms of god, but treating some of them as impure, just because they are born in a particular caste . . . The elite have committed a heinous crime thereby, by approving the orthodox notion that Untouchables are impure and contact with them pollutes. There is no doubt that the people who did and supported this purification function have insulted the Untouchables. It also leads to the question as to why a legal action should not be taken against them.[21]

He reiterated that his movement at Mahad was towards equality. He stated:

We do not feel bad at all for the Untouchables having got wounded in the Mahad riots. If we feel bad, it is because the Untouchables have lost an opportunity there. If they had decided, it was a great opportunity to teach the attackers a lesson. But we never looked at this issue as a riot. We consider it as the first battle in the war for establishing equality.[22]

In the second article addressed to the British government, Dr Ambedkar presented the case of the Untouchables, arguing that they have civil rights and that they have done nothing wrong by taking water from the tank in Mahad. He invoked the conceptions of human rights and natural rights to make his point, i.e., everyone has certain inherent rights, which cannot be taken away. He noted:

The custom of untouchability is not lawful. This custom has neither granted any rights to the touchable community against the untouchable community nor has it abolished any rights of the untouchables. Human rights in public life cannot be established by issuing an ordinance by someone. It is inherent in every human being. Just because it was not used or there was a gap in its usage, it does not cease to exist. It is as foolish to forbid a person from using a water source just because he had not used before, as it is to say that a person cannot walk on a particular road because he had not done it before.[23]

Dr Ambedkar argued that it was the duty of the government to
protect the law and rights, and gave an interesting suggestion:
'. . . the government will also have to obtain surety from the
orthodox leaders. This is very important. Because, it is usually
experienced that some orthodox elements incite gullible people
in the society by exploiting their religious sentiments and keep
themselves aloof.'[24] However, Dr Ambedkar was sceptical
about the British government's approach, as he remarked: 'We
have little doubt about whether the government will accept
our suggestion and implement it without delay. Although our
British government is not reactionary, it is extremely slow. It
has developed an attitude of marking time instead of marching
on. And when a social issue is involved, it invariably gets
paralytic.'[25] Dr Ambedkar also expressed surprise that instead
of implementing the Bole resolution by itself, the government
had delegated it to the local boards and municipalities, which
were not implementing it.[26]

In his third article addressed to the Untouchables,
Dr Ambedkar highlighted that the Untouchables had to mark
their opposition to the unjust caste system. He wrote: 'The
importance of the Mahad conference precisely lies in the fact
that it communicated the objection of the untouchables to
being treated as such.'[27] He appealed that the Untouchables
ought to start taking similar actions everywhere as they did
in Mahad. He believed: 'Things will not happen without such
resistance. Otherwise the thoughtless touchable people will
not be pushed to think about the custom of untouchability
whether it is good or bad.'[28] However, he was also conscious
of the reaction from the oppressor castes, who would try to
safeguard their interests. He thus noted:

There is a big difference between bringing about change
in public opinion and in the behaviour of powerful
people. Where there is no connection between opinion

and self-interest, the change in the former can be brought about through peaceful means like debates, discussions, negotiations, etc. But where such connection exists, the change in opinion cannot be brought about merely through amicable means, without denting self-interest.

He thus highlighted that the Untouchables need to struggle to make their voices heard and change the social narrative. It was his message that:

> It is true that the option of resistance that we suggested is difficult. We also know that when you resist there will be response from the Touchables too. That does not mean the Untouchables should get scared of that. They should rather be prepared to fight back if they attack. It will not work without that. The Untouchables have to show their prowess. If they abide by this advice, they can be rest assured about the success of the option we suggested.[29]

Dr Ambedkar's point about the reaction from the oppressor castes was true. Even after attacking the gathering of Untouchables in Mahad, the caste hatred among the oppressor castes against the Untouchables was so great that a meeting was called to consider the question of the purification of the tank, which according to them had been defiled by the touch of the Untouchables. They then performed a purification drive by chanting, while taking out the water from the tank in one hundred and eight pots.[30] This was done to demoralize the Depressed Classes and show them their place. This raised a new issue for Dr Ambedkar. If the Mahad Satyagraha had been left at that moment, 'it might have been misconstrued as a failure and demoralized the Untouchables, neutralizing the gains from the Conference'.[31] Dr Ambedkar therefore decided to launch another Satyagraha on a larger scale to show the consistent resilience of the Untouchables to exercise their rights. It was a struggle for the vindication of his people's rights.

Dr Ambedkar decided to launch the struggle under the aegis of the Bahishkrit Hitakarini Sabha. Through an announcement in *Bahishkrit Bharat* on 26 June 1927, Dr Ambedkar called on the Depressed Classes to do two things: first, extinguish the stigma of pollution attached to them by the caste Hindus of Mahad, who had purified the Chavdar tank, and, second, denounce the act of assaults committed by the oppressor castes on their representatives for having taken water from the Chavdar tank. The announcement also required the interested members of the Depressed Classes to register themselves at the office of the Bahishkrit Hitakarini Sabha in Bombay.[32]

The Sabha then convened a public meeting in Mumbai on 3 July 1927, where Dr Ambedkar announced his intention to conduct a Satyagraha in Mahad. This announcement was widely publicized in *Bahishkrit Bharat* (15 July 1927).[33] Dr Ambedkar also made efforts to unite all Untouchable castes within the nomenclature of 'Depressed Classes'. In a public gathering in Pune on 20 July 1927, he emphasized that he was working for all Untouchables. He gave an example in support of his stand:

> The critics also say that all the benefits of the government schemes are being grabbed by Mahars. Mr. Nikalje of Mahar Caste was nominated for Mumbai Corporation. But when I found that he is unable to perform to my satisfaction, I did not hesitate to nominate Mr. P. Balu, who is a famous cricketer belonging to Chamar [c]ommunity.[34]

Under pressure from the oppressor castes, the Mahad Municipality on 4 August 1927 withheld its previous resolution of 1924 under which it had declared the Chavdar tank open to the Depressed Classes.[35] This was done to prevent the agitation

announced by Dr Ambedkar, by taking away the legal basis of
his demand for access to the Tank. Dr Ambedkar then decided
to continue with the struggle. In *Bahishkrit Bharat* on 12 August
1927, Dr Ambedkar noted:

> The khadi-wearing elitist lot wanted to escape the
> responsibility of the assault at Mahad by blaming it on
> the illiterate people of the touchable castes. But this
> resolution tears off their mask and exposes their true colour
> to the world. Needless to say, if they had been conscious
> of the lawful rights of the excluded and if the attack of
> the illiterate goons on the Untouchables had been really
> unacceptable to them, they would not have indulged in the
> intrigue of retracting the previous resolution.[36]

Consequently, a meeting of a thousand Untouchables was
held under the presidency of Dr Ambedkar on October 30,
where he explained the incidents at Mahad. A resolution
was then passed to hold a conference at Mahad on 25 and
26 December with the objective of asserting their right to
use water from a public tank and to agitate (Satyagraha)
if they were not allowed to exercise their right.[37] As the
fervour around the Mahad Satyagraha grew, some activists
from the Untouchable community proposed parallel temple-
entry movements.[38] One such suggestion was regarding the
Ambadevi Temple at Amravati (in present-day Maharashtra).[39]
The 30 October meeting also included a decision to launch a
temple entry campaign at Amravati temple in the middle of
November 1927.[40]

A conference was then organized on 13 November 1927
in Amravati, at which Dr Ambedkar gave the presidential
address, highlighting the importance of the method of
satyagraha for equal rights. Dr Ambedkar connected the rights
of the Untouchables with the conception of nation-building.

He spoke: 'If Untouchables come out of that stigma and participate in nation-building, they will only contribute to the progress of the nation. Therefore, this movement for removal of Untouchability is in true sense a movement for nation-building and fraternity.'[41]

He asserted that the issue of temple entry or access to public resources is an issue of equality. He stated:

> Another argument these Touchables give is that even if they do not allow the Untouchables into their temples, all are free to build a temple for themselves. I would like to ask those so-called learned ones why they object to Railways for having separate coaches for Whites and Indians? . . . There is only one answer to this and that is: it is not a matter of travel only, it is a matter of equality! . . . The Untouchables have the same reason for demanding the right to worship God in the same temple. They want to prove that the temple is not defiled by their entry . . . The Untouchables are not servants . . . On the basis of this alone they should accept the rights of the Untouchables. And when there are rights there is no question of custom of usage.[42]

He further added that public property cannot be used as the private property of the oppressor castes. He noted:

> Legally, the right to public property is not required to be established by any deed; it is available automatically to everybody. Even if he has no usage or it was not continuous, it does not deprive him of that right. Suppose, somebody did not walk on a particular road, does that mean he can never use that road? Therefore, it would be quite idiotic to say that since Untouchables never went to the temple or never drew water from the public wells, so now they cannot do that.[43]

Dr Ambedkar also dismissed the contention of the oppressor castes that the Untouchables should wait for them to change and allow equal rights. He referred to the Thirteenth Amendment to the American Constitution, which abolished slavery, to demand accountability and action from the oppressor castes. He stated:

> I am aware that some Touchables are suggesting that the matter of equal rights for the Untouchables should be allowed to be resolved by the Touchables amongst themselves. It cannot be resolved by the movement of the Untouchables. The Untouchables should wait till the Touchables willingly allow them such equal rights. How can it be trusted that they will willingly grant such rights to the Untouchables? It will be sheer stupidity to wait for such a miracle to happen . . . Another section of the Touchables tells us that even if we launch our movement, we will not succeed. If we launch a struggle, whatever few Touchables who have sympathy with our cause will feel offended and we will lose their sympathy. The progressive Touchables will then join the orthodox Hindus against us. I want to tell them that if they have sympathy for us, if they feel anguished about the injustice caused to us, then they should support us wholeheartedly like the Whites supported the Blacks in America to end slavery. Otherwise, it does not matter whether you have sympathy or hatred towards us.[44]

Similar criticism had been directed at Dr Martin Luther King Jr during the Civil Rights Movement in the US. Some White clergymen argued that African Americans should wait for White society to change. In response, Dr King wrote a letter in 1963 from an Alabama jail, where he was imprisoned for leading non-violent protests against racial injustice.[45] Dr King wrote:

We know through painful experience that freedom is never voluntarily given by the oppressor; it must be demanded by the oppressed. Frankly, I have never yet engaged in a direct-action movement that was 'well timed' according to the timetable of those who have not suffered unduly from the disease of segregation. For years now I have heard the word 'wait'. It rings in the ear of every Negro with a piercing familiarity. This 'wait' has almost always meant 'never'. It has been a tranquilizing thalidomide, relieving the emotional stress for a moment, only to give birth to an ill-formed infant of frustration. We must come to see with the distinguished jurist of yesterday that 'justice too long delayed is justice denied'. We have waited for more than three hundred and forty years for our God-given and constitutional rights. The nations of Asia and Africa are moving with jet-like speed toward the goal of political independence, and we still creep at horse-and-buggy pace toward the gaining of a cup of coffee at a lunch counter. I guess it is easy for those who have never felt the stinging darts of segregation to say 'wait'. But when you have seen vicious mobs lynch your mothers and fathers at will and drown your sisters and brothers at whim; when you have seen hate-filled policemen curse, kick, brutalize, and even kill your black brothers and sisters with impunity; when you see the vast majority of your twenty million Negro brothers smothering in an airtight cage of poverty in the midst of an affluent society; when you suddenly find your tongue twisted and your speech stammering as you seek to explain to your six-year-old daughter why she cannot go to the public amusement park that has just been advertised on television, and see tears welling up in her little eyes when she is told that Funtown is closed to colored children, and see the depressing clouds of inferiority begin to form in her little mental sky, and see her begin to distort her little personality by unconsciously developing a bitterness toward white people; when you have to concoct an answer for a five-year-old son asking in agonizing pathos, 'Daddy, why do white people treat colored people so mean?'; when you take a cross-country drive and find it necessary to sleep night after night in the uncomfortable corners of your automobile because no motel will accept you; when you are humiliated day in and day out by nagging signs reading 'white' and 'colored'; when your first name becomes 'nigger' and your middle name becomes 'boy' (however old you are) and your last name becomes 'John,' and when your wife and mother are never given the respected title 'Mrs.'; when you are harried by day and haunted by night by the fact that you are a Negro, living constantly at tiptoe stance, never knowing what to expect next, and plagued with inner fears and outer resentments; when you are forever fighting a degenerating sense of 'nobodyness'—then you will understand why we find it difficult to wait. There comes a time when the cup of endurance runs over and men are no longer willing to be plunged into an abyss of injustice where they experience the bleakness of corroding despair. I hope, sirs, you can understand our legitimate and unavoidable impatience.[46]

Both Dr Ambedkar and Dr King believed in immediate action, knowing well that the argument that the oppressed should keep waiting for a change in society is a tool to maintain the status quo of oppression.

Caste Hindus in Mahad wanted the district magistrate to issue an order prohibiting the Untouchables from taking water from the Chavdar tank, but he refused (7 December). The leaders of the oppressor castes then filed a suit in the Mahad Civil Court for an injunction against Dr Ambedkar and his colleagues on 12 December 1927. The court *ex parte* issued a temporary injunction on 14 December against the defendants, pending the decision of the suit, and prohibited Dr Ambedkar and his colleagues from going to the Chavdar tank.[47]

However, Dr Ambedkar convened the meeting at Mahad as planned. On 25 December 1927, he addressed the gathering, announcing that the Mahad Satyagraha was the foundational moment for equality in India. He said:

> The Touchables of Mahad are opposing Untouchables to draw water from Mahad Lake not because its water will get polluted or it will vanish into thin air. They oppose it because they do not want to accept that the Untouchables are equal to them. Gentlemen, you will understand the significance of the movement of Satyagraha we have launched. Please do not be under the impression that the Satyagraha Committee has invited you for drinking of water of this Mahad Lake. You have never used its water in the past. It is not that if we do not use it we are going to die. Our objective is to prove that we are human beings just like others. Therefore, this Conference is arranged to lay a foundation for establishing the social equality. And, therefore, this Conference is unique and historical. There is no parallel to this event in the entire history of India.[48]

Dr Ambedkar added that the only similar social revolutionary moment was the French Revolution of 1789. He stated that it was only 'because of the French Revolution of 1789 that not only France but all the countries in the whole of Europe today are enjoying prosperity and peace.'[49] He then explained how the principle of non-discrimination was in the interest of the country. Linking discrimination to the 'poverty, wretchedness and humiliating status' suffered by the Depressed Classes, he held that social reform was in the interest of the nation at large.[50]

Dr Ambedkar further emphasized the equality principle, by noting:

Some people laugh at the concept of equality. They argue that every person has different physical and mental capabilities. How can they be treated equal? But these people have not fully understood the meaning of equality. They do not realize that the power to control others cannot be granted on the basis of birth, it should be granted only on the basis of qualities. But all should be treated equally till they are trained and educated to become capable for the grant of powers.[51]

Dr Ambedkar had also prepared a few resolutions to be taken up at the Conference. These resolutions were passed on the very first day (25 December). The language of these resolutions took into account the following international events: the French Revolution, where the French people had ended monarchy and established a Republic based on liberty, equality and fraternity; the then-recent revolution in Russia that established the rule of equality and destroyed the rule of the priests and czars, and the ongoing movement for a socialist government in England.[52] The Marathi translations of these resolutions were read by Dr Ambedkar's colleagues.[53]

The starting point in the first resolution incorporated the basic cardinal rule of equality stating that all human beings were equal from birth to death and that no policy ought to violate this principle of equality. The next point highlighted what is now considered the principle of non-discrimination on the use of public roads, public schools, public water sources and temples. It contended that those who opposed this were the 'enemies of a well-organized social structure and justice'.

Another point that the first resolution highlighted was what is now the modern constitutional principle of 'equal protection of laws'. It noted:

Law is not the limits determined by any particular class. The right to determine how the law should be, must be vested in people or their representatives. This law should be equally applicable to all, irrespective of whether it is related to defence or governance. And since social structure is to be based on the principle of equality, caste should not come in the way of exercising dignity, authority or vocation. If at all discrimination is inevitable, it should be based on attributes of a person; it should not be just by birth. Therefore, this Conference condemns the prevailing custom of caste discrimination and the inequality stemming from it.

Another resolution prepared by Dr Ambedkar rejected the authority of the *Manusmriti*. It said:

It is the firm opinion of this Conference that *Manusmriti*, taking into consideration its verses (statements) which undermined the Shudra caste, thwarted their progress, and made their social, political, and economic slavery permanent . . . is not worthy of becoming a religious or a sacred book. And in order to give expression to this opinion, this Conference is performing the cremation rites of such a religious book which has been divisive of people and destroyer of humanity.[54]

After passing these resolutions, Dr Ambedkar proceeded to burn the *Manusmriti* ceremoniously on a pyre. As biographer Ashok Gopal notes:

Dr Ambedkar had previously spoken of burning Hindu scriptures in his speech at Nipani in April 1925. The targeting of the *Manusmriti* also had a precedent. In 1927-28, the non-Brahmin leader of the Madras province, 'Periyar' E.V. Ramaswamy Naicker, had repeatedly called for its burning, and copies had been burnt at several places. But no one had previously organised such an event in the Bombay province.[55]

The burning of the *Manusmriti* was a radical moment in the history of India. The oppressed had directly challenged the authority of religious documents that sanctioned their discrimination and oppression. It demonstrated that the Untouchables were no longer willing to abide by the religious confinements propagated by the oppressor castes. After burning the *Manusmriti*, the gathering walked peacefully on the roads of Mahad (as they were prohibited by the court to go to the tank) to show their willpower to exercise their rights.[56]

In the next two days, Dr Ambedkar decided to postpone the agitation while the suit awaited settlement before the civil court. He had already achieved what he wanted. He had awakened the conscience of the Untouchables, successfully converted the struggle of Mahad into a fight for the rights of the Untouchables, as well as laid down the foundations of equality in the Indian constitutional discourse.

Later, Dr Ambedkar won the case before the civil court. The court accepted the arguments, long emphasized by Dr Ambedkar, that the oppressor castes had no right to exclude Untouchables from taking water from the tank. Dr Ambedkar was also able to successfully prove that the tank was not private property and that the Touchables had no ownership rights over it.[57] The judgment of the trial court was also upheld by the Bombay High Court.[58]

The equality provisions of the future Indian Constitution carry the imprint of the Mahad struggle in their reference to equal access to public services. Article 15(2) of the Indian Constitution prohibits discrimination with regard to 'the use of wells, tanks, bathing ghats, roads and places of public resort'—a point which was constantly highlighted by Dr Ambedkar for several decades.

7

Equal Voting Rights
(Universal Adult Franchise)

A provision in the GOI Act of 1919 had stated that the British government would appoint a Royal Commission at the end of ten years to examine the workings of the Act and recommend changes as may be found necessary. In November 1927, a Royal Commission under the chairmanship of Sir John Simon was appointed. The Commission comprised British parliamentarians but did not include any Indian member. In protest, the Indian National Congress and the Muslim League refused to cooperate with the Commission and decided to boycott it. However, the representatives of minority social groups, including Dr Ambedkar, decided to participate in the proceedings to make their points in drafting the future Constitution.

The Simon Commission came on its first visit to India on 3 February 1928. Simultaneously, an All Parties Conference, convened by the Congress party in February and May 1928, appointed a committee under Motilal Nehru to draft a Swaraj Constitution for India.[1] For this Conference, all political parties and individuals, except for Dr Ambedkar and his organization, were invited.[2] The Nehru Committee began its work in June and took a couple of months to come up with a draft.[3]

In the meantime, Dr Ambedkar submitted two statements dated 29 May 1928 to the Simon Commission on behalf of the Bahishkrit Hitakarini Sabha to highlight the concerns of the Depressed Classes. These statements highlighted the larger constitutional principle of universal adult franchise for the future Constitution, and seem to be built on the constitutional resolutions prepared by Dr Ambedkar during the Mahad Satyagraha.

The statement concerning the safeguards for the Depressed Classes began by noting that it would have been satisfactory if Indians representing various social groups and interests of the country had been appointed to the statutory Commission.[4] It then pointed out the promise made to the Depressed Classes in the Montagu–Chelmsford Report, 'So with the Depressed classes, we intend to make the best arrangements we can for their representation in order that they too may ultimately learn the lesson of self-protection.'[5] However, it noted with regret that 'all these promises were thrown to the wind by the Southborough Committee'. It was noted that the Southborough Committee was 'grossly indifferent . . . to the problem of making adequate provision for safeguarding the interests of the Depressed Classes'.[6] The Sabha noted its protest against the non-recognition of the right of the Depressed Classes in the Legislative Assembly in 1919.

The Sabha noted that the Southborough Committee had actually reduced the strength of the Depressed Classes in the legislature. Hence, in the new arrangement, it demanded that extra representation be given to the Depressed Classes. It noted, 'The standing of the community must mean its power to protect itself in the social struggle. That power would obviously depend upon the educational and economic status of the community.' As the Depressed Classes are backward, they must be 'entitled to some electoral advantage over what they are entitled to on the basis of their strength'. Another reason why the Sabha wanted an increment in representation was, 'The representation of a minority, if it is to protect the minority, must also be effective. If not, it would be a farce.'

The Sabha was opposed to the system where the members of the Depressed Classes in the legislature were nominated. It wanted its members to be directly elected. The Sabha reiterated what Dr Ambedkar had submitted before the Southborough Committee: 'Election is not only correct in principle from the standpoint of responsible Government, but is also necessary in practice from the standpoint of political education. Every community must have an opportunity for political education which cannot well be secured otherwise than by the exercise of the vote.' The Sabha also demanded ministership in the cabinet government noting that no 'great benefit can come to them from the introduction of political reforms unless they can find a place in the cabinet of the country, from where they can influence the policy of the government.'

Interestingly, the Sabha argued against communal electorates and demanded reserved seats in general constituencies for the Depressed Classes. In the case of candidates from the Depressed Classes, it urged 'the total abandonment of the residential qualification and a partial relaxation in the condition as to deposit'.[7]

The Sabha highlighted the importance of universal franchise, and submitted that the weaker sections of society must be given the right to franchise so that they could negotiate with the systems of power, stating,

So vital is this question of the franchise that upon its determination alone can depend on the degree of the transfer of political power . . . Franchise means the right to determine the terms of associated life . . . If that is the meaning of franchise, then it follows that it should be given

to those who by reason of their weak power of bargaining
are exposed to the risk of having the terms of associated life
fixed by superior forces in a manner unfavourable to them.

It therefore demanded that the condition to become part of
the franchise should be lowered 'to bring it within the reach
of the large majority of the poor and the oppressed sections
of society'.

The Sabha believed that apart from the demand for
adequate representation, it was necessary that the future
constitution must include, in its fundamental rights segment,
specific clauses guaranteeing the civil rights of the Depressed
Classes and that the Depressed Classes must be treated as a
protected minority. The Sabha also submitted a tentative list
of rights for the Depressed Classes for the future constitution:

(1) An equitable and just proportion of the total grant
    for education be earmarked for the benefit of the
    Depressed Classes

(2) The right of the Depressed Classes to unrestricted
    recruitment in the army, navy, and the police without
    any limitation as to caste

(3) For a period of 30 years the right of the Depressed
    Classes for priority in the matter of the recruitments
    to all posts, gazetted as well as non-gazetted in all
    civil services

(4) The right of the Depressed Classes to the appointment
    of a special inspector of police from amongst themselves
    for every district

(5) The right of the Depressed Classes to effective
    representation (as defined above) in Local Bodies

(6) The right of the Depressed Classes to appeal to the
    Government of India in cases of violation of these rights
    by the Provincial Government and the Government

of India be given the power to compel the Provincial Government to conform to the law in the matter.

The premise of these demands was that the Depressed Classes needed mandatory inclusion in services to assert themselves and protect themselves from social tyranny. The submission note prepared by Dr Ambedkar for the Sabha also included a lengthy justification for posting these demands. It noted:

> So rigorous is the enforcement of the social code against the Depressed Classes that any attempt on the part of the Depressed Classes to exercise their elementary rights of citizenship only ends in provoking the majority, to practice the worst form of social tyranny known to history. It will be admitted that when society is itself a tyrant, its means of tyrannizing are not restricted to the acts which it may do by the hands of its functionaries and it leaves fewer means of escape, penetrating much more deeply into the details of life, and enslaving the soul itself. Protection against such tyranny is usually to be found in the police power of the state. But unfortunately in any struggle in which the Depressed Classes are on the one side and the upper class of Hindus on the other, the police power is always in league with the tyrant majority, for the simple reason that the Depressed Classes have no footing whatsoever in the police or in the Magistracy of the country.[8]

The submissions also argued that it is always better to safeguard the minorities through legal safeguards, rather than leaving them unprotected and to the whims of the majority. It also added that constitutional guarantees are a must if the government wants the Depressed Classes to have faith in the future constitution. The note submitted by Dr Ambedkar also included annexures documenting how various instances of discrimination affect the rights and daily lives of the Depressed Classes.[9]

As mentioned in a previous chapter, Dr Ambedkar believed that the issue of universal franchise and adequate representation was interlinked with the issue of education for the Depressed Classes. This was because the Depressed Classes were lagging in education, which was used as a criterion to be a part of the franchise. Therefore, Dr Ambedkar submitted another statement to the Simon Commission, which was about the state of education of the Depressed Classes in the Bombay Presidency, on behalf of the Bahishkrit Hitakarini Sabha on 29 May 1928.

The statement questioned the long silence of the British on the issue of promoting education among the native population. It noted that the oppressed castes, who were at the receiving end of the casteist policies of the Peshwas, had hoped for a change in approach with the coming of the British.

> It must be admitted that under the Peshwa Government the Depressed Classes were entirely out of the pale of education. They did not find a place in any idea of state education, for the simple reason that the Peshwa Government was a theocracy based upon the canons of Manu, according to which the Shudras and Atishudras (classes corresponding to the Backward Classes of the Education Department), if they had any right to life, liberty and property, had certainly no right to education. The Depressed Classes who were labouring under such disabilities naturally breathed a sigh of relief at the downfall of this hated theocracy.

However, it argued that the British had failed to focus on the education of the oppressed castes, as they were only focused on promoting education among the high-caste Brahmins.

The statement quoted the Report of the Board of Education of the Bombay Presidency 1850–51, which stated that 'only a small section of the population can be brought under the influence of Government education in India, and . . . this section should consist of the "upper classes"', which were said to include 'landowners and jaghirdars' and 'Brahmins'.

The submitted statement acknowledged that only Christian missionaries took charge of the education of the Depressed Classes. It argued that: 'Unless compulsion in the matter of primary education is made obligatory and unless the admission to primary schools is strictly enforced, conditions essential for educational progress of the Backward Classes will not come into existence.'

What the Bahishkrit Hitakarini Sabha, speaking through Dr Ambedkar, had already submitted on the issues of universal adult franchise, rights and education was echoed in the draft report of the Nehru Committee finalized in August 1928. Like the Sabha, the Nehru Report recommended universal adult suffrage along with a parliamentary system of government.[10] It also included a section on the Bill of Rights, including that of education. On this point, credit must go to Dr Ambedkar, who was the first one to highlight the universal language of rights in the Indian constitutional discourse. However, with reference to the Depressed Classes, the Nehru Committee Report stated: 'In our suggestions for the Constitution we have not made any special provision for the representation of the "Depressed" Classes in the legislatures.'[11] The Committee considered the methods of separate electorates or nomination as harmful and unsound and did not make any provision for the representation of Depressed Classes, even though it recommended reserved seats in joint electorates for Muslims. On this aspect, Dr Ambedkar criticized the Report and argued that it did not embody the views of the Non-Brahmins and the Depressed Classes.[12] He later wrote an editorial in

Bahishkrit Bharat to express his views on the Report, stating, '[T]he scheme prepared by the Nehru Committee regarding the planning of electorates is not fair and just. It is an effort of the caste Hindus to acquire power without disturbing the power of Brahminical caste hierarchy.'[13]

The viceroy had established a national-level committee to coordinate the work of the Commission; every state legislative council elected a provincial committee to work with the Simon Commission.[14] Consequently, the Bombay government established the Bombay Province Committee to facilitate the work of the Commission. Dr Ambedkar, already a nominated member of the Bombay Legislative Council and now a professor at Government Law College, Bombay, from June 1928, was elected as a member of the Bombay Province Committee on 3 August 1928.[15] Further, Dr Ambedkar was called to submit evidence and was examined before the Simon Commission on 23 October 1928 in Pune (then Poona). He answered the questions posed by the members of the Commission. He demanded that the Depressed Classes be regarded as 'a distinct and independent minority' in the constitutional sense. His rationale was, 'A minority which is oppressed, or whose rights are denied [by] the majority, would be a minority that would be fit for consideration for political purposes.' He argued, 'The Depressed Classes minority needs far greater political protection than any other minority in British India, for the simple reason that it is educationally very backward, that it is economically poor, socially enslaved, and suffers from certain grave political disabilities, from which no other community suffers.' When asked about proportional representation to minorities, he demanded a far greater say in the affairs of the legislature. He argued,

I do not quite accept the principle of representation of minorities according to population of the legislature as though it was a museum in which we have only to keep so many specimens of so many communities. A Legislative Council is more than a museum, it is a place where, for instance, social battles have to be fought, privileges have to be destroyed, and rights have to be won. Now, if that is the conception of a Legislative Council, I do not think it at all in the fitness of things to confine the minority to proportional representation according to population, that means you are condemning a minority to be perpetually a minority without the power necessary to influence the actions in the majority.

Dr Ambedkar consistently demanded universal adult franchise for all communities. If the government was not going to provide that, then the alternative for the Depressed Classes would be special electorates, along with 'certain safeguards either in the [future] Constitution' regarding the education of the Depressed Classes and their entry into public services. On being asked the reason for the insistence on the inclusion of the Depressed Classes in public services, he shared the experiences of the community with 'the administration of the law' as being 'very bitter'. He narrated that 'in many cases the law is administered to the disadvantage of the depressed class man'. He gave an example of how the government officials from oppressor castes allotted land, which was rocky and unfit for cultivation, to the Depressed Classes, while showing 'absolute favouritism to the caste Hindu' by allotting them rich and fertile land. Dr Ambedkar called this the 'most fragrant abuse of the administrative power' and argued, 'I personally attach far more importance to good administration of law than to more efficient administration of law.'

Dr Ambedkar was also asked about the criminal tribes and the aboriginal (indigenous) community. His view seems to be unclear, as he was reluctant to speak on behalf of the criminal tribes and aboriginals, and was only presenting the demands of the Untouchables. However, Dr Ambedkar was a part of larger social movements demanding justice for criminal tribes.[16] He submitted that in some parts of the country, members of criminal tribes and aboriginal communities were treated as Untouchables. When asked whether these communities 'stand midway between touchability and untouchability', he responded that 'they were lower down than the untouchables'. He also expressed his reluctance to speak on the issue, as he noted, 'My point is this, that with respect to the criminal tribes we have no data for forming an opinion as to whether they are untouchable or not, because there is very little intercourse between the main body of Hindus and the criminal tribes.' He was also posed with a question on the protection of the indigenous communities such as the Bhils. To this, he responded, 'I think that they also should be allowed some protection by representation.'

In those days, there was a major labour strike.[17] Dr Ambedkar stated that the Untouchable labourers faced discrimination at the hands of workers from oppressor castes. He further submitted that he was supporting adult franchise for both men and women. On being questioned about the lack of political conscience among the masses, he submitted that 'the depressed classes will exercise their vote in a most intelligent manner'. He submitted that the conditions of the Untouchables had not changed at all in the last two decades. He gave an example, 'Even in the case of rivers they can take water only from a portion of the river. A point on the river is appointed for them', i.e., the Depressed Classes draw water at a point lower down the river path from where the caste Hindus draw water.

The Simon Commission continued its proceedings till the winter of 1928, after which it worked on its report. After its deliberations, the Bombay Province Committee submitted the 'Report on the Constitution of the Government of Bombay Presidency' on 7 May 1929.[18] It did not endorse universal adult franchise. Dr Ambedkar fundamentally differed with the Committee and thus did not sign that report. Instead, he submitted a separate report criticizing the main report, while highlighting his concerns and recommendations on 17 May 1929.[19] Interestingly, Dr Ambedkar's report was lengthier than the main report submitted by the Bombay Province Committee.[20]

Among other things, Dr Ambedkar critiqued his colleagues on the Committee for putting prerequisites to attain franchise and for not recommending universal adult franchise. He reiterated the meaning and importance of franchise, by stating that:

> My colleagues look upon the question of franchise as though it was nothing but a question of competency to put into a ballot box a piece of paper with a number of names written thereon . . . Such a view of the franchise is undoubtedly superficial and involves a total misunderstanding of what it stands for . . . [F]ranchise, far from being a transaction concerned with the marking of the ballot paper, stands for direct and active participation in the regulation of the terms upon which associated life shall be sustained and the permit of good carried on . . . For, associated life is shared by every individual and as every individual is affected by its consequences, every individual must have the right to settle its terms. From the same premises it would further follow that the poorer the individual the greater the necessity of enfranchising him.[21]

He criticized the property requirement of voting rights in the following terms:

> [For] in every society based on private property the terms of associated life as between owners and workers are from the

start set against the workers. If the welfare of the worker is to be guaranteed from being menaced by the owners the terms of their associated life must be constantly resettled. But this can hardly be done unless the franchise is dissociated from property and extended to all propertyless adults.[22]

Dr Ambedkar further submitted that the blame for illiteracy among the masses lay not on the masses themselves, but on those who have been ruling society. He stated:

No one can deny the existence of illiteracy among the masses of the country . . . First of all, illiteracy of the illiterate is no fault of theirs. The Government of Bombay for a long time refused to take upon itself the most important function of educating the people, and, when it did, it deliberately confined the benefit of education to the [higher] classes and refused to extend it to the masses[23] . . . If the responsibility for illiteracy falls upon the Government, then to make literacy a condition precedent to franchise is to rule out the large majority of the people who, through no fault of their own, have never had an opportunity of acquiring literacy provided to them.[24]

He submitted that the denial of the right to vote to the masses was a situation of full injustice. He noted,

To keep people illiterate and then to make their illiteracy the ground for their non-enfranchisement is to add insult to injury. But the situation indeed involves more than this. It involves an aggravation of the injury. For to keep people illiterate and then to deny them franchise which is the only means whereby they could effectively provide for the removal of their illiteracy is to perpetuate their illiteracy and postpone indefinitely the day of their enfranchisement.[25]

Dr Ambedkar also rejected the argument that voting rights should be granted slowly as it has been done in other countries such as England. He submitted,

> My reply is that there is no reason why we should follow in the footsteps of the English nation in this particular matter. Surely the English people had not devised any philosophy of action in the matter of franchise. On the other hand, if the extension was marked by such long intervals it was because of the self-seeking character of the English ruling classes. Besides, these is no reason why every nation should go through the same stages and enact the same scenes as other nations have done. To do so is to refuse to reap the advantage which is always open to those who are born later.[26]

Hence, Dr Ambedkar was advancing a comparative constitutional law perspective for developing the constitutional discourse in India. (A comparative constitutional law perspective from the US will be discussed in a subsequent chapter.)

It is clear that though Dr Ambedkar cooperated with the Simon Commission, he questioned the British approach and policies on several fronts. While he emphasized the demands of the Depressed Classes, he did so by endorsing and defending the larger constitutional principles of universal adult franchise and representative form of government. Dr Ambedkar was negotiating with the colonial power to lay down the constitutional foundations for all demands.

8

Historical Reservation for the Oppressor Castes v. Affirmative Action for Oppressed Castes[*]

When Dr Ambedkar was making a demand before the Simon Commission for reservation in services for the backward communities, he also responded to the objections raised by Indian leaders from oppressor castes against his demand. It was argued by these leaders who were a part of the British administration that providing reservation for backward communities in services would dilute the 'efficiency of administration'.

Dr Ambedkar pointed out that it was not long ago when Indian leaders from oppressor castes would raise concerns before the British for excluding Indians from their administration on the same grounds of 'efficiency of administration'. According to Dr Ambedkar, the notion of 'efficiency of administration' was an exclusionary construct in the colonial and pre-colonial era. He also pointed out how 'the Brahmins and the allied castes' enjoyed historical reservations in their favour in all aspects of social and political power.

[*] This is a revised version of a portion of my article published in *Economic and Political Weekly*. Anurag Bhaskar, 'Reservations, Efficiency, and the Making of Indian Constitution', *Economic and Political Weekly*, Vol. 56, Issue No. 19 (2021).

Double Standards of Oppressor Castes

Dr Ambedkar narrated how Indian leaders from the 1890s had appealed to the British to include Indians (indirectly oppressor castes) within their services and administration. It was only after such continuous demands that the case for 'Indianization of services'[1] was accepted by the Royal Commission on Public Services in India, also known as the Islington Commission, in 1915. The proportion between the Indians and the Europeans in the different services was thereafter given effect.[2]

When the same oppressor castes, who got the benefit of the opening of services and became part of the British administration, thereafter used this notion of 'efficiency of administration' against the inclusion of oppressed castes within the services, Dr Ambedkar criticized their hypocritical conduct in his submissions before the Simon Commission in 1928. He noted: 'It is notorious that the public services of the country in so far as they are open to Indians have become by reason of various circumstances a close preserve for the Brahmins and allied castes. The Non-Brahmins, the Depressed Classes and the Mohamedans are virtually excluded from them.'[3]

Dr Ambedkar further noted that 'the Brahmins and the allied castes' relied upon 'educational merit' and 'competitive examinations' as the 'only test which can be taken to guarantee efficiency' in order to exclude the backward castes from becoming a part of the power system.[4] Dr Ambedkar stated unequivocally that the education system in India has been overwhelmingly undemocratic, thereby disadvantaging the oppressed castes. He noted:

> The system of competitive examination relied upon may result in fairness to all castes and creeds under a given set of circumstances. But those circumstances presuppose that the educational system of the State is sufficiently democratic

and is such that facilities for education are sufficiently widespread and sufficiently used to permit all classes from which good public servants are likely to be forthcoming to compete. Otherwise even with the system of open competition large classes are sure to be left out in the cold. This basic condition is conspicuous by its absence in India, so that to invite Backward Classes to rely upon the results of competitive examination as a means of entry into the Public Services is to practise a delusion upon them and very rightly the Backward Classes have refused to be deceived by it.[5]

Thus, in Dr Ambedkar's view, the education system strengthens inequalities, if it does not address the already existing social disparities.

Moral Case and Administrative Utility

Dr Ambedkar destroyed the myth of 'efficiency' with several arguments. Before the Simon Commission, he presented a case of 'administrative utility' and a 'moral case' for the Backward Classes to have a 'favoured treatment' for their inclusion in the public services. He gave examples from the past of how so-called upper caste officers acted 'to the aggrandizement of their community and to the detriment of the general public'.[6] For this reason, Dr Ambedkar argued: '[The] disadvantages arising from the class bias of the officers belonging to Brahmin and allied castes has outweighed all the advantages attending upon their efficiency and that on the total they have done more harm than good.'[7] The remedy, he thus suggested, was 'a proper admixture of the different communities in the public service', which will supply 'a most valuable corrective to the evils of class bias'.[8]

Dr Ambedkar then argued that the case of exclusion of the Backward Classes from the administrative services was morally wrong and evil in the same way as the exclusion of Indians from public services. He posed several questions to the opponents of the inclusion of the Backward Classes within public services:

> Now what one would like to ask those who deny the justice of the case of the Backward Classes for entry into the Public Service is whether it is not open to the Backward Classes to allege against the Brahmins and allied castes all that was alleged by the late Mr Gokhale[9] on behalf of Indian people against the foreign agency? Can [the Backward Classes] not complain that as a result of their exclusion they are obliged to live all the days of their lives in an atmosphere of inferiority, and that the tallest of them has to bend in order that the exigencies of the existing system may be satisfied?

He further asked:

> Can [the Backward Classes] not assert that the upward impulses which every school-boy of the Brahmanical community feels that he may one day be a Sinha, a Sastri, a Ranade or a Paranjpye, and which may draw forth from him the best efforts of which he is capable is denied to them? . . . Can they not lament that the moral elevation which every self-governing people feel cannot be felt by them and that their administrative talents must gradually disappear owing to sheer disgust till at last their lot as hewers of wood and drawers of water in their own country is stereotyped?[10]

The answers to all these questions, Dr Ambedkar said, are in the 'affirmative'. What Dr Ambedkar explained through the above questions was the system of exclusion against Backward Classes, which had been in existence even before the British regime began in India. The construct of 'efficiency' was a repackaging of the caste traditions of stereotypes, prejudices and subsequent ostracism.

Historical Reservations for the Oppressors

In a later work[11] (which will be discussed in a subsequent chapter), Dr Ambedkar reminded the oppressor castes that they had received their privileges and social advancement not because of any merit.[12] He stated that the Brahmin, Banias and allied castes have historically controlled power as the 'governing class', and have treated the backward castes as a 'servile class'. He thus stated:

> The governing class does not bother to inquire into the ways and means by which it has acquired its supremacy. It does not feel the necessity of doing so, partly because it believes that it acquired its supremacy by dint of merit and partly because it believes that no matter how it acquired its power it is enough that it is in a position to dictate its policy on the servile classes.[13]

Dr Ambedkar noted that the oppressor castes 'acquired their political power not by force of intellect—for intellect is nobody's monopoly—but by sheer communalism',[14] a kind of absolute reservation since ancient times. They exercised control of social conduct and administration.[15]

Dr Ambedkar stated that Manusmriti, the ancient socio-legal code, had provided that the important administrative, military and ministerial posts 'were all reserved for the Brahmins'.[16] Not only this, but the chances of oppressed castes being able to gain upward social mobility were shot down. Because of the Manusmriti and other laws, 'education was made the monopoly and privilege of Brahmins', while 'to acquire learning' was criminalized for the oppressed lower castes and resulted in 'cruel and inhuman punishment such as cutting the tongue of the criminal and filling his ear with hot molten lead'.[17] He added, 'India is the only country where the intellectual class, namely, the Brahmins not only made education their monopoly but declared acquisition of education by the lower classes, a crime punishable by cutting off of the tongue or by the pouring of molten lead in the ear of the offender.'[18] While these reservations for Brahmins did not exist during British rule, Dr Ambedkar pointed out that 'the advantages derived from their continuance over several centuries have remained'.[19]

Dr Ambedkar further noted that if the marginalized and oppressed castes are 'so fallen, so degraded, so devoid of hope and ambition, it is entirely due to the Brahmins and their philosophy'.[20] This philosophy was based on

(1) graded inequality between the different classes; (2) complete disarmament of the Shudras and the Untouchables; (3) complete prohibition of the education of the Shudras and the Untouchables; (4) ban on the Shudras and the Untouchables occupying places of power and authority; (5) ban on the Shudras and the Untouchables acquiring property and (6) complete subjugation and suppression of women.[21]

Dr Ambedkar also noted how the Banias (Vaishyas) controlled the resources and businesses to keep the marginalized communities entrenched in economic slavery. As he noted,

[The Bania] lives on interest and as he is told by his religion that money lending is the occupation prescribed to him by Manu, he looks upon it as both right and righteous . . . Interest, interest on interest, he adds on and on and thereby draws families perpetually into his net: Pay him as much as a debtor may, he is always in debt . . . His grip over the nation is complete. The whole of poor, starving, illiterate India is mortgaged to the Bania.[22]

Dr Ambedkar thus concluded: 'To sum up, the Brahmin enslaves the mind and the Bania enslaves the body. Between them, they divide the spoils which belong to the governing classes.'[23]

In Dr Ambedkar's view, the argument of 'efficiency' has been a method used by oppressor castes to protect their own interests and structural advantages. Dr Ambedkar stated that instead of making any sacrifice of their interests for an inclusive India, the upper castes made a 'cry of "nationalism in danger"' and 'efficiency' against reservations.[24] He noted,

> Whenever the servile classes ask for reservations in the Legislatures, in the Executive and in public services, the governing class raises the cry of 'nationalism in danger'. People are told that if we are to achieve national freedom, we must maintain national unity, that all questions regarding reservations in the Legislatures, Executives and the public services are inimical to national unity and therefore for anyone interested in national freedom it is a sin to stand out for such reservations and create dissensions. That is the attitude of the governing class.[25]

Dr Ambedkar also attacked the tendency of the oppressor castes to leave 'no occasion to deprecate and to ridicule reservations'.[26] He noted,

> The governing class in India does not merely refuse to surrender its power and authority; it never loses an opportunity to pour ridicule on the political demands of the servile classes. Some members of the governing classes [including those pretending to be liberals] have gone to

the length of composing lampoons and parodies in order
to make the demand of the servile classes appear absurd
and ridiculous.[27]

Dr Ambedkar argued that this tendency of oppressor castes to
parody and ridicule the demands of the marginalized castes is
also a tool to maintain their power.[28] He made a sharp comment
in response:

> The governing classes [oppressor castes] are bent on giving
> the reservations a bad name in order to be able to hang those
> who are insisting upon them[29] . . . If the governing class in
> India stands on the principle of efficiency and efficiency
> alone it is because it is actuated by the selfish motive of
> monopolizing the instrumentalities of government[30] . . .
> Efficiency combined with selfish class interests instead of
> producing good government is far more likely to become a
> mere engine of suppression of the servile classes.[31]

He further argued that the responsibility of the oppressor castes
cannot go away by merely saying 'that these privileges no longer
exist'. He noted, 'They must admit that while the privileges
have gone the advantages derived from their continuance
over several centuries have remained.'[32] Thus, Dr Ambedkar
rejected the stereotypes against affirmative action, which have
been advanced by the oppressor castes.

'Good Governance' versus 'Efficient Administration'

Dr Ambedkar argued that to undo the reservation of oppressor
castes, the conception of 'good governance' needs to be
emphasized. In a couple of his writings, he had consistently
distinguished the construct of 'efficiency of administration'

from that of 'good governance'. He asserted that a good administration or government is one that is truly representative. In one of the articles, he had noted:

> [The] view that good Government was better than efficient Government . . . must also be made applicable to the field of administration. It was through administration that the State came directly in contact with the masses. *No administration could do any good unless it was sympathetic* . . . As against this the Brahmins have been taking their stand on efficiency pure and simple. They know that this is the only card they can play successfully by reason of their advanced position in education. But they forget that if efficiency was the only criterion then in all probability there would be very little chance for them to monopolize State service in the way and to the extent they have done. For if efficiency was made the only criterion there would be nothing wrong in employing Englishmen, Frenchmen, Germans and Turks instead of the Brahmins of India.[33]

Dr Ambedkar elaborated on this point by asserting that the 'Indianization' of public services was also based on the notions of representation and inclusiveness, and not on an exclusionary notion of 'efficiency'. Therefore, a good government would require the inclusion of Backward Classes, which must not be opposed. He argued:

> The case for Indianization, it must be remembered, did not rest upon efficient administration. *It rested upon considerations of good administration* . . . It is therefore somewhat strange that those who clamoured for Indianization should oppose the stream flowing in the direction of the Backward Classes, forgetting that the case for Indianization also includes the case for the Backward Classes.[34]

Dr Ambedkar further noted that 'the question of entry into the Public Service is . . . a question of life and death' for the Scheduled Castes, as they did not have openings for a career in trade and industry because of untouchability and biases against them.[35] Since 'it is only in government service that they can find a career',[36] this created, Dr Ambedkar argued, a 'natural idealism of the backward communities' and 'aspirations' to contribute to governance.[37] In his view, reservations for the backward communities 'makes available for the national service such powerful social forces, in the absence of which any Parliamentary government may be deemed to be poorer'.[38] Thus, for Dr Ambedkar, giving due representation would have enhanced efficiency. In other words, Dr Ambedkar's conception of 'good government' meant that efficiency would be measured by the test of representation and inclusion of under-represented social groups.

Dr Ambedkar strongly asserted that reservations, by providing representation to Backward Classes, would act as a system of counterchecks to protect political democracy from being subverted by particular privileged groups.[39] According to Dr Ambedkar, reservations 'are only another name for what the Americans call checks and balances which every constitution must have, if democracy is not to be overwhelmed by the enemies of democracy'.[40]

Later Influence on Constitution-Drafting

Dr Ambedkar reiterated the above-mentioned points during the deliberations on the Constitution. He had written a letter to Jawaharlal Nehru, charging that 'the administration was unsympathetic to Scheduled Castes because it was manned' wholly by 'Caste Hindu officers' who 'practiced tyranny and oppression' on the Scheduled Castes.[41] The best way to remedy this situation, Dr Ambedkar argued, was for the Scheduled Castes to 'become members of the various governments in India and thereby to ensure that [Scheduled Castes] also became members of the civil services'.[42] These views of Dr Ambedkar on representation and inclusion also found an echo in the speeches given by Jaipal Singh Munda, a leader from the Adivasi community, and Dharanidhar Basu Matari, a member from Assam. Both of them highlighted how the indigenous Adivasi communities had suffered because of the exclusionary system created by the oppressor castes. In fact, Munda was one of Dr Ambedkar's strongest supporters in the Constituent Assembly and openly supported the constitutional safeguards introduced by Dr Ambedkar for socially oppressed communities.[43]

Munda highlighted that the ruling establishments need to learn from Adivasis, rather than teaching them about democracy and freedom. He said:

> Sir, I am proud to be a *Jungli*, that is the name by which we are known in my part of the country . . . Sir, if there is any group of Indian people that has been shabbily treated it is my people. They have been disgracefully treated, neglected for the last 6,000 years. This [Objective] Resolution is not going to teach *Adibasis* democracy. You cannot teach democracy to the tribal people; you have to learn democratic ways from them. They are the most democratic people on earth.[44]

Matari, on 23 November 1949, remarked that the 'advanced communities will have to make special efforts, particular sacrifices if the backward classes are to come up'.[45] He added that the tribals, who have been neglected and exploited in the past, will continue to be suppressed, 'unless there is special arrangement made for their advancement'. This can be done, Matari said, only when tribals are recruited: 'to all branches of service, from the lowest to the highest'; 'not only in the provinces but also at the Centre'; and 'not only should there be a minimum quota fixed for their appointments, but their promotion must equally be seen to, so that they do not stick where they begin'. 'For this to happen', Matari further added, 'the advanced classes must make a sacrifice' and 'recede'. Matari discarded the arguments about 'efficiency of administration' as 'just dodges to perpetuate class or territorial interests'. He alluded that the so-called upper castes benefited from the 'jobs, the contacts and the privileges' during the British regime and that these 'sections that have captured the services will see to it that their superiority is never threatened or endangered'. He, however, hoped that the rights of the tribals would be protected under the new constitutional regime.

It is for these reasons that Dr Ambedkar made a consistent case before the British government that the moral wrong of excluding oppressed lower castes from public offices and services must be corrected through reservations. He continuously argued for the provisions of representation in the public services and legislatures to be included in the future Constitution, so that the historical reservations of oppressor castes could be stopped. Several provisions of the Constitution came to be as a result of these efforts, and thus Dr Ambedkar's ideas are relevant for understanding the vision behind the incorporation of these provisions.

9

Drafting of the Government
of India Act 1935

The Simon Commission Report of 1930 was not accepted by Indians. In order to discuss the future political constitution of India, the British government decided to hold Round Table Conferences in London consisting of representatives from India, the British government and British political parties to frame a constitution for India with a view to satisfying the demands of the people of India.[1]

The Round Table Conference was a monumental event in the history of India. Though the Conference was not a Constituent Assembly entrusted with the work of drafting a constitution, it was significant as Indian representatives were being consulted in the framing of the future Constitution of India. The Conference attempted to develop a consensus over the main issues regarding the constitutional framework. Dr Ambedkar played a key role in the three Round Table Conferences and in the drafting of the Government of India Act 1935.

First Round Table Conference (RTC)

The first RTC consisted of 'eighty-nine members, out of which sixteen were representatives of the three British parties, fifty-three Indian members of the delegation representing various interests except the non-cooperating Congress, and twenty of the Indian States'.[2] Dr Ambedkar received the invitation to the first RTC through the viceroy on 6 September 1930. At the first RTC, Dr Ambedkar and Rao Bahadur Srinivasan represented the Depressed Classes. After Dr Ambedkar arrived in London, he immediately started building contacts with important politicians in Britain in 'connection with the problem of the Depressed Classes'.[3] He also visited the London School of Economics to meet some of his old professors and former classmates.[4]

For the first Round Table Conference, Ramsay MacDonald, then prime minister of Britain, was unanimously elected as the chairman.[5] When Dr Ambedkar rose to speak in the plenary session on 20 November 1930, he surprised everyone with his sharp views on the British Empire and the constitutional framework. He unequivocally asserted, 'The bureaucratic form of government in India should be replaced by a government which will be a government of the people, by the people and for the people.'[6] Dr Ambedkar spoke in two capacities: first, as a representative of the Depressed Classes, and second, as an Indian.[7]

In the first capacity, he reproved the British for the fundamentally unchanged condition of the Depressed Classes in Indian society even during their administration, declaring the colonial machinery to be 'quite incompetent'.[8] He observed that 'the British Government has accepted the social arrangements [and practices] as it found them'[9] and put forth a demand for the establishment of a government that would 'not be afraid to amend the social and economic code of life which the dictates of justice and expediency so urgently called for'—a role, in his words, 'the British Government will never be able to play'.[10] For him, a share in political power for the Depressed

Classes was a necessity, and only 'a Swaraj constitution' with special political representation for them would be efficient in providing them with the power to address their grievances.[11]

In his second capacity as an Indian, he warned the British against the use of force against Indians or implementing a Constitution without the consent of Indians.[12] Quoting Edmund Burke, he reminded the British that *power and authority are sometimes bought by kindness* and not necessarily with brute force.[13] Dr Ambedkar had a clear message for the British, 'The time when you were to choose and India was to accept is gone, never to return. Let the consent of the people and not the accident of logic be the touchstone of your new constitution, if you desire that it should be worked.'[14]

Pointing out the exclusion of the Depressed Classes and the injustices committed against them, Dr Ambedkar said that the new Constitution must be considerate of social realities, and must not be prepared without taking into consideration the concerns of the Depressed Classes. He stated:

It must also be recognized that while the intelligentsia is a very important part of Indian society, it is drawn from its upper strata and although it speaks in the name of the country and leads the political movement, it has not shed the narrow particularism of the class from which it is drawn. In other words what the Depressed Classes wish to urge is that the political mechanism must take account of and must have a definite relation to the psychology of the society for which it is devised. Otherwise you are likely to produce a constitution which, however symmetrical, will be (a) truncated one and a total misfit to the society for which it is designed.[15]

Therefore, he demanded that the issue of political representation of the Depressed Classes could 'not be left to the shifting sands of sympathy and goodwill of the rulers of the future'.[16] He further noted:

> We know that political power is passing from the British into the hands of those who wield such tremendous economic, social and religious sway over our existence . . . We are prepared to take the inevitable risk of the situation in the hope that we shall be installed, in adequate proportion, as the political sovereigns of the country along with our fellow countrymen.[17]

For Dr Ambedkar, 'Swaraj' also meant that the Depressed Classes were given political power to lead a dignified life.

Dr Ambedkar's speech was appreciated in both British and Indian newspapers. They seemed to be convinced that 'Dr. Ambedkar was a nationalist; and so they began to whisper that he also was one of the revolutionary leaders of India'.[18]

Nine sub-committees were appointed after the discussion in the plenary session of the first RTC to examine different issues. Dr Ambedkar was made a member of all these committees, except the Federal Structure Committee.[19]

In the sub-committee on the provincial Constitution, Dr Ambedkar's submissions were noteworthy. He argued that the Union government must have a say in matters of all-India character. He added that the minorities must get safeguards in the Constitution itself 'against anything likely to injure their interests being done or left undone by the Cabinet'.[20] On the point of the powers of the governor, he submitted that no system 'can permit the Governor the power to interfere in the day-to-day administration of the country'. Instead, 'The Ministry must be allowed to carry on the day-to-day administration on the basis of joint responsibility.'[21] He added, 'I cannot understand how there can be responsible Government in a Province in which the Governor is allowed to do a thing without a Ministry.'[22] Dr Ambedkar was also in favour of provinces managing their services: 'I quite agree in principle that with provincial autonomy the power of regulating the Services in a Province should belong to that Province, and that the Provinces should have full liberty to Indianize the Services as they desire and according to their means and circumstances.'[23] The British prime minister, who was chairing the provincial constitution sub-committee, listened to Dr Ambedkar keenly.[24]

Though Dr Ambedkar was not a member of the Federal structure sub-committee, he wrote a letter to its Chairman, Lord Sankey,[25] expressing his views and concerns on the issue. When Dr Ambedkar inquired from Lord Sankey about the status of the letter, he replied: 'I am not only going to place your letter before the Committee. I am going to draw the Committee's attention to it myself'.[26] He added, 'not a word of the letter shall be left out'.[27]

For the consideration of the Minorities sub-committee, Dr Ambedkar prepared a document titled 'A Scheme of Political Safeguards for the Protection of the Depressed Classes in the Future Constitution of a Self-governing India'.[28] The Scheme consisted of a Declaration of Fundamental Rights, safeguarding the cultural, religious and economic rights of the Depressed Classes. Several provisions in this draft were inspired by American civil rights legislation, such as those on non-discrimination, and other foreign legislations such as the Burma Anti-Boycott Act, 1922.[29] This was perhaps the first time that such provisions on non-discrimination against fellow citizens were tabled before the British government in India. Dr Ambedkar's draft also included a prohibition on social boycotts. All these provisions were re-emphasized by him in two separate documents ('Communal Deadlock' and 'States and Minorities') in the mid-1940s, just before the framing of India's Constitution. These documents are the subject of subsequent chapters.

Before the Minorities sub-committee, Dr Ambedkar submitted that:

> the minorities shall have representation in the Legislature and the Executive, that they shall have representation in the public services of the country, and that the constitution shall provide that there shall be imposed on the future legislatures of India, both Central and Provincial, certain limitations on their legislative power which will prevent the majorities from abusing their legislative power in such a manner as to enact laws which would create discrimination between one citizen and another.[30]

Dr Ambedkar added that the Depressed Classes are prepared to accept joint electorates and reserved seats, 'barring a short transitional period which they want for their organization', if they were granted adult universal suffrage.[31] That transitional period would be of ten years of separate electorates.[32]

For the finalization of the draft report, the chairman of the sub-committee decided to form a smaller committee, adding, 'We must include Dr. Ambedkar'.[33] In the preparation of the report, the members of the sub-committee referred to Dr Ambedkar's draft as a reference point.[34] Dr Ambedkar also 'urged that untouchability, with all its consequent disabilities, should be abolished by law, and that they should be guaranteed free and unfettered enjoyment of their rights'.[35] He further appealed that 'the constitution should also provide ways and means by which we shall be protected in the exercise of those rights'.[36] The final report of the Minorities sub-committee included points to this effect.[37]

In the sub-committee on franchise, Dr Ambedkar again emphasized that 'you cannot have in India any system of suffrage short of adult suffrage which will give equality of representation to all the castes and communities in India'.[38] The franchise sub-committee later recommended:

> that an expert Franchise Commission should be appointed with instructions to provide for the immediate increase of the electorate so as to enfranchise not less than ten per cent of the total population and indeed a larger number—but not more than twenty-five per cent of the total population—if that should, on a full investigation, be found practicable and desirable'.[39]

Dr Ambedkar expressed his dissent, and argued that the 'immediate introduction of adult suffrage is both practicable and desirable'.[40]

In fact, before the provincial constitution sub-committee, Dr Ambedkar said, 'I should not have anything to do with a constitution which did not provide the franchise for my community.'[41]

Dr Ambedkar's preparedness, scholarship and intellect impressed the delegates and the British statesmen.[42] Dr Ambedkar's view that the future Indian government or constitutional framework ought not to be a rule of classes over the masses found echo in the Labour Party circles of Britain.[43] The Round Table Conference was adjourned on 19 January 1931. This was done to give the delegates more time to think about several key issues, including the question of representation of different communities in the proposed legislature. Furthermore, the British wanted to speak with the leaders of the Congress party—the major political party in India, which had not participated in the proceedings of the first Round Table Conference.[44] However, Dr Ambedkar was confident that the Conference, though in a limited sense, laid the foundation of self-government in India.[45] The Conference was significant as it discussed the conception of India as a federal entity. Moreover, it established the cause of the Depressed Classes and Dr Ambedkar 'before the bar of world opinion'.[46]

Second Round Table Conference

The names of the delegates to the second Round Table Conference were announced in the third week of July 1931. Dr Ambedkar and Gandhi were invited to attend the Conference.[47] Mahatma Gandhi wrote to Dr Ambedkar on 6 August 1931, that he would like to meet him. Accordingly, the meeting was held on 14 August 1931, at Mani Bhavan, Mumbai, where Dr Ambedkar came to see Mahatma Gandhi.[48] It was the first meeting between them. Gandhi was the undisputed leader of the Congress party. Dr Ambedkar confronted him on the reluctance of the Congress to take down untouchability as a condition for independence.[49] When Dr Ambedkar asked Gandhi about his stand on political safeguards for the Depressed Classes, the latter replied: 'I am against the political separation of the Untouchables from the Hindus. That would be absolutely suicidal.'[50] This was the beginning of the clash between the two.

The second Round Table Conference commenced on 7 September 1931. The main work of the Conference was going to be done in the Federal Structure Committee and the Minorities Committee. This time, Dr Ambedkar was included in the Federal Structure Committee.[51] Dr Ambedkar's knowledge and articulation made him indispensable for discussing the future Indian constitutional framework. Dr Ambedkar was in favour of direct democracy, where representatives were elected, rather than nominated. He argued for a similar condition for the representatives of the princely states. This was a direct defence of the civil and political rights of people residing in the princely states. Furthermore, Dr Ambedkar contested the demand of the landlords for special representation, arguing that 'they should not be given special representation as they sided with the orthodox, and thereby defeated the ends of freedom and progress'.[52] Such was the character of his speech that 'every speaker devoted some part or other of his speech to refuting or supporting Dr Ambedkar's speech as a majority of them thought that his views were radical and revolutionary'.[53] This made Dr Ambedkar the focal point of the discussion.[54] Dr Ambedkar also raised the point of the time frame as to when the Indian Federation would start.[55] In his turn, Gandhi opposed any special representation for the Depressed Classes.[56]

In the meetings of the Minorities committee, Dr Ambedkar publicly contradicted Gandhi's statement.[57] He told the Committee that 'the Depressed Classes were not anxious about the transfer of power under the present circumstances'.[58] Rather,

> if the Government wanted to transfer power, it should be accompanied by such conditions and by such provisions that the power should not find itself into the hands of a clique, into the hands of the oligarchy, or into the hands of a group of people whether Mohammedans or Hindus; the solution should be such that the power should be shared by all communities in their respective proportions.[59]

Dr Ambedkar also participated in the debates on the federal system, where he made 'a very thought-provoking and illuminating speech on the composition of the Federal Court'.[60]

After these proceedings, Dr Ambedkar submitted a supplementary memorandum on the claims of the Depressed Classes for special representation. Perhaps disturbed by the stand taken by Gandhi and to strengthen his negotiations,

Dr Ambedkar made a new proposal: 'The Depressed Classes shall have the right to elect their representatives to the Provincial and Central Legislatures through Separate Electorates of their voters.'[61] This was a change in his stance in comparison to his submissions before the Simon Commission, where he had advocated for joint electorates. Further, he proposed that the system of separate electorates for the Depressed Classes shall not be liable to be replaced by a system of joint electorates and reserved seats, unless (a) 'A referendum of the voters held at the demand of majority of their representatives in the Legislatures concerned and resulting in an absolute majority of the members of the Depressed Classes having the franchise'; (b) 'No such referendum shall be resorted to until after twenty years and until universal adult suffrage has been established'.[62] Keer notes: 'In one of his letters Dr. Ambedkar said that the Depressed Classes leaders, who supported Gandhi, did not understand that Gandhi was opposed not only to the Special Electorate but also to the Special Representation for the Depressed Classes: otherwise the problem would have been solved long before.'[63]

As there was no unanimous solution to the Minorities issue and the sharing of seats, the British prime minister decided to arbitrate and settle the communal problem.[64] The second Round Table Conference was then adjourned on 1 December 1931. In the same month, based on the recommendation of the Franchise Sub-Committee in the first Round Table Conference, the Indian Franchise Committee ('Lothian Committee') was appointed.[65] Dr Ambedkar was made a member of this committee.[66]

Archival sources show that Dr Ambedkar left London and sailed for New York on 5 December 1931, a few days after the conclusion of the second Round Table Conference.[67] While in New York, he spent some time near Columbia University and made efforts to get in touch with Jane Addams, American social reformer, internationalist and Nobel Peace Prize recipient, by sending a letter dated 15 December 1931. He wrote to Addams: 'Your life of devotion to the submerged of the world has been the inspiration and encouragement for us all even in darkest India.'[68] Dr Ambedkar could not get a response from Addams though, and returned to London on 4 January 1932.

Lothian Committee Report

Dr Ambedkar was keenly involved in the proceedings of the committee.[69] In its report of May 1932, the committee came to the conclusion that the machinery to deal with millions of voters was inadequate. It stated:

> [It] seems to us to be the course of wisdom and statesmanship not to attempt to launch the new constitution on the basis of adult franchise, but to seek a more manageable basis, at the same time providing that the system of franchise will give reasonable representation to the main categories of the population.[70]

The report added: 'It will then be for the legislatures themselves, after a definite period has passed, to determine at what pace the electorate should be expanded and the date when they may wish to introduce adult suffrage.'[71] As he expressed before the Franchise Sub-Committee, Dr Ambedkar wanted the immediate introduction of adult franchise. In his separate note in the Lothian Committee report, Dr Ambedkar expressed reservations that 'the allocation of seats to labour, women, and other special interests must not affect the proportion of seats which the Depressed Classes have claimed in the Minorities Pact submitted to the Round Table Conference'.[72] The Lothian

Committee report was submitted to the British Parliament in
May 1932. In the last week of the same month, Dr Ambedkar
undertook a voyage to Britain to meet the British prime minister
and other cabinet ministers before the decision on the communal
issue and minority representation was announced.[73] He met
every senior British official, and passionately put forward his case
for the rights of the Depressed Classes.

Poona Pact

The Communal Award was announced in August 1932,
and provided for separate electorates for the Depressed
Classes.[74] Contrary to popular perception, Dr Ambedkar had
disagreements with the Communal Award. On 23 August 1932,
he issued a public statement that '[T]he Communal Award has
ruthlessly scaled down their representation in the Provincial
Legislatures to quite insignificant proportions. The result is that
the Communal Award creates positive grievances by refusing
them adequate representation.'[75] As Gandhi was opposed to
any form of special electorates for the Depressed Classes, he
began a fast unto death against the Award in Yerawada prison
where he was imprisoned at that time. The British government
declined to give in to Gandhi's demands without the consent of
Dr Ambedkar as the representative of the Depressed Classes.[76]
Consequently, Dr Ambedkar had to negotiate with him for
several days. Dr Ambedkar was under immense pressure to save
Gandhi's life.[77] As Galanter notes, Dr Ambedkar was subject to
'the sense of the cataclysm that might engulf the untouchables
if Gandhi were to die'.[78] Eventually, both agreed to a settlement
which is popularly known as the 'Poona Pact' of September
1932. The Pact adopted the system of joint electorates with
reserved constituencies. Dr Ambedkar was able to scale the
proportion of seats reserved for Depressed Classes through the
Pact. This agreement was accepted by the British government[79]

and was to be considered as a legal electoral framework for the subsequent constitutional framework.

Third Round Table Conference

The third Round Table Conference was held in November–December 1932.[80] While Gandhi and the Congress did not participate, Dr Ambedkar went to London once again to build on the previous discussions. Dr Ambedkar was being seen as someone who was 'writing new pages of Indian history.'[81] The third conference considered the Report of the Lothian Committee.[82] Some of the discussions were indeed significant. For instance, the members of the Conference were 'unanimously in favour of accepting the proposals of the Franchise Committee [Lothian Committee] that women should be enfranchised in respect of the same property qualification as that prescribed for men.'[83] Similarly, the Conference

> was of opinion that a special provision should be made to enfranchise a larger number of voters belonging to the Depressed Classes and that the standard to be aimed at should, as proposed by the Franchise Committee, be 10 per cent, of the Depressed Class population in each Province, such of the differential qualifications suggested by the Franchise Committee being adopted as might be necessary to secure this result in the light of the varying conditions in each Province.[84]

However, as most members were not present at the third Conference, there could not be a consensus on larger issues. The recommendations of the third Conference were then published in the form of a White Paper (Command Paper 4238)[85] in January 1933. The Paper was submitted to the British Parliament for discussion.[86]

Joint Committee on Indian Constitutional Reform

In considering the White Paper, the British Parliament appointed a joint committee of select members from the House of Lords and the House of Commons called the Joint Committee on Indian Constitutional Reform. The Joint Committee was empowered to examine the White Paper and the issue of the future constitutional framework in consultation with the representatives from British India and the princely states.[87] It was entrusted with the task of formulating a new Act for India.[88] Dr Ambedkar was one of the few Indian members invited to participate as a delegate in the proceedings of the committee.[89] He was active in these proceedings, as he cross-questioned a number of individuals on key issues.

Dr Ambedkar raised important questions that helped in deciding the scope of various possible provisions for future legislation. This included cross-questioning about bringing civil servants under the control of the Indian legislature,[90] the scope of powers of the governor,[91] Centre-state finance,[92] Reserve Bank,[93] the jurisdiction of the Federal Court[94] and women's franchise,[95] among others. He also made British officials acknowledge that they were reluctant to interfere in social reforms for fear of a possible backlash from orthodox leaders. One British official stated, '. . . legislation can never be too much in advance of public opinion in a country like India'.[96] Dr Ambedkar also secured a clarification from the British that there could be further advancement in the political status and constitutional reforms in India beyond what was discussed at the Round Table Conferences.[97] This was significant as Dr Ambedkar was setting the tone for the narrative of constitutional reforms. The most interesting exchange in the proceedings of the committee happened between Dr Ambedkar and Rajkumari Amrit Kaur, the latter representing the All India Women's Conference.[98]

Dr Ambedkar constantly quizzed her on the issue of reservation of seats in the legislature for women, to which Kaur responded in the negative: 'We have always been opposed to reservation.'[99] But the way in which Dr Ambedkar was insisting on the question of reservations for women demonstrated his concern about the participation of women in politics. With Kaur's opposition, the issue of women's reservation was dismissed—only to reappear as an important issue decades after India's independence.[100]

Some notable individuals, including Rabindranath Tagore, wanted a modification of the Poona Pact to the effect that it should be inapplicable in Bengal, i.e., there should be no reserved seats for Depressed Classes in Bengal.[101] Tagore sent a cable to the then advocate general of Bengal, Sir N.N. Sircar:

> Upon the immediate settlement of [Poona Pact] question Mahatmaji's life depended and the intolerable anxiety caused by such a crisis drove me precipitately to a commitment which I now realise as a wrong done against our country's permanent interest... [J]ustice had been sacrificed in case of Bengal. I have not the least doubt now that such an injustice will continue to cause mischief for all parties concerned keeping alive the spirit of communal conflict in our Province in an intense form making peaceful government perpetually difficult.'[102]

It was argued by some political individuals: 'The award of His Majesty's Government is much more acceptable to us than the Poona Pact.'[103] Dr Ambedkar rebutted in much detail all these arguments against the reservation of seats for the Depressed Classes.[104] In a discussion in the Joint Committee on the Poona Pact on 31 July 1933, Dr Ambedkar gave a stern warning: 'I do not think that it would be possible for me to take any further part in the Proceedings of the Committee, if, for instance, the whole question was reopened with regard to the representation of the Depressed Classes.'[105]

When M.K. Acharya, representing the All-India Varnashram Swarajya Sangha, proposed that the legislature should not have the competence to pass laws affecting the fundamentals of religion, Dr Ambedkar posed several questions to him. When Dr Ambedkar insisted that Acharya define the extent of his proposal in legal terms, the latter responded: 'Dr Ambedkar is now trying to heckle me into some kind of answer in three words. I cannot.'[106] In a way, Dr Ambedkar was making his way on the point of social reform through law.

Dr Ambedkar also cross-questioned Winston Churchill (a member of the Joint Committee) on why the masses should not be given adult franchise. Churchill opposed the demand, arguing: 'Because I think it quite impracticable.'[107]

Dr Ambedkar was strongly in favour of the inclusion of what the British called 'primitive tribes' (sic) in the political system. He contradicted the claims of British officials, who were opposed to such a thought. Dr Ambedkar argued that if the tribes became a part of the political system, then they would find friends in the Depressed Classes.[108]

Government of India Act 1935

Based on these proceedings, the Joint Committee on Indian Constitutional Reform prepared a Bill, which was later enacted as the GOI Act 1935. Several provisions in the Bill reflected the discussions in the Round Table Conferences and the proceedings of the Joint Committee. For instance, the Act created the Federal Court, Public Service Commission, regulatory provision over the Reserve Bank, etc. The provisions of the Poona Pact were also incorporated in the Act. Thus, the Act for the first time recognized 'Scheduled Castes' as a political group in need of legal protection in the form of reserved seats.[109]

As seen in this chapter, Dr Ambedkar participated in all the proceedings which led to the drafting of the Act of 1935. He was the key figure who was setting the narrative—be it at the Round Table Conferences, Communal Award, Poona Pact, or questions in the Joint Committee. Dr Ambedkar was constantly focusing on the conceptions of responsible government, adult franchise, minority rights, powers of constitutional institutions like the governor and the Federal Court, etc. He was so unhappy with the behaviour of Indian leaders at the Round Table Conferences that he later noted: 'Believe me when I say that some of your national leaders were thoroughly unprepared for the job of constitution-making. They went to the Round Table Conference without any comparative study of constitutions and could propound no solutions to problems with which they were presented.'[110] Critical of Gandhi's approach, he stated: 'Mr. Gandhi also forgot that he was going to a political conference.'[111]

The future Constitution would rely on the GOI Act 1935, which had a clear imprint of Dr Ambedkar's contributions and foresight. However, contrary to the belief of some individuals, it must also be noted that the future Constitution, prepared under the leadership of Dr Ambedkar, was a deviation from the GOI Act of 1935 on many fronts. It added so many significant aspects of constitutionalism, which Dr Ambedkar advocated: full citizenship, fundamental rights, abolition of untouchability, affirmative action, entrenched minority rights, universal adult franchise, protection of Scheduled Tribes, judicial review, etc. In that sense, the future Constitution of 1950 departed from the culture of colonialism.

Furthermore, a lot of significant features would be adopted into the Constitution of 1950 because of the political pressure exerted by Dr Ambedkar. In the mid-1940s, Gandhi and Sardar Patel exchanged several letters to discuss how to deal with Dr Ambedkar's demands.[112] In that way, Dr Ambedkar brought the rights-based discourse to the mainstream.

10

Annihilation of Caste—
From a Constitutional Perspective

In 1935, Dr Ambedkar was invited to deliver a public address at a conference organized by Jat Pat Todak Mandal, a Lahore-based organization of caste Hindu social reformers with the aim of eradicating the caste system. However, when the organizers came to know about the radical content of the address, they requested Dr Ambedkar to alter some of it. In protest, Dr Ambedkar refused to change the nature of his address, leading to the event being cancelled by the organizers. The address prepared by Dr Ambedkar, titled 'Annihilation of Caste', was later published by him in the form of a book in 1936.

While it is commonly understood that Dr Ambedkar's *Annihilation of Caste* was a direct attack on the caste system, it also needs to be emphasized that the book presented a clear understanding of how caste survives in political, constitutional and legal systems. It gives us an idea about the kind of constitutionalism which Dr Ambedkar was endorsing for a future India. As scholar Aishwary Kumar notes:

> Ambedkar would begin to develop a distinctive understanding of freedom, at once republican in its vision, ontological in its depth, and phenomenological in its

sensitivity to the morals—or rather, religiosity—of everyday life. For Ambedkar, only a democratization of the innermost recesses of faith could transcend—if need be, by force—the artificial division between civic virtue and personal conviction, between the political and religious.[1]

In the book, Dr Ambedkar reimagined not only the constitutional aspects of India's political struggle but also how caste threatens the various constitutional rights that every individual ought to have. Several values propounded in the book were later referenced by Dr Ambedkar during the framing of India's Constitution.

Social Aspects of Constitutionalism

Written against the backdrop of political resistance against colonialism, Dr Ambedkar argued in *Annihilation of Caste* that the demand for political change could not come about in isolation. He emphasized that political reform could not happen unless it was accompanied by social reform. According to him: 'Political reform cannot with impunity take precedence over social reform in the sense of reconstruction of society is a thesis which, I am sure, cannot be controverted.'[2] To buttress his point, he quoted Ferdinand Lassalle, 'the friend and co-worker of Karl Marx', who said, before a Prussian audience in 1862, that:

The constitutional questions are in the first instance not questions of right, but questions of might. The actual constitution of a country has its existence only in the actual condition of force which exists in the country: hence political constitutions have value and permanence only when they accurately express those conditions of forces which exist in practice within a society.[3]

Resonating with this, Dr Ambedkar too propounded that political constitutions cannot be written without addressing social issues. A constitution must have necessary provisions to deal with social differences, otherwise those differences will continue to affect the working of any political constitution. Leaving out social problems could result in significant challenges to governance for future political leaders. Dr Ambedkar used examples from history in which political revolutions had been preceded by social revolutions. It was therefore essential, he stated, that 'political constitution must take note of social organization'.[4] Thus, Dr Ambedkar was showing a mirror to the existing discourse on drafting India's Constitution that had long nullified the social inequalities that overwhelmed Indian society and polity.

Taking things further, he added that if the social and religious minorities of India were trying to cooperate and negotiate with the dominant nationalist discourse, then instead of ridiculing them, their demands had to be considered. He argued that if the minorities wanted, they would have refused to accept majority rule on any terms. Providing an example, Dr Ambedkar brought up the case of Ireland:

> It is well-known that in the course of the negotiations between the representatives of Ulster and Southern Ireland, Mr Redmond, the representative of Ireland, in order to bring Ulster in a Home Rule Constitution common to the whole of Ireland said to the representatives of Ulster: 'Ask any political safeguards you like and you shall have them.' What was the reply that Ulstermen gave? Their reply was, 'Damn your safeguards, we don't want to be ruled by you on any terms.' People who blame the minorities in India ought to consider what would have happened to the political aspirations of the majority if the minorities had taken the

attitude which Ulster took. Judged by the attitude of Ulster to Irish Home Rule, is it nothing that the minorities agreed to be ruled by the majority, which has not shown much sense of statesmanship, provided some safeguards were devised for them?'[5]

Dr Ambedkar then turned to the economist interpretation of history and constitutionalism. The economic proponents argue that 'political and social reforms are but gigantic illusions and that economic reform by equalization of property must have precedence over every other kind of reform'.[6] Dr Ambedkar disagreed with such assertions. The basic flaw in such an understanding, he highlighted, was that economic power is not the only power that governs society. Rather, the social status of an individual is a source of power in a deeply divided society. He added,

> If liberty is the ideal, if liberty means the destruction of the dominion which one man holds over another then obviously it cannot be insisted upon that economic reform must be the one kind of reform worthy of pursuit. If the source of power and dominion is at any given time or in any given society social and religious then social reform and religious reform must be accepted as the necessary sort of reform.[7]

That is to say, power is not just economic or political, it is also social. Dr Ambedkar noted that mere self-declaration of being casteless is not enough. Instead, what is needed is that there are efforts by proponents of economic equality that attack the systems of social inequality.[8] His message was clear, 'Turn in any direction you like, caste is the monster that crosses your path. You cannot have political reform, you cannot have economic reform, unless you kill this monster.'[9]

Structural Discrimination

Dr Ambedkar questioned the structural discrimination and exploitation that took away the liberty of the Untouchables. He linked the exploitation of caste, with the denial of one's dignity and a withholding of the liberty of changing one's fortune. He noted: 'Caste System is not merely division of labour. It is also a division of labourers . . . It is a hierarchy in which the divisions of labourers are graded one above the other . . . This division of labour is not spontaneous, it is not based on natural aptitudes.'[10] The kind of work that Untouchables can do is limited. The Untouchables are denied the chance to move outside their designated roles, thus violating their liberty. He noted, 'The division of labour brought about by the caste system is not a division based on choice. Individual sentiment, individual preference has no place in it. It is based on the dogma of predestination.' The basis of such exploitation is not scientific at all. Rather, it 'is a social system which embodies the arrogance and selfishness of a perverse section of the Hindus who were superior enough in social status to set it in fashion and who had authority to force it on their inferiors'.[11] This system, which resulted in the restricting of the liberty of the Untouchables and other Backward Classes, is the antithesis of liberty and leads to bonded labour. Such clear arguments naturally would have led to a constitutional thought, where bonded labour ought not to be accepted.

Dr Ambedkar highlighted how the system of caste and its manifestations created an absence of fraternity. It was his belief: 'The caste system prevents common activity and by preventing common activity it has prevented the Hindus from becoming a society with a unified life and a consciousness of its own being.'[12] Caste leads to an 'anti-social spirit', where self-proclaimed superior castes enjoy hating other castes.

Dr Ambedkar stated, 'The literature of the Hindus is full of caste genealogies in which an attempt is made to give a noble origin to one caste and an ignoble origin to other castes.'[13]

Dr Ambedkar further added that by suffocating any voice of reform, the system of caste again denies individuals their liberty to lead a life of their choice. This is evidenced in its mechanism of social boycott, which is used to maintain the hierarchies of caste, by denying the freedom to choose and thus individual liberty. He highlighted,

> The assertion by the individual of his own opinions and beliefs, his own independence and interest as over against group standards, group authority and group interests is the beginning of all reform. But whether the reform will continue depends upon what scope the group affords for such individual assertion . . . Now a caste has an unquestioned right to excommunicate any man who is guilty of breaking the rules of the caste and when it is realized that excommunication involves a complete cesser of social intercourse it will be agreed that as a form of punishment there is really little to choose between excommunication and death.

That is why it has been difficult for individuals to 'assert their independence by breaking the barriers of caste'. Dr Ambedkar thus demanded that 'such a nefarious act as an attempt to excommunicate a person for daring to act contrary to the rules of caste' should be made an offence punishable by law. At that time, as British courts allowed caste groups to regulate their affairs and punish their members with excommunication, Dr Ambedkar questioned such discretion given to caste groups, by noting: 'Caste in the hands of the orthodox has been a powerful weapon for persecuting the reforms and for killing all reform.'[14]

What Kind of Constitutionalism?

Dr Ambedkar proposed that an ideal society, devoid of caste hierarchy, 'would be a society based on liberty, equality and fraternity'.[15] This was not the first time he was referring to this phrase. He had invoked the terms during the Mahad Satyagraha. Here, Dr Ambedkar elaborated on what 'liberty', 'equality' and 'fraternity' would mean.

He linked the idea of fraternity with the conception of democracy. As he noted:

> An ideal society should be mobile, should be full of channels for conveying a change taking place in one part to other parts. In an ideal society there should be many interests consciously communicated and shared. There should be varied and free points of contact with other modes of association. In other words, there must be social endosmosis. This is fraternity, which is only another name for democracy. Democracy is not merely a form of Government. It is primarily a mode of associated living, of conjoint communicated experience. It is essentially an attitude of respect and reverence towards fellowmen.[16]

For Dr Ambedkar, there are two aspects of liberty. Firstly, liberty does not mean the freedom to discriminate against others.[17] Secondly, liberty was significant not just in the context of individual rights. It was not merely a right to free movement, in the sense of a right to life and limb, and property. It was also about one's freedom to choose one's conduct and fate and decide one's own profession.[18] If such liberty is not allowed, then the result—Dr Ambedkar noted—would be 'to perpetuate slavery'. One would be forced to carry forward one's occupation from generation to generation. He explained:

> For slavery does not merely mean a legalized form of subjection. It means a state of society in which some men

are forced to accept from other the purposes which control their conduct. This condition obtains even where there is no slavery in the legal sense. It is found where, as in the caste system, some persons are compelled to carry on certain prescribed callings which are not of their choice.[19]

In the conception of equality, Dr Ambedkar argued that 'social inheritance or endowment in the form of parental care, education, accumulation of scientific knowledge, everything which enables him to be more efficient' needs to be considered.[20] He noted, 'It is obvious that those individuals also in whose favour there is birth, education, family name, business connections and inherited wealth would be selected in the race. But selection under such circumstances would not be a selection of the able. It would be the selection of the privileged.'[21] Thus, for him, equality meant equality of opportunity for everyone. It would not be right to treat unequals equally. Rather, efforts are needed to bring everyone on an equal level playing field. Dr Ambedkar noted, 'It is good for the social body to get the most out of its members, it can get most out of them only by making them equal as far as possible at the very start of the race.'[22] Dr Ambedkar's assertions were a reflection of emerging affirmative action frameworks, which would facilitate equality.

Challenging Caste as Law

Dr Ambedkar argued that the system of Chaturvarna (four varnas) successfully survived because the system of caste worked as a form of law or 'the maintenance of the penal system which could maintain it by its sanction'.[23] That is, if someone tried to transgress the rules of caste, then they were punished by the law of caste. To explain his assertion, he gave the following example:

That, without penal sanction the ideal of Chaturvarna cannot be realized, is proved by the story in the Ramayana

of Rama killing Shambuka. Some people seem to blame
Rama because he . . . without reason killed Shambuka. But to
blame Rama for killing Shambuka is to misunderstand the
whole situation. Ram Raj was a Raj based on Chaturvarna.
As a king, Rama was bound to maintain Chaturvarna. It
was his duty therefore to kill Shambuka, the Shudra, who
had transgressed his class and wanted to be a Brahmin.
This is the reason why Rama killed Shambuka. But this also
shows that penal sanction is necessary for the maintenance
of Chaturvarna. Not only penal sanction is necessary, but
penalty of death is necessary. That is why Rama did not
inflict on Shambuka a lesser punishment.'[24]

Dr Ambedkar again criticized Manusmriti, which prescribed
'such heavy sentences as cutting off the tongue or pouring of
molten lead in the ears of the Shudra, who recites or hears
the Vedas'.[25]

The subjugation of Untouchables and the Shudras was so
deep that they did not have any medium to revolt against an
unjust system. The structural discrimination and oppression
against them denied them even their own self-dignity.
Dr Ambedkar highlighted this as follows:

The three classes, Brahmins, Kshatriyas and Vaishyas although
not very happy in their mutual relationship managed to work
by compromise. The Brahmin flattered the Kshatriya and
both let the Vaishya live in order to be able to live upon him.
But the three agreed to beat down the Shudra. He was not
allowed to acquire wealth lest he should be independent of the
three Varnas. He was prohibited from acquiring knowledge
lest he should keep a steady vigil regarding his interests.
He was prohibited from bearing arms lest he should have
the means to rebel against their authority. That this is how

the Shudras were treated by the Tryavarnikas is evidenced by
the Laws of Manu. There is no code of laws more infamous
regarding social rights than the Laws of Manu. Any instance
from anywhere of social injustice must pale before it. Why
have the mass of people tolerated the social evils to which
they have been subjected? There have been social revolutions
in other countries of the world. Why have there not been
social revolutions in India, is a question which has incessantly
troubled me. There is only one answer, which I can give and
it is that the lower classes of Hindus have been completely
disabled for direct action on account of this wretched system
of Chaturvarna. They could not bear arms and without arms
they could not rebel. They were all ploughmen or rather
condemned to be ploughmen and they never were allowed to
convert their ploughshare into swords. They had no bayonets
and therefore everyone who chose could and did sit upon
them. On account of the Chaturvarna, they could receive no
education. They could not think out or know the way to their
salvation. They were condemned to be lowly and not knowing
the way of escape and not having the means of escape, they
became reconciled to eternal servitude, which they accepted
as their inescapable fate.[26]

The acts of resistance would thus demand a challenging of the
law of caste.

Freedom to Choose

It was Dr Ambedkar's emphasis that the walls of caste would
be broken, if individuals were given full liberty to choose their
partners beyond the sanctions of caste. Merely allowing people
to marry within sub-castes or to hold inter-caste dinners would
not take away the basis of the caste system. The right to make

one's own life choice without the dictums of caste was crucial in Dr Ambedkar's analysis, as he argued:

> I am convinced that the real remedy is inter-marriage. Fusion of blood can alone create the feeling of being kith and kin and unless this feeling of kinship, of being kindred, becomes paramount the separatist feeling—the feeling of being aliens—created by Caste will not vanish. Among the Hindus inter-marriage must necessarily be a factor of greater force in social life than it need be in the life of the non-Hindus. Where society is already well-knit by other ties, marriage is an ordinary incident of life. But where society [is] cut asunder, marriage as a binding force becomes a matter of urgent necessity. *The real remedy for breaking caste is inter-marriage. Nothing else will serve as the solvent of caste.*[27] (sic)

The Urgency of Social Reforms

Dr Ambedkar noted that for the annihilation of caste, it is not just necessary that political reforms happen but there is a need for a change in social discourse. The obstacles that one faces while advancing social reforms are manifold as compared to someone demanding political reforms. He highlighted, 'Political tyranny is nothing compared to social tyranny and a reformer, who defies society, is a much more courageous man than a politician, who defies government.'[28] The reason why caste has survived is because it is much more than individual conduct. Dr Ambedkar argued that caste as a notion has been entrenched as 'a state of the mind'. Therefore, any legal or constitutional change must be supported by a powerful social discourse. According to Dr Ambedkar:

> Why is it that a large majority of Hindus do not inter-dine and do not inter-marry? Why is it that your cause is not

popular? There can be only one answer to this question and
it is that inter-dining and inter-marriage are repugnant to
the beliefs and dogmas which the Hindus regard as sacred.
Caste is not a physical object like a wall of bricks or a line of
barbed wire which prevents the Hindus from co-mingling,
and which has, therefore, to be pulled down . . . The
destruction of caste does not therefore mean the destruction
of a physical barrier. It means a *notional* change.[29]

Dr Ambedkar further emphasized that the reason why the
caste barriers have not weakened is because of 'the attitude
of hostility, which the Brahmins have shown towards this
question'.[30] The Brahmins, who were the beneficiaries of
the caste system, were a part of the movement for political
reform and in some cases also of economic reform, but not
so much 'to break down the barricades of caste'. According to
Dr Ambedkar, the oppressing castes, as they enjoyed privileges
coming out of social oppression, would not have been ready to
throw away those privileges and battle for social reforms.[31] (On
a similar note, Dr Martin Luther King wrote in 1963: 'History
is the long and tragic story of the fact that privileged groups
seldom give up their privileges voluntarily. Individuals may see
the moral light and voluntarily give up their unjust posture;
but, as Reinhold Niebuhr has reminded us, groups are more
immoral than individuals.'[32])

The Need for a Broader Constitutional Framework

Dr Ambedkar therefore argued that the system of caste should
not be considered as a religious system or religion. Rather, it is
nothing more than a set of rules governing society.[33] It must,
he argued, be brought under State regulation. A new legal or
constitutional framework ought to come in place, where the
sanctity of socio-religious texts such as the Vedas, Shastras

and Puranas, which are treated as sacred and authoritative, must by law cease to be. He added that 'the preaching of any doctrine, religious or social, contained in these books should be penalized'.[34] Thus, he was in favour of constitutional regulation of religious affairs, so that religion cannot be used as grounds to discriminate against marginalized groups. In other words, one's fundamental rights ought not to be regulated or diluted by religious beliefs.

On that note, Dr Ambedkar demanded that the priesthood among Hindus should either be abolished or should be regulated by the State. This was because priesthood was seen as providing higher social status, and was a self-declared hereditary domain of the Brahmins. That is, only a Brahmin could become a priest. Dr Ambedkar stressed that priesthood must cease to be hereditary and that every person who professes to be a Hindu must be eligible to be a priest. He noted:

> It should be provided by law that no Hindu shall be entitled to be a priest unless he has passed an examination prescribed by the State . . . A priest should be the servant of the State and should be subject to disciplinary action by the State in the matter of his morals, beliefs and worship, in addition to his being subject along with other citizens to the ordinary law of the land.[35]

He added that the number of priests should be limited by law according to the requirements of the State as is done in the case of the civil services. There is nothing revolutionary in such a proposal, as every profession in India is regulated.[36]

Thus, it was Dr Ambedkar's thesis that only with a 'new doctrinal basis'—in consonance with liberty, equality and fraternity—could democracy be envisaged in India. Without such a realization, the demand for swaraj 'may turn out to be only a step towards slavery', i.e., the oppressed caste would be subjected to slavery.[37] These values of liberty, equality, fraternity would be later emphasized by Dr Ambedkar in his last address in the Constituent Assembly.

II

An Enhanced Version of
Separation of Power

By the mid-1940s, efforts were being made to resolve the issue
of communal altercations in undivided India. While the focus
was on Hindu–Muslim issues, there were communities such
as Scheduled Castes and Sikhs, whose interests were also at
stake. In March 1942, the Cripps Mission suggested that the
British should retain power for the present but offer India
dominion status and a constitutional assembly after the Second
World War. The proposal contained no mention of Dalit
representation or separate electorates.[1] Following this, in 1944,
the Sapru Conciliation Committee was set up 'to examine the
whole communal and minorities question from a constitutional
and political point of view, put itself in touch with the different
parties and their leaders, including the minorities interested in
the question, and present a solution'. However, Dr Ambedkar
strongly criticized the proposal for the severe burdens that it
imposed on Scheduled Castes.[2] He found both proposals—
Cripps Mission and Sapru Committee—unsatisfactory.[3]

In 1945, Dr Ambedkar wrote 'Communal Deadlock and
How to Solve It', after the Cripps Proposal and the Sapru
Proposals were out. He also used the opportunity to dismiss the

charge thrown at Scheduled Castes[4] of 'being selfish, interested only in themselves', by emphasizing that they have been important stakeholders in the solution of the country's political problems. Through 'Communal Deadlock', Dr Ambedkar was trying to solve the Hindu–Muslim dispute by proposing a new constitutional framework, which deviated from the traditional Westminster model of government.

According to the English doctrine of 'Separation of Power', each organ of the State has to perform separate functions, and thereby maintain a system of checks and balances on each other. Power is thus divided between different institutions and office-holders. However, in a deeply divided society, it may happen that power is concentrated in the hands of the majority community. For power to be divided equally among different communities, the constitutional framework ought to devise such a system. What could such a system be? Dr Ambedkar in 'Communal Deadlock' proposed a constitutional framework which, in my view, resembles a new version of the 'Separation of Power' principle. That is, power would be divided and shared not just by different institutions but also between different communities in a divided society, so that the rule of power does not end up becoming the rule of the majority community or the historical oligarchy. I call this an enhanced version of the separation of power principle.

That is why the first important issue that Dr Ambedkar highlighted, with reference to the framing of the Indian Constitution, was that it must be framed with the consensus of different communities and not by the British. He argued: 'A Constitution, framed by the British Government and imposed upon Indians, sufficed in the past. But if the nature of the future Constitution Indians are clamouring for, is borne in mind it will be clear that an imposed Constitution will not do.'[5] What was this nature, which Dr Ambedkar referred to? He answered:

> The Constitution must be so made that it will not only command the obedience but also the respect of all; and all or if not all, at any rate, all important elements in the national life of India shall be prepared to uphold it and to give it their support. This can happen only if the Constitution is framed by Indians for Indians and with the voluntary consent of Indians. If the Constitution is imposed by the British Government and is not accepted by one section and is opposed by another, there will arise in the country an element, hostile to the Constitution, and which will devote its energies not to working the Constitution but to breaking it.'[6]

It was Dr Ambedkar's proposal that power must be distributed between different institutions—not only the legislature but equally the executive. Furthermore, the quantum of the representation of the minorities was very important in his scheme.[7] Dr Ambedkar was not in favour of any token or minimal representation, but wanted as much share in representation, such that without the support of the minorities, no important decision could be made by the government.

Power-Sharing in the Services

Dr Ambedkar reiterated a principle, well accepted by the British government, that 'all communities should be represented in the Public Services in a prescribed proportion and no single community should be allowed to have a monopoly has been accepted by the Government of India'.[8] This principle was part of the Government of India resolutions of 1934 and 1943.[9] Furthermore, there was an administrative practice of the British that any appointment made contrary to the Government of India resolutions would be deemed null and void. Dr Ambedkar wanted to incorporate the resolutions and the administrative practice of maintaining representation in the services as part of constitutional principles and in the text of the Constitution. That is to say, the future Constitution should include a provision for the representation of all communities and the consequent division of power in a prescribed proportion.

Nature of the Executive

The British System of government by a majority party rests on the premise that the majority is a political majority. However, Dr Ambedkar underscored that in a divided society like India, 'there is a perpetual antipathy between the majority and the minorities'.[10] This can result in 'the danger of communal discrimination by majority against minorities', thereby forming 'an ever-present menace to the minorities'. More particularly because, 'the majority in India is a communal majority and not a political majority', i.e., the majoritarian religion decides the political majority. For Dr Ambedkar, 'minority' did not mean numerical or religious minority, but also social groups who have been excluded and ostracized even if they had a large population.[11] Explaining later, he added:

> In India the majority is born; it is not made. That is the difference between a communal majority and a political majority. A political majority is not a fixed or a permanent majority. It is a majority which is always made, unmade and remade. A communal majority is a permanent majority fixed in its attitude. One can destroy it, but one cannot transform it.[12]

To prevent such a situation from happening, Dr Ambedkar proposed that the nature of the executive should be designed in such a way as to prevent the communal majority from becoming a majority. This is because 'the executive power assumes far greater importance than the legislative power' in managing the everyday decisions of the government. He thus reached the conclusion that the English style of executive would not suit the Indian political situation. As he noted, 'The system under which a party which has secured a majority at the poll is deemed entitled to form a Government on the presumption that it has the confidence of the majority is untenable in Indian conditions.'[13] A couple of years later, Dr Ambedkar repeated this principle in his document 'States and Minorities'. There he emphasized that, 'No matter what social and political programme it may have the majority will retain its character of being a communal majority. Nothing can alter this fact. Given this fact it is clear that if the British System was copied it would result in permanently vesting executive power in a communal majority.'[14] He also stated that the 'British System of Government imposes no obligation upon the majority party to include in its cabinet the representatives of the minority party'. He further added, 'If applied to India the consequence will be obvious. It would make the majority community a governing class and the minority community a subject race. It would mean that a communal majority will be free to run the administration according to its own ideas of what is good for the minorities.' He declared that such a functioning of the administration cannot be a 'democracy', rather it is 'imperialism'. In strong words, he again noted, 'In the light of these consequences it is obvious that the introduction of British type of the executive will be full of menace to the life, liberty and pursuit of happiness of the minorities in general and of the Untouchables in particular'.[15]

What would be the fate of the Untouchables if the administration was biased and communal? Dr Ambedkar summarized thus:

> The problem of the Untouchables is a formidable one for the Untouchables to face. The Untouchables are surrounded by a vast mass of Hindu population which is hostile to them and which is not ashamed of committing any inequity or atrocity against them. For a redress of these wrongs which are matters of daily occurrence, the Untouchables have to call in the aid of the administration. What is the character and composition of this administration? To be brief, the administration in India is completely in the hands of the Hindus. It is their monopoly. From top to bottom it is controlled by them. There is no Department which is not dominated by them. They dominate the Police, the Magistracy and the Revenue Services, indeed any and every branch of the administration. The next point to remember is that the Hindus in the administration have the same positive anti-social and inimical attitude to the Untouchables which the Hindus outside the administration have. Their one aim is to discriminate against the Untouchables and to deny and deprive them not only of the benefits of law, but also of the protection of the law against tyranny and oppression. The result is that the Untouchables are placed between the Hindu population and the Hindu-ridden administration, the one committing wrong against them and the other protecting the wrong-doer, instead of helping the victims.[16] Thus, there would be 'the administration unbridled in venom and in harshness, uncontrolled by the Legislature and the Executive', which 'may pursue its policy of inequity towards the Untouchables without any curb'.[17]

In 'Communal Deadlock', Dr Ambedkar came up with the following framework:

- The Executive should cease to be a Committee of the majority party in the Legislature. It should be so constituted that it will have its mandate not only from the majority but also from the minorities in the Legislature.
- The Executive should be non-Parliamentary in the sense that it shall not be removable before the term of the Legislature.
- The Executive should be Parliamentary in the sense that the members of the Executive shall be chosen from the members of the Legislature and shall have the right to sit in the House, speak, vote and answer questions.[18]

It seems that Dr Ambedkar's proposal was batting for a larger accountability of the executive so that it could be prevented from committing administrative excesses. If the members of the executive were given certain safeguards, they could act independently of the government.[19] He further proposed a reservation in the Cabinet (at least one seat) for minorities with less population.[20] In *States and Minorities,* he succinctly described that such a form of the executive is intended to give effect:

(i) To prevent the majority from forming a Government without giving any opportunity to the minorities to have a say in the matter; (ii) To prevent the majority from having exclusive control over administration and thereby make the tyranny of the minority by the majority possible; (iii) To prevent the inclusion by the Majority Party in the Executive representatives of the minorities who have no confidence of the Minorities; (iv) To provide a stable Executive necessary for good and efficient administration.[21]

Dr Ambedkar stated that his model was an evolved version of the American form of the executive designed to suit Indian conditions 'especially to the requirements of minorities'.[22] He later added: 'The Constitution of the USA is full of such checks and balances which are embodied in clauses relating to Fundamental Rights and Separation of Powers.'[23] The style of electing the prime minister proposed by Dr Ambedkar is dealt with in the next heading.

Selection of the Cabinet and Principles of 'Confidence in Executive'[24]

As per the British parliamentary model, the prime minister is the leader of the ruling party in the parliament. Each cabinet minister is appointed in accordance with the discretion of the prime minister in the ruling party. But Dr Ambedkar proposed that the prime minister as the executive head of the Government 'should have the confidence of the whole House'. That is, s/he should be selected by the entire house including the opposition parties.[25] Furthermore, he proposed that 'the person representing a particular minority in the Cabinet should have the confidence of the members of his community in the Legislature'. It was also suggested that a cabinet minister shall not be liable to be removed except on impeachment by the House on the grounds of corruption or treason.

Based on the above propositions, Dr Ambedkar provided for the method of selecting the prime minister and the cabinet ministers. As he noted,

> My proposal is that the Prime Minister and the members of the Cabinet from the majority community should be elected by the whole House by a single transferable vote and that the representatives of the different minorities in the

Cabinet should be elected by a single transferable vote of the members of each minority community in the Legislature.[26]

Principle of 'Relative Majority' and 'Balanced Representation'[27]

Dr Ambedkar believed that in order to put the executive under control, the nature and the composition of the legislature also needs to be such that no religion/social group commands an absolute majority. He advanced a system of 'relative majority', where a group with a large population can have the highest number of elected representatives, but that strength should not cross a maximum cut-off of 40 out of 100 seats. That is, the Hindu majority in India cannot have an absolute majority in the legislature.

Dr Ambedkar's proposed system had a weightage system in the legislature, in which there would be a reduction of seats in the Central legislature for the Hindu majority (while it remained a majority) and a subsequent increase in the seats for minorities (while they remained a minority or minorities). The number of seats cut from the Hindus was supposed to be distributed among the minorities, including Scheduled Castes and Tribes, on the criteria of economic, educational and social backwardness of minorities, 'so that a minority which is large and which has a better social, educational and economic standing gets a lesser amount of weightage than a minority whose numbers are less and whose educational, economic and social position is inferior to that of the others'.[28] Similarly, in a Provincial legislature with a Muslim majority, the seats for Muslims would be reduced to a relative majority, leading to an increase in seats for other minorities in the province.[29]

Thus, in Dr Ambedkar's formulation, such a scheme represented the principle of relative majority and ensured a balanced representation of the majority and minorities.[30] In this system, no one community would be placed in a position to dominate others by virtue of its numbers.[31]

The purpose of having such a system was clear: to prevent majority rule in India. As Dr Ambedkar himself explained:

- Majority Rule is untenable in theory and unjustifiable in practice.
- A majority community may be conceded a relative majority of representation but it can never claim an absolute majority.
- The relative majority of representation given to a majority community in the legislature should not be so large as to enable the majority to establish its rule with the help of the smallest minorities.
- The distribution of seats should be so made that a combination of the majority and one of the major minorities should not give the combine such a majority as to make them impervious to the interest of the minorities.
- The distribution should be so made that if all the minorities combine they could, without depending on the majority, form a government of their own.

Thus, Dr Ambedkar's proposal would have made sure that the majority community is not able to exercise any power without obtaining the consent of the social and religious minorities. It was a strong constitutional safeguard proposed for the minorities in India, which was unique in the world.

Dr Ambedkar stated that this proposal would even address the demand for the creation of Pakistan. He noted, 'The Muslim objection to the Hindu majority and the Hindu and Sikh objections to the Muslim majority are completely eliminated [in my proposal], both in the Central as well as in the Provinces.'[32] He further noted, 'My proposals are for a United India. They are made in the hope that the Muslims will accept them in preference to Pakistan as providing better security than Pakistan does.'[33]

Electorates for Minorities

Dr Ambedkar argued that the minorities should be able 'to select candidates to the Legislature who will be real and not nominal representatives of the minority'. This can only happen when there is a system that guarantees this representation. He noted that while a 'separate electorate gives an absolute guarantee to the minority, that its representatives will be no others except those who enjoy its confidence', a system of joint electorates may be equally good if it provides certain safeguards. Dr Ambedkar provided for qualified joint electorates with reserved seats, i.e., only those members could be elected as the representative of the minorities, who secured a minimum prescribed percentage of minority votes.[34] This demand was later raised by him in the Constituent Assembly, as will be discussed in a subsequent chapter.

Mandatory Safeguards in Place of a Rule of Unanimity

Dr Ambedkar dismissed the demand of the Hindus to have the rule of absolute majority. He argued that the rule of majority is not sacrosanct. In contrast, he posed before the Hindus another accepted principle of decision-making called the 'rule of unanimity', which was applicable in several institutions. He describes the rule as follows:

> The Hindu does not seem to be aware of the fact that there is another rule, which is also operative in fields where important disputes between individual and nations arise and that rule is a rule of unanimity. If he will take the trouble to

examine the position he will realize that such a rule is not a
fiction, but it does exist. Let him take the Jury System. In the
jury trial the principle is unanimity. The decision is binding
upon the judge only if the verdict of the jury is unanimous.
Let him take another illustration of the League of Nations.
What was the rule for decisions in the League of Nations?
The rule was a rule of unanimity.[35]

That is to say, the majority could not take any decision without
having a consensus with the minorities. He noted, 'It is obvious
that if the principle of unanimity was accepted by the Hindus as
a rule of decision in the Legislature and in the Executive there
would be no such thing as a Communal Problem in India'.[36]

Dr Ambedkar then argued that since the rule of unanimity
was not being demanded by the minorities, the majority
Hindus should concede mandatory constitutional safeguards
to the minorities. As he noted, '[The minorities] are prepared
to accept freedom and the dangers in which they likely to be
involved; provided they [are] granted satisfactory safeguards.'
Thus, the majority Hindus should be grateful for this gesture
of the minorities. Dr Ambedkar appealed to the Hindus to
abandon the principle of absolute majority rule and be satisfied
with a relative majority rule proposed by him.

From the Perspective of the Untouchables

Dr Ambedkar also highlighted why the proposed safeguards
were necessary even from the perspective of the Untouchables:

The purpose of these guarantees demanded by the
Untouchables is not to fill the Legislature, the Executive
and the Administration by the representatives of the
Untouchables. These guarantees are really floorings below

which the Untouchables will not fall under the crushing pressure of the Hindu Communal Majority. They are intended to keep the Hindu Communal Majority within bounds. For, if there were no such guarantees to the Untouchables, the result will be that the Hindu Communal Majority will not only capture the Legislature, the Executive and the Administration, but the Legislature, the Executive and the Administration will be over-run by the Hindu Communal Majority and these powerful organs of the State, instead of protecting the minorities, will become the tools of the Hindu Communal Majority doing its biddings . . . In other words, the Untouchables are anxious to make India safe for democracy . . .'[37]

Dr Ambedkar's proposal was foresighted. He was proposing a system which provided for greater accountability and could have prevented majoritarian rule in all situations. His proposal was that of ensuring minorities of their rightful share in the governance of the country with the help of mandatory constitutional safeguards and checks on the exercise of power by the majority. Unfortunately, Dr Ambedkar's proposal was not taken seriously by any other stakeholder. He would later bring some of the proposals back to the Constituent Assembly.

12

Learning from Global
Constitutional Evolution

In several of his writings, Dr Ambedkar draws reference to the historical developments or principles in other countries. The purpose does not seem to be only to draw parallels between India and other countries. Rather, what Dr Ambedkar does is attempt to refine global ideas to suit Indian conditions and to learn from the evolution of history in other countries. For instance, he often invoked the concept of 'liberty, equality and fraternity' from the French Revolution to reflect on social conditions in India. In the previous chapter, it was seen how Dr Ambedkar tweaked the Westminster model of parliamentary democracy to evolve a system suitable for the Indian social composition.

While India was on the cusp of framing its own Constitution, Dr Ambedkar reflected on the constitutional history of other countries to highlight important constitutional principles. At the same time, he argued that the future Indian Constitution should not repeat the mistakes or moments of legally sanctioned injustices that took place in other countries. These lessons from global history were best captured in *What Congress And Gandhi Have Done To The Untouchables: A False Claim* which Dr Ambedkar published in May 1945. This book was written by him with the main purpose of appealing to the foreign audience about the situation of the Untouchables of India, along with raising concerns over the attitude of inaction of the Congress party and in particular, Gandhi towards them. However, the book provides an answer in advance as to why the Indian Constitution, adopted in 1950, had a mandatory provision of affirmative action in the form of quotas, as well as why it has so many detailed provisions. The answer lies in Dr Ambedkar's analysis of American and Greek constitutional history.

American Constitutional History

Since his time in America in the early 1910s, Dr Ambedkar constantly read about American society and its constitutional history. He had 'been a fan of the Fourteenth Amendment to the US (United States) Constitution which helped guarantee freedom for African Americans'.[1] Dr Ambedkar found a natural connection with the problems of African Americans. He would make references to American slavery and the Civil Rights Act to comment on the situation of the Untouchables in India and to propose legal solutions. For instance, during the negotiations at the Round Table Conference, he had submitted that the Indian Constitution should have a provision on the lines of the Civil Rights Protection Acts of 9 April 1868, and of 1 March 1875—'passed in the interest of the Negroes after their emancipation'.[2] The said provision provided:

> Whoever denies to any person except for reasons by law applicable to persons of all classes and regardless of any previous condition of Untouchability the full enjoyment of any of the accommodations, advantages, facilities, privileges of inns, educational institutions, roads, paths, streets, tanks, wells and other watering places, public

conveyances on land, air or water, theatres or other places
of public amusement, resort or convenience whether they
are dedicated to or maintained or licensed for the use of
the public shall be punished with imprisonment of either
description for a term which may extend to five years and
shall also be liable to fine.[3]

In *Slavery and Untouchability*, he noted that 'Neither slavery nor
untouchability is a free social order.'[4]

In *What Congress and Gandhi Have Done,* Dr Ambedkar stated
that his demand for mandatory constitutional safeguards for
Untouchables as a prerequisite for the support to the drafting
of the future Constitution comes from the story of the
'betrayal of the Negroes [African Americans] in the United
States after the Civil War'.[5] He noted: 'The Untouchables say
that the experience of the world does not justify the hope that
when the "Fight for Freedom" ends, the stronger elements
have shown the generosity to give security to the weaker
elements.'[6] Dr Ambedkar then recounted what happened
to the African Americans, despite the progressive promises
made to them during the 1860s in the US.

The American Civil War was fought in the 1860s to save
the disintegration of the American Union and to end slavery.
Dr Ambedkar quoted American historian Herbert Aptheker
to highlight how lakhs of African Americans served in the
Federal American Army and fought 'notwithstanding shameful
discriminations and disadvantages' within a country which
treated them as 'slaves'.[7] He further quoted Aptheker: '. . . let
it always be remembered that in the war to save the republic
thirty-seven thousand Negro soldiers were killed in action'.[8]

Dr Ambedkar posed a question: 'What happened to
the Negroes after the Civil War was over?' He noted that
though the Thirteenth Amendment to the US Constitution,
enacted by the Republican Party through the US Congress,

abolished slavery, it did not give the 'Negroes . . . any right
to participate in the government as voters or officials'. Later,
the Republicans enacted the Fourteenth Amendment 'to
make the Southern States accept that the Negroes were to be
treated as the political equals of the Whites'. The Fourteenth
Amendment conferred citizenship on all persons, including
Negroes born or naturalized in the US. Subsequently,
'the Republicans carried another amendment called the
Fifteenth Amendment, forbidding the voting right of a
citizen to be denied or abridged on account of race, colour or
previous condition of servitude which also became by similar
acceptance part of the Constitution and binding on all the
States'. But these amendments were not enough for the rescue
of the African Americans.

Dr Ambedkar narrated that the Whites in the southern
states of America 'had no intention to admit the Negroes to equal
citizenship'. To bypass the Fifteenth Amendment, the White
lawmakers of the southern states framed franchise laws which
denied the Negroes the right to vote on grounds other than
race or colour. Literacy tests and other conditions were adopted,
which effectively excluded the Negroes but fully included the
Whites. Violent racist organizations such as Ku Klux Klan
carried out activities 'to suppress the Negroes and prevent
them from exercising their political rights'. Dr Ambedkar
further narrated how the 'purposes of the Southern States and
the Southern Whites were facilitated by the decisions of the
Supreme Court of the United States'. He narrated that the US
Supreme Court upheld the State laws disfranchising the Negroes
on the grounds that it was not based on race or colour as per the
Fifteenth Amendment.[9] Furthermore, the US Supreme Court
refused to give any remedy against the activities of the Ku Klux
Klan on the grounds that it was a private body not covered by
the Fifteenth Amendment.[10]

Dr Ambedkar then posed another question, 'What did the Republicans do?' He highlighted that instead of 'amending the Constitution to give better and more effective guarantees to the Negroes' at that time, the Republicans agreed to recognize the Southern States and withdrew their military troops stationed therein 'leaving the Negroes to the tender mercy of their masters'.[11]

Such a profound understanding of American history and his own experiences of untouchability made Dr Ambedkar reflect on the issues of the Untouchables back in India. He remarked: 'The Untouchables cannot forget the fate of the Negroes.'[12] In fact, the connection that Dr Ambedkar felt with the African Americans made him write a letter in July 1946 to the prominent African American intellectual W.E.B. Du Bois. Dr Ambedkar wrote to inquire from Du Bois about the National Negro Congress petition to the United Nations (UN), which attempted to secure minority rights through the UN Council. Dr Ambedkar explained that he had been a 'student of the Negro problem', and that '[t]here is so much similarity between the position of the Untouchables in India and of the position of the Negroes in America that the study of the latter is not only natural but necessary'.[13] In a letter dated 31 July 1946, Du Bois responded by telling Dr Ambedkar he was familiar with his name, and that he had 'every sympathy with the Untouchables of India'.[14]

The experience of African Americans with politics in the US was thus a learning for Dr Ambedkar. It made him cautious of the 'story of the betrayal', where African Americans lost their lives in the Civil War, yet they had to battle for every inch of equality at every moment even several decades after the War.[15] Dr Ambedkar would not have wanted the same fate for the Untouchables. For this reason, Dr Ambedkar remained sceptical his entire life about the nationalist movement in India, which focused on political independence from British rule.

It is for this reason that Dr Ambedkar sought mandatory constitutional safeguards, especially representation in the legislature and services, as a condition to support the Congress party. A mandatory constitutional provision on representation would have prevented even the judiciary from striking down the rights of social minorities. Furthermore, he argued that marginalized communities cannot be left to the whims and fancies of future politicians. When the inevitable query came up as to what ought to be done, Dr Ambedkar invoked the concept of 'constitutional morality' derived from the history of Greece.

'Constitutional Morality' and the History of Greece[16]

Dr Ambedkar was well aware of the reality of Indian society. He knew that there existed a wide gap between the ideal of a possible transformative Constitution and the social reality. As he once popularly said: 'Democracy in India is only a top-dressing on an Indian soil, which is essentially undemocratic'.[17] As discussed in the previous chapters, he argued that Indian society was not suited for an exact imitation of the Western constitutional models or principles. He thus demanded the tweaking of Western principles. One such conception which Dr Ambedkar invoked a number of times was that of constitutional morality.

For its constitutional democracy to bring about a social transformation in Indian society, Dr Ambedkar emphasized the adoption and practice of constitutional morality—an idea originally propounded by the English historian George Grote, in the nineteenth century. Grote had conceptualized this idea in his A History of Greece (1851) on the establishment of democracy in Athens in ancient Greece.

In the fifth century BCE, Kleisthenes, an Athenian lawmaker, had initiated democratic reforms in Athens by introducing a new constitution, which included franchise for excluded masses, free speech and equality before the law. But there was a major problem: how to educate the Athenian noble class in such a manner that they respected the sanctity of the constitution? After all, what was to stop them from vying for personal power and disrupting the newly enshrined freedoms? Grote explains that the inculcation of a new sense of passionate attachment and paramount reverence for the Constitution and its sense of goodwill was as necessary as the writing of the Constitution. He termed this 'rare and difficult sentiment' as 'constitutional morality', which would force the leading ambitious men to respect the Constitution and its forms.

Grote defined constitutional morality as habits of

'paramount reverence for the form of the constitution, enforcing obedience to the authorities acting under and within those forms, yet combined with the habit of open speech, of action subject only to definite legal control, and unrestrained censure of those very authorities as to all their public acts—combined, too, with a perfect confidence in the bosom of every citizen, admits the bitterness of party contest, that the forms of constitution will be not less sacred in the eyes of his opponents than in his own.'[18]

The democratic process, for Grote, could not be used to undermine a constitution's broad principles. He listed 'freedom' as well as 'self-imposed restraint' as the bases of constitutional morality. He emphasized the diffusion of such morality in both the political majority and the minority as an indispensable condition for the 'free and peaceful' working of a government and its institutions. Another scholar suggests that Grecian democracy was ultimately overthrown 'not by the spears of conquerors, but through the disregard of constitutional morality by her own citizens'.[19]

Dr Ambedkar noted that it would be misleading to assume that people in a country would naturally follow constitutional morality. He noted, 'Habits of constitutional morality may be essential for the maintenance of a constitutional form of government. But the maintenance of a constitutional form of government is not the same thing as a self-government by the people.'[20] Dr Ambedkar argued that conceptions like constitutional morality and democracy cannot work on their own in a deeply divided country like India, where oppressor castes own power and are not ready to share it. This power has to be restricted through constitutional principles.

In Dr Ambedkar's view, since the element of constitutional morality was missing from the people at the time of Independence, it became necessary that a detailed structure of administrative provisions be incorporated into the Constitution, i.e., administrative power and who shall own it had to be controlled. Dr Ambedkar explained that the 'forms' of a constitution—which constitutional morality seeks to protect—had two essential ingredients. The first, in his words, is that 'the form of administration has a close connection with the form of the Constitution'.[21] The second ingredient, Ambedkar recognized, is that even without altering its form, the Constitution can be perfectly perverted 'by merely changing the form of the administration' and making it 'inconsistent and opposed to the spirit of the Constitution'. He was thus warning against the possibility of abuse of power, which could undermine the processes and values established by the Constitution. Those in office could misuse power and authority for selfish motives and damage the functioning of the constitutional democracy.

Dr Ambedkar's belief that 'it is wiser not to trust the Legislature to prescribe forms of administration' at the time of constitution-making, reveals his larger goal. He wanted to institutionalize every step that constitutional functionaries would take in the future. The lesser the discretion left, the better the chances of power being regulated. In laying down an administrative blueprint, the Constitution institutionalized fairness and non-arbitrariness in governance and politics for future regimes. In other words, Dr Ambedkar was prescribing a constitutional design that would prevent arbitrariness by laying down legal procedures to regulate the exercise of power.

Dr Ambedkar further emphasized a functioning moral order in society, which would then necessitate the existence of ethics in political and social life. The most glaring dysfunction he diagnosed was the proclivity of 'the majority to deny the existence of minorities'.[22] Since the rule of the majority in India, in his words, was 'basically a communal majority and not a political majority', it was onerous on the majority 'to realize its duty not to discriminate against minorities'.[23] Protection of minorities from the excesses of the majority thus forms an essential habit of Dr Ambedkar's constitutional morality. Thus, Dr Ambedkar broadened the scope of Grote's conception of constitutional morality by institutionalizing it in the form of mandatory provisions and larger accountability principles.

While Dr Ambedkar emphasized the cultivation and inculcation of constitutional morality by society, he was of the view that the diffusion of constitutional morality among the public as well as the State authorities cannot be presumed. He underlined the importance of informed and reasoned public engagement, and famously remarked that constitutional morality is 'not a natural sentiment' and that the people of India are 'yet to learn it'.[24] That is, the quality of administration would be improved through public discourse and scrutiny. Dr Ambedkar stated that the text of the Constitution was 'only a skeleton', and its 'flesh' was to be a robust constitutional morality.[25] The task, it is clear today, remains unfinished.

Dr Ambedkar's references to American and Greek history in *What Congress and Gandhi Have Done* demonstrate his ability to learn from global history and constitutional practices. As also recounted in the previous chapters as well as in the proceedings of the Constituent Assembly, Dr Ambedkar often referred to constitutional systems and practices in other countries such as Ireland, Japan, South Africa, Canada, etc. This shows his deep understanding of comparative learning. This not only helped in the drafting of India's Constitution but it also presented us with the option to refine our systems and principles by tweaking the comparative practices to suit Indian soil, thereby ensuring that mistakes committed in other countries could be avoided in India.

13

Foundations of the Indian Constitution

The aspirations of a newly emerging nation were vested in the exercise undertaken by the Constituent Assembly, to speak and act for India. The Assembly's authority rested on a strange balance—while it was created by the Cabinet Mission Plan, the Assembly claimed to derive its powers from the people of India.[1] The Assembly was represented by the majority with Hindus occupying 94.6 per cent of seats. Further, only fifteen members of the whole Constituent Assembly were women.[2] The Assembly largely consisted of dominant interests—through the Congress party. They had a nearly 70 per cent majority before, and 82 per cent composition after Partition. But the Scheduled Castes Federation, through Dr Ambedkar, and the Communists had a small, hard-fought contingent within the Assembly.[3]

Dr Ambedkar was elected as a member of the Constituent Assembly from undivided Bengal before the Partition. Muslim League members and representatives of the princely Indian states were not a part of this assembly.

The first speech of Dr Ambedkar in the Constituent Assembly shows his statesmanship and political and constitutional wisdom in solving nascent India's major problems. The speech also demonstrates that Dr Ambedkar was much more concerned about the future of India's Constitution and its minorities than any other leader/member of the Constituent Assembly. Let us

now look at the background against which Dr Ambedkar made
his first speech in the Constituent Assembly.

The first meeting of the Constituent Assembly of India
took place in Constitution Hall, New Delhi on 9 December
1946.[4] A few days later, on 13 December 1946, Jawaharlal
Nehru presented the Objectives Resolution to define the
scope and direction of the proceedings of the Constituent
Assembly and the drafting of the Constitution.[5] The
Resolution stated:

(1) This Constituent Assembly declares its firm and solemn
resolve to proclaim India as an Independent Sovereign
Republic and to draw up for her future governance a
Constitution;

(2) WHEREIN the territories that now comprise British
India, the territories that now form the Indian States,
and such other parts of India as are outside British
India and the States as well as such other territories
as are willing to be constituted into the Independent
Sovereign India, shall be a Union of them all; and

(3) WHEREIN the said territories, whether with
their present boundaries or with such others as may
be determined by the Constituent Assembly and
thereafter according to the Law of the Constitution,
shall possess and retain the status of autonomous Units,
together with residuary powers, and exercise all powers
and functions of government and administration, save
and except such powers and functions as are vested in
or assigned to the Union, or as are inherent or implied
in the Union or resulting therefrom; and

(4) WHEREIN all power and authority of the Sovereign
Independent India, its constituent parts and organs of
government, are derived from the people; and

(5) WHEREIN shall be guaranteed and secured to all the people of India justice, social, economic and political; equality of status, of opportunity, and before the law; freedom of thought, expression, belief, faith, worship, vocation, association and action, subject to law and public morality; and

(6) WHEREIN adequate safeguards shall be provided for minorities, backward and tribal areas, and depressed and other backward classes; and

(7) WHEREBY shall be maintained the integrity of the territory of the Republic and its sovereign rights on land, sea, and air according to Justice and the law of civilised nations, and

(8) THIS ancient land attains its rightful and honoured place in the world and make its full and willing contribution to the promotion of world peace and the welfare of mankind.

Nehru noted that the Resolution was 'in the nature of a pledge', a 'firm and solemn resolve to have a sovereign Indian republic', 'something that breathes life in human minds', and a 'declaration' that India was ready for the world. He further noted that even though the word 'democratic' did not appear in the Resolution, the Constituent Assembly was certainly 'aiming at democracy' and that the Resolution gave 'the content of democracy'. Nehru added,

> Others might take objection to this Resolution on the ground that we have not said that it should be a Socialist State. Well, I stand for Socialism and, I hope, India will stand for Socialism and that India will go towards the constitution of a Socialist State and I do believe that the whole world will have to go that way.

Nehru hoped that the Resolution presented by him would be passed by the Assembly without any addition or subtraction to convey the message that the Constituent Assembly was speaking in a united voice. He clarified, 'Later on, we can frame our Constitution in whatever words we please.' The Objective Resolution was a refined version of the resolution passed in the Karachi session of the Congress.[6]

However, on 17 December 1946, Dr M.R. Jayakar (a member of the Assembly) moved a proposal to put the proceedings of the Assembly on hold until the Muslim League and the princely Indian states joined the proceedings.[7] He noted: 'My real purpose in moving this amendment is to save the work of this Assembly from frustration. I fear that all the work we shall be doing here is in imminent danger of being rendered infructuous.' Many members opposed the proposal of Dr Jayakar.

On 17 December, Dr Rajendra Prasad (chairman of the Constituent Assembly) invited Dr Ambedkar to speak on the Resolution long before his turn.[8] This may be because the former wanted to hear the latter's views on the subject. On being called out of turn, Dr Ambedkar expressed his surprise, noting,

> I thought that as there were some 20 or 22 people ahead of me, my turn, if it did come at all, would come tomorrow. I would have preferred that as today I have come without any preparation whatsoever. I would have liked to prepare myself as I had intended to make a full statement on an occasion of this sort.

Therefore, what Dr Ambedkar spoke on that day was in all likelihood on issues closest to his heart, as he was giving the speech with less preparation.

Dr Ambedkar began by appreciating the Resolution for its clauses emphasizing justice, equality, liberty and adequate safeguards for minorities, backward and tribal areas, and Depressed and other Backward Classes. However, he found the Resolution to be 'very disappointing', as it did not provide details as to how the vision of the Constitution would be achieved. He noted that the Resolution is a semblance of the 'Declaration of the Rights of Man' pronounced by the French Constituent Assembly. However, he added that while the Resolution 'enunciates certain rights', it 'does not speak of remedies'. The system of remedies is one of the underlying themes consistently reiterated by Dr Ambedkar in several of his writings. He therefore noted, 'Rights are nothing unless remedies are provided whereby people can seek to obtain redress when rights are invaded.' If remedies are not provided, then 'we do not know what exactly would be the position with regard to fundamental rights, if this matter is left to the Executive of the day'.

Dr Ambedkar further emphasized the need to lay down more clauses to bring justice. He stated:

Sir, there are here certain provisions which speak of justice, economic, social and political. If this Resolution has a reality behind it and a sincerity, of which I have not the least doubt, coming as it does from the Mover of the Resolution, I should have expected some provision whereby it would have been possible for the State to make economic, social and political justice a reality and I should have from that point of view expected the Resolution to state in most explicit terms that in order that there may be social and economic justice in the country, that there would be nationalization of industry and nationalization of land, I do not understand how it could be possible for any future Government which believes in doing justice socially, economically and politically, unless its economy is a socialistic economy.

The most important aspect of Dr Ambedkar's speech was his interpretation of the word 'Republic' in the context of that time, when there was a Hindu–Muslim problem dominating the discourse of Constitution-framing and nation-building. In this regard, he commented on the proposal of Dr Jayakar to have representatives from the Muslim League join the Assembly. He made an impassioned appeal and demonstrated the spirit of statesmanship, as he noted:

> I have got not the slightest doubt in my mind as to the future evolution and the ultimate shape of the social, political and economic structure of this great country. I know today we are divided politically, socially and economically; We are a group of warring camps and I may go even to the extent of confessing that I am probably one of the leaders of such a camp. But, Sir, with all this, I am quite convinced that given time and circumstances nothing in the world will prevent this country from becoming one. (*Applause*). With all our castes and creeds, I have not the slightest hesitation that we shall in some form be a united people. (*Cheers*).

He therefore emphasized the need to accommodate the concerns of even those who were opposing the Constituent Assembly and bring them on board to draft India's future Constitution together. He supported the proposal of Dr Jayakar and appealed to everyone to show an act of statesmanship, by noting:

> Our difficulty is not about the ultimate future. Our difficulty is how to make the heterogeneous mass that we have today

take a decision in common and march on the way which leads us to unity. Our difficulty is not with regard to the ultimate, our difficulty is with regard to the beginning . . . I should have thought that in order to make us willing friends, in order to induce every party, every section in this country to take on to the road it would be an act of greatest statesmanship for the majority party even to make a concession to the prejudices of people who are not prepared to march together and it is for that, that I propose to make this appeal. *Let us leave aside slogans, let us leave aside words which frighten people. Let us even make a concession to the prejudices of our opponents, bring them in, so that they may willingly join with us on marching upon that road, which as I said, if we walk long enough, must necessarily lead us to unity.* If I, therefore, from this place support Dr Jayakar's amendment, it is because I want all of us to realize that . . . We should leave aside all legal considerations and make some attempt, whereby those who are not prepared to come, will come. Let us make it possible for them to come, that is my appeal. (emphasis added)

Dr Ambedkar stated if the members of the Constituent Assembly did not show statesmanship in accommodating their political opponents (the Muslim League) at that time, then it would affect the fate of the Muslims deciding to stay in India. It is necessary to reproduce what he said:

It seems to me there are only three ways by which the future will be decided. Either, there shall have to be surrender by the one party to the wishes of the other—that is one way. The other way would be what I call a negotiated peace and the third way would be open war. Sir, I have been hearing from certain members of the Constituent Assembly that they are prepared to go to war. I must confess that I am appalled at the idea that anybody in this country should think of solving the political problems of this country by the method of war. I do not know how many people in this country support that idea. A good many perhaps do and the reason why I think they do, is because most of them, at any rate a great many of them, believe that the war that they are thinking of, would be a war on the British. Well, Sir, if the war that is contemplated, that is in the minds of people, can be localized, circumscribed, so that it will not be more than a war on the British, I probably may not have much objection to that sort of strategy. But will it be a war on the British only? I have no hesitation and I do want to place before this House in the clearest terms possible that if war comes in this country and if that war has any relation to the issue with which we are confronted today, it will not be a war on the British. It will be a war on the Muslims.

In the hope that the founders of the future Indian Constitution would realize the significance of his moral appeal, Dr Ambedkar quoted the same excerpt from Edmund Burke's speech, which he had earlier quoted to the British during the first Round Table Conference. 'Power and authority are sometimes bought by kindness,' he quoted, and this does away with the need to use force, violence and strength. He noted that if the Muslims are 'subjugated' and 'made to surrender to the Constitution that might be prepared without their consent', then the 'country would be involved in perpetually conquering them'. He gave a clear warning: 'The conquest [to subjugate Muslims] would not be once and *for ever*.' He therefore appealed that the Constituent Assembly should exercise its sovereign power with wisdom because that is 'the only way by which we can carry with us all sections of the country' and 'can lead us to unity'. Thus, Dr Ambedkar's hope was for a united India, which would respect its minorities.

Ashok Gopal, biographer of Dr Ambedkar, calls it 'a commanding performance'.[9] Gopal quotes N.V. Gadgil, a member of the Constituent Assembly, who stated: 'His speech was so statesmanlike, so devoid of bitterness and so challenging that the whole Assembly listened to it in abrupt silence . . . The speech was greeted with a tremendous ovation, and he was smothered with congratulations in the lobby.'[10] Gopal also quotes an English-language newspaper from that time, which called Dr Ambedkar's address the 'weightiest speech in the Constituent Assembly.'[11]

The Objective Resolution was adopted on 22 January 1947.[12] Later, Nehru pointed out that the Objective Resolution could be adopted, with certain changes, as the Preamble.[13] As the chairman of the Drafting Committee, Dr Ambedkar played a crucial role in drafting the final version of the Preamble. The Drafting Committee, headed by Dr Ambedkar, felt that the Preamble should be restricted to defining the essential features of the new State and its basic sociopolitical objectives and that the other matters dealt with in the resolution could be more appropriately provided for in the substantive parts of the Constitution.[14] Credit must go to Dr Ambedkar for bringing the phrase 'Fraternity' in the final draft of the Preamble.[15] As discussed in previous chapters, 'Fraternity' was one of the core constitutional ideas consistently invoked by Dr Ambedkar to emphasize the need for goodwill among the people of India. The Preamble was then adopted by the Constituent Assembly in November 1949.

14

Interrelation between Civil–Political and Socio-Economic Rights

After it had become clear that a Constituent Assembly would be formed to frame the future Constitution, the All-India Scheduled Castes Federation (SCF) entrusted Dr Ambedkar with the task of preparing 'a memorandum on the safeguards for the Scheduled Castes for being submitted to the Constituent Assembly'.[1] The memorandum prepared by him defined the nature and scope of fundamental rights, minority rights and safeguards for the Scheduled Castes.

When Dr Ambedkar later became a part of the Fundamental Rights Sub-Committee of the Constituent Assembly (as mentioned in the previous chapter), he refined his earlier memorandum, prepared on behalf of SCF, in the form of a draft constitution for the 'United States of India'. While he submitted the document for the consideration of the members of the Constituent Assembly, he also circulated it publicly under the title 'States and Minorities' in March 1947 for the benefit of the larger public. The draft also included explanatory notes for each provision to make it easy for people to understand why that provision was included.

Set of Rights

Dr Ambedkar's draft constitution was a restatement of civil–political as well as socio-economic rights and provided a mechanism for enforcing these rights. The unique part was that Dr Ambedkar discussed the interrelationship between fundamental rights (civil–political rights) and socio-economic rights as a matter of constitutional principle. Again, Dr Ambedkar was expanding the conception of constitutional rights to address the social inequalities in a deeply divided society. Furthermore, Dr Ambedkar's draft also drew from constitutional principles and provisions from other countries, 'particularly from those wherein the conditions are more or less analogous to those existing in India'.[2] This yet again demonstrated his wide reading of global comparative constitutionalism.

The preamble of Dr Ambedkar's draft constitution provided for the establishment of a 'body politic' which would ensure 'good government' and 'maintain the right of every subject to life, liberty and pursuit of happiness and to free speech and free exercise of religion'. It further provided for the removal of 'social, political and economic inequality by providing better opportunities to the submerged classes' and assurance of 'freedom from fear'.[3]

His draft included a set of fundamental provisions like due process of the law, equal protection of the law and equality before the law. In this set of fundamental rights, he ensured that the principle of non-discrimination was written explicitly. For instance, his draft provided: 'Any existing enactment, regulation, order, custom or interpretation of law by which any penalty, disadvantage or disability is imposed upon or any discrimination is made against any citizen shall, as from the day on which this Constitution comes into operation, cease to have any effect.'[4] This was a significant departure from the approach of British courts, where they respected social 'customs', even when they jeopardized the rights of the marginalized.

Another provision declared it to be a criminal offence to deny any person

> the full enjoyment of any of the accommodations, advantages, facilities, privileges of inns, educational institutions, roads, paths, streets, tanks, wells and other watering places, public conveyances on land, air or water, theatres or other places of public amusement, resort or convenience, whether they are dedicated to or maintained or licensed for the use of the public.

While the wording of the provision seems to be derived from the American Civil Rights Act, it also reflected the content of Dr Ambedkar's struggle towards access to public resources. As the labour of the oppressed castes was exploited and a kind of slavery was maintained, Dr Ambedkar's draft penalized 'subjecting a person to forced labour or to involuntary servitude'. Interestingly, Dr Ambedkar provided for a fundamental right to privacy[5] (as understood now) as well as a fundamental right to vote.

Judicial Protection

Dr Ambedkar argued that '[r]ights are real only if they are accompanied by remedies'.[6] He added, 'It is no use giving rights if the aggrieved person has no legal remedy to which he can resort when his rights are invaded.' Thus, his draft Constitution provided for provisions which would 'prevent the Legislature and the Executive from overriding' the rights. He assigned this function to the judiciary, adding 'the Courts have been made the special guardians of the rights guaranteed by the Constitution'. The draft included a provision providing the Supreme Court with the power to issue writs against violation of fundamental rights.[7] In Dr Ambedkar's words, 'The clause proposes to give protection to the citizen against Executive tyranny by investing the Judiciary with certain powers of inquisition against the abuse of authority by the Executive.'[8]

Freedom from Discrimination

Dr Ambedkar was clear in his ideas that in an unequal country like India, the oppressed communities may face unequal treatment from those in authority who do not belong to their community.[9] For instance, he noted, 'Unequal treatment has been the inescapable fate of the Untouchables in India . . . Many other minority communities may be suffering from similar treatment at the hands of the majority community.'[10] Therefore, Dr Ambedkar included a provision to ensure that all citizens shall have equal benefit of laws, rules and regulations.

Similar to what he submitted during the Round Table Conference in the 1930s, Dr Ambedkar proposed a clause drawing from the Civil Rights Protection Act, 1866, and of 1875, enacted in the US to protect the Negroes from unequal treatment. The clause prohibited discrimination in the actions of the legislature and the executive. In effect, it provided that no citizen shall be discriminated against by the State in relation to 'the full and equal enjoyment' of services and natural resources, such as 'accommodations, advantages, facilities, educational institutions, privileges of inns, rivers, streams, wells, tanks, roads, paths, streets, public conveyances on land, air and water, theatres and other places of public resort or amusement'. This was significant because the Scheduled Castes, like the African Americans in the US, were denied equal access to the mentioned services and resources.

The clause further provided that all citizens shall have an equal share in 'the benefits of any religious or charitable trust dedicated to or created, maintained or licensed for the general public or for persons of the same faith and religion'. The clause also provided that no law, rule or regulation can restrict citizens in their efforts 'to claim full and equal benefit of all laws and proceedings for the security of persons and property as is enjoyed by other subjects regardless of any usage or custom or usage or custom based on religion'. This, in effect, prohibited the religious custom-based restrictions on the caste-oppressed communities. In addition, it was provided that no law or regulation could restrict the ability of all citizens 'to make and enforce contracts, to sue, be parties, and give evidence, to inherit, purchase, lease, sell, hold and convey real and personal property'. This was done, as oppressed castes were even denied property rights. Lastly, the clause allowed all citizens 'to be eligible for entry into the civil and military employ and to all educational institutions except for such conditions and limitations as may be necessary to provide for the due and adequate representation of all classes of the subjects of the State'. In other words, the State would not discriminate in the exercise of its power.[11]

State and Private Discrimination

Another provision (Article II, Section II, Clause 3) targeted '[d]iscrimination against citizens by Government officers in public administration or by private employers in factories and commercial concerns on the grounds of race or creed or social status' and declared it to 'be treated as an offence'. Dr Ambedkar's explanatory note to this provision noted,

Discrimination is another menace which must be guarded against if the Fundamental Rights are to be real rights.

In a country like India where it is possible for discrimination to be practised on a vast scale and in a relentless manner Fundamental Rights can have no meaning. The remedy follows the lines adopted in the Bill which was recently introduced in the Congress of the USA the aim of which is to prevent discrimination being practised against the Negroes.[12]

This provision by Dr Ambedkar was unique in the sense that it not only prohibited discrimination by State officials but also by private employers. Discrimination by private entities is an emerging field of law, but Dr Ambedkar had thought about it in his draft. To give effect to this proposed provision, Dr Ambedkar provided that the Union legislature 'shall have the right as well as the obligation to give effect to this provision by appropriate legislation'.[13]

The Link between Political Rights and Economic Equality

Dr Ambedkar proposed that the Constitution of India should prescribe an economic structure in its written text. It was provided that 'as a part of the law of its Constitution', the key industries should be owned, run and managed by the State.[14] He prescribed that: 'Insurance shall be a monopoly of the State and that the State shall compel every adult citizen to take out a life insurance policy commensurate with his wages as may be prescribed by the Legislature'; and 'agriculture shall be State Industry'. Furthermore, it was provided that the agricultural industry should be organized on the basis of collective farming for a period of ten years.[15] This clause was much more expansive than the traditional understanding of constitutional law or constitutionalism. For it moved beyond the imagination of a liberal constitution and laid emphasis on prescribing a particular socialistic economic structure in constitutional law.

Dr Ambedkar was well aware that this proposal may seem to be radical to those who see constitutional law in a particularly limited sense. Therefore, he wrote a detailed note explaining the relevance and the proposed impact of his proposal. He noted, 'The main purpose behind the clause is to put an obligation on the State to plan the economic life of the people on lines which would lead to the highest point of productivity without closing every avenue to private enterprise, and also provide for the equitable distribution of wealth.'[16] It placed on the shoulders of the State the obligation to supply capital both for agriculture as well as for industry.

As the proposal had recommended the nationalization of key industries, Dr Ambedkar believed that state socialism was essential for the rapid industrialization of India. Private enterprise did not have the resources and even if it did, it would produce inequalities of wealth which capitalism had produced in Europe. His proposal had two special features. One was that it proposed state socialism in important fields of economic life. The second was that it did not leave the establishment of state socialism to the will of the legislature. Instead, it established state socialism by the law of the Constitution and thus made it unalterable by any act of the legislature and the executive.[17]

As this proposal was an expansive view of constitutional law, Dr Ambedkar defended his proposal in the following terms:

Students of Constitutional Law will at once raise a protest. They are sure to ask: Does not the proposal go beyond the scope of the usual type of Fundamental Rights? My answer is that it does not. If it appears to go beyond it is only because the conception of Fundamental Rights on which such criticism is based is a narrow conception.[18]

He then stated that such a provision was based on the interrelation between liberty and the economic structure of society. He argued,

For what is the purpose of prescribing by law the shape and form of the economic structure of society? The purpose is to protect the liberty of the individual from invasion by other individuals which is the object of enacting Fundamental Rights. The connection between individual liberty and the shape and form of the economic structure of society may not be apparent to everyone. Nonetheless the connection between the two is real.[19]

Dr Ambedkar further argued that conceptions of constitutional law, economic structure and political democracy are interlinked. He thus provided a framework to understand this phenomenon:

Political Democracy rests on four premises which may be set out in the following terms: (i) The individual is an end in himself; (ii) That the individual has certain inalienable rights which must be guaranteed to him by the Constitution; (iii) That the individual shall not be required to relinquish any of his constitutional rights as a condition precedent to the receipt of a privilege; (iv) That the State shall not delegate powers to private persons to govern others.[20]

He stated that if the economic structure was allowed to be governed by private enterprises, then the last two points in this framework would be violated, i.e., people are forced to give away their rights.

To explain this, Dr Ambedkar gave the following example:

How many have to relinquish their constitutional rights in order to gain their living? . . . Ask those who are unemployed whether what are called fundamental rights are of any value to them. If a person who is unemployed is offered a choice between a job of some sort, with some sort of wages, with no fixed hours of labour and with an interdict on joining a union and the exercise of his right to freedom of speech, association, religion, etc., can there be any doubt as to what his choice will be? How can it be otherwise? The fear of starvation, the fear of losing a house, the fear of losing savings if any, the fear of being compelled to take children away from school, the fear of having to be a burden on public charity, the fear of having to be burned or buried at public cost are factors too strong to permit a man to stand out for his Fundamental Rights.[21]

He thus concluded that the unemployed and marginalized are 'compelled to relinquish their Fundamental Rights for the sake of securing the privilege to work and to subsist'. In simple words, the fundamental rights of the poor and the marginalized are done away with if economic equality is not brought in. Therefore, it is clear that fundamental rights are interconnected with the socio-economic rights of citizens. Dr Ambedkar highlighted the impact of socio-economic factors on the ability of individuals to assert their fundamental rights.

Furthermore, Dr Ambedkar argued that the function of fundamental rights is not limited to providing liberty by restraining State power, but it is also to make the State accountable if private citizens or entities violate the rights of other citizens. He noted:

Constitutional lawyers assume that the enactment of Fundamental Rights is enough to safeguard their liberty and that nothing more is called for. They argue that where the State refrains from intervention in private affairs—economic and social—the residue is liberty. What is necessary is to make the residue as large as possible and State intervention as small as possible ... [But one] more question remains to be answered. To whom and for whom is this liberty? Obviously, this liberty is liberty to the landlords to increase rents, for capitalists to increase hours of work and reduce the rate of wages . . . For in an economic system employing armies of workers, producing goods *en masse* at regular intervals some one must make rules so that workers will work and the wheels of industry run on. If the State does not do it the private employer will . . . In other words what is called liberty from the control of the State is another name for the *dictatorship of the private employer*.[22]

To prevent the violation of the rights of individuals by private enterprises, Dr Ambedkar said that his proposal

seeks to limit not only the power of government to impose arbitrary restraints but also of the more powerful individuals or to be more precise to eliminate the possibility of the more powerful having the power to impose arbitrary restraints on the less powerful by withdrawing from the control he has over the economic life of people.

The overall purpose of this provision, Dr Ambedkar noted, was 'an attempt to establish state socialism without abrogating parliamentary democracy' and by making it a part of constitutional law—thereby a 'constitutional socialism'.[23] By including it as a part of the Constitution, this provision would gain permanency, thereby preventing it from being done away with by the majority, Dr Ambedkar argued.[24] He further added that in the existing constitutions of other countries, which only prescribe the form of the political structure of society leaving the economic structure untouched, the result is that the 'political structure is completely set at naught by the forces which emerge from the economic structure'. That is, the political structure is controlled by the economic forces. In Dr Ambedkar's view, this is contrary to the conception of democracy, where every person ought to have a say in the social and political structure, and not just the powerful. He thus argued that the understanding of constitutional law and constitutions needed to be expanded beyond the fundamental rights (civil–political rights), and should also include enforceable socio-economic rights arising out of a constitutional economic structure.[25] He demanded that the future constitutions of emerging democracies ought to learn from the fallouts of liberal constitutionalism and adopt a stronger version of rights, which also manages the economy based on the rights of citizens.[26]

Prohibiting Social Boycott

The draft included a specific provision on 'social boycott' and declared it to be a criminal offence. Dr Ambedkar defined 'social boycott' in the following terms:

> A person shall be deemed to boycott another who— (a) refuses to let or use or occupy any house or land, or to deal with, work for hire, or do business with another person, or to render to him or receive from him any service, or refuses to do any of the said things on the terms on which such things should commonly be done in the ordinary course of business, or (b) abstains from such social, professional or business relations as he would, having regard to such existing customs in the community which are not inconsistent with any fundamental right or other rights of citizenship declared in the Constitution, ordinarily maintain with such person, or (c) in any way injures, annoys or interferes with such other person in the exercise of his lawful rights.

According to the draft, whoever instigates or threatens to boycott 'with intent to cause harm to such person in body, mind, reputation or property, or in his business or means of living, boycotts such person or any person in whom such person is interested, shall also be guilty of the offence of boycotting'.

The reason why Dr Ambedkar drafted this provision was that 'Social boycott [has been] always held over the heads of the Untouchables by the Caste Hindus as a sword of D[a]mocles'. He quoted from a report made by a Government of Bombay-appointed committee in 1928[27] to highlight how the poor economic condition of the Untouchables was used by the oppressor castes to maintain social hierarchy and prevent any mobility. The report stated:

> The Depressed Classes have no economic independence in most parts of the Presidency . . . We have heard of numerous instances where the orthodox classes have used their economic power as a weapon against those Depressed Classes in their villages, when the latter have dared to exercise their rights, and have evicted them from their land, and stopped their employment and discontinued their remuneration as village servants. This boycott is often planned on such an extensive scale as to include the prevention of the Depressed Classes from using the commonly used paths and the stoppage of sale of the necessaries of life by the village Bania.[28]

Dr Ambedkar noted that the weapon of social boycott is a form of enhanced violence upon the Untouchables. He further noted that social boycott was being used against other minorities as well. Therefore, such a provision, which Dr Ambedkar drew from the Burma Anti-Boycott Act, 1922, becomes necessary in Indian society. Again, this provision demonstrates linkages between economic conditions and social hierarchies of caste, which Dr Ambedkar tried to resolve through a solid constitutional system.

Financial Assistance for Foreign Education

Dr Ambedkar's draft Constitution provided that 'Governments—
Union and State—shall be required to assume financial
responsibility for the higher education of the Scheduled Castes
and shall be required to make adequate provisions in their
budgets'. The State governments shall fulfil the responsibility
'for finding money for secondary and college education of
the Scheduled Castes in India'. Dr Ambedkar provided that
'[t]he responsibility for finding money for foreign education of
the Scheduled Castes shall be the responsibility of the Union
Government'.

The Constitutional Protection of Safeguards

Dr Ambedkar also included a provision to the effect that
the future Constitution would incorporate all safeguards
in its text explicitly so that these safeguards gain permanent
stature. He gave examples of other countries such as South
Africa and Canada where the arrangement of sharing political
power between different groups was incorporated into the
Constitution. Dr Ambedkar criticized the approach of those
who opposed this proposal and noted:

> Unfortunately for the minorities in India, Indian nationalism
> has developed a new doctrine which may be called the Divine
> Right of the Majority to rule the minorities according to
> the wishes of the majority. Any claim for the sharing of
> power by the minority is called communalism while the
> monopolizing of the whole power by the majority is called
> Nationalism[29] (sic).

It was often asked by the oppressor castes how long the
constitutional safeguards for the oppressed castes would

continue. Dr Ambedkar faced the same question even in the days before the enactment of the Constitution when the level of safeguards was negligible. In this regard, Dr Ambedkar proposed the following provision:

> The provisions for the Scheduled Castes shall not be altered, amended or abrogated except in the following manner:
>
> Any amendment or abrogation of . . . any part thereof relating to the Scheduled Castes shall only be made by a Resolution passed in the manner prescribed below by the more Popular Chamber of the Union Legislature:
>
> (i)   Any proposal for amendment or abrogation shall be initiated in the form of a Resolution in the more Popular Chamber of the Union Legislature.
>
> (ii) No such Resolution shall be moved—
>   (a) unless 25 years have elapsed after the Constitution has come into operation and has been worked; and
>   (b) unless six months' notice has been given to the House by the mover of his intention to move such a Resolution.
>
> (iii) On the passing of such a Resolution, the Legislature shall be dissolved and a new election held.
>
> (iv) The original Resolution in the form in which it was passed by the previous Legislature shall be moved afresh in the same House of the newly elected Union Legislature.
>
> (v)   The Resolution shall not be deemed to have been carried unless it is passed by a majority of two-thirds of the members of the House and also two-thirds of members of the Scheduled Castes who have been returned through separate electorates.[30]

This was a rigid procedure which required the approval of 'two-thirds of members of the Scheduled Castes who have been returned through separate electorates'. In that sense, such safeguards were an arrangement made by and for the Scheduled Castes. Those safeguards (such as affirmative action or quotas) could not be diluted without their consent. *It was an enhanced version of the separation of power principle.* In his explanatory note, Dr Ambedkar noted:

> This is not a new demand. It replaces Clause 6 of the Poona Pact which provides that the system of representation for the Scheduled Castes by reserved seats shall continue until determined by mutual consent between the communities concerned in the settlement. Since there is no safe method of ascertaining the will of the Scheduled Castes as to how to amend and alter the safeguards provided for them it is necessary to formulate a plan which will take the place of Clause 6 of the Pact.

Dr Ambedkar also stated that 'provisions with similar objectives' are contained in the Constitutions of Australia, America and South Africa.[31]

The Contemporary Lesson

Several of these provisions were considered radical by others, as they were not endorsed by members of the Fundamental Rights Sub-Committee and other members of the Constituent Assembly. However, some provisions proposed by Dr Ambedkar were later incorporated into the Constitution, e.g., the provision of non-discrimination. Several other provisions (next chapter) were shaped by his inputs.

But what is most important is that these ideas contemplated by Dr Ambedkar later became well-accepted doctrines of constitutional interpretation. For instance, the Supreme

Court of India held that civil–political rights (Part III of the Constitution) and sociopolitical rights (Part IV) need to be read together in harmony.[32] Another constitutional idea of Dr Ambedkar that the State must have an obligation to protect citizens' rights against private actors became the law of the land through another judgment of the Supreme Court of India.[33] Though these judgments do not credit Dr Ambedkar, the intellectual origin of these judgments has to be credited to Dr Ambedkar. He was consistent in giving a broader meaning to the principles of constitutional law. Thus, reflecting on these constitutional ideas of Dr Ambedkar carries lessons for contemporary constitutionalism.

15

Being Chosen as Chairman
of the Drafting Committee

Dr Ambedkar was elected as the chairman of the Drafting Committee on 29 August 1947. The Committee was entrusted with the task of preparing the draft of the Indian Constitution. Historians have stated different reasons for the selection of Dr Ambedkar as the Drafting Committee chairman. But there are several reasons which show that Dr Ambedkar was the obvious choice to guide the members of the Constituent Assembly.

Education and Involvement in Constitution-Drafting

To begin with, Dr Ambedkar was well qualified and had attained a foreign degree in law. Such was the significance of his education that he was offered a judgeship on his return from London in the 1920s.[1] His knowledge of law and political theory was profound. Furthermore, Dr Ambedkar was present on all the occasions of constitutional deliberations in the three decades before 1947, when crucial decisions were made. In that sense, he was aware of the evolution of how Constitutions were framed. For instance, he was involved in the constitutional negotiations for the GOI Act 1919, as well as in the Round

Table Conferences (RTC), which led to the enactment of the GOI Act 1935. Dr Ambedkar was present at all three RTCs in London and the Cabinet Mission proceedings, thereby showing his deep interest in the constitutional drafting process. Even Sir B.N. Rau, who was later appointed constitutional adviser to the Constituent Assembly, was not involved in the drafting of these Acts, which were equivalent to a domestic constitution for India drafted by the British.[2] Dr Ambedkar was the one who was most prepared during the initial meetings of various sub-committees of the Constituent Assembly. For instance, he alone had prepared a list of fundamental rights before the initial meeting of the Fundamental Rights Sub-Committee.[3]

Expert on Constitutional Law

Dr Ambedkar was an expert in English law, especially English constitutional law. It is the quality of a good teacher that they are able to explain complex principles in easy language to their students. Dr Ambedkar gave several lectures on the English Constitution as a professor at Government Law College, Bombay in 1934–35. For instance, he explained, in simple language, the principles underlying the English Constitution— what is the power of the British Crown, the House of Lords, the concept of legislative supremacy, separation of power, etc.[4] As he noted,

> I am merely trying to make Dicey's English Constitution easier for Indian students to follow and to understand. From the standpoint of Indian students, Dicey's treatise suffers from two defects. It presupposes a knowledge of certain parts of the English Constitution. For instance, it presupposes a knowledge of what is Parliament, how it is constituted and how it functions. This presupposition, howsoever justifiable

it may be in the case of English students, would be without warrant in the case of Indian students who are called upon to take up the study of Dicey for the first time (sic).

Furthermore, while explaining the commentary of Dicey, he would invoke his principles to examine Indian social problems.[5] For instance, he stated that the exercise of power such as sovereign power by the oppressor castes 'is far more likely to become a mere engine of suppression of the servile classes'.[6]

He simplified concepts while updating students about developments in English constitutional law which happened through legislations or conventions. He explained the principle of 'separation of power' in the following words:

The English Constitution certainly does not recognize the principle of the separation of powers. The King is a part of the legislature, the head of the judiciary and the supreme executive authority in the land. The Ministry which carries on the executive Government of the country in the name of the King are members of Parliament. There is, therefore, no separation between the executive and the legislature. The Lord Chancellor is the working head of the Judicature. He is also a member of the Cabinet. There is, therefore, no separation between the executive and the judiciary. Not only is there no separation between the three organs of the State, but there is no foundation for the statement that their authority is limited by the Constitution for the simple fact that there is no Constitution in the American sense of the word which allocates the functions of the different organs of the State and delimits their authority.[7]

Dr Ambedkar was also clear about the concept of parliamentary or legislative supremacy. He explained how

Parliament had the authority to legislate not only on public issues but also on private rights. He noted:

> Most legislative assemblies confine their legislative powers to the regulation of the rights of the public in general. Private rights and domestic rights are deemed either to be too particular and too sacred to be interfered with by Parliament. But the British Parliament has never accepted these limitations upon its legislative authority. In the case of the lives of the Duke of Clarence and Gloucester, Parliament passed an Act declaring that their daughters and wives should inherit their property although they were alive.[8]

Regulating the private sphere was an idea that appealed to Dr Ambedkar, as he was fighting a battle to regulate Indian social discrimination, which had a basis in inherent personal beliefs and biases, through the legal system. Dr Ambedkar also prepared lecture notes on the common law,[9] dominion status,[10] law of specific relief,[11] law of trust,[12] etc.

Dr Ambedkar was so impactful in his teaching that his achievements were publicly acknowledged. When he was appointed the principal of Government Law School, Bombay, in June 1935,[13] the college magazine (8 January 1936 issue) published the following note in his honour:

> We however note with satisfaction that Mr. Fyzee has handed over charge to no less a person than Dr. Ambedkar. A lawyer of repute, he is a close student of Economics, an authority on Constitutional Law and a personality known throughout India and elsewhere. To write more about him would be otiose. Expecting much from our Principal we shall not embarrass him now. We prefer to wait and see.[14]

Expertise in the Government of India Act 1935

As mentioned before, the 1935 Act, which was being relied upon by the Constituent Assembly, was a subject about which Dr Ambedkar was well-equipped as he had thoroughly examined the Act. In June 1939, he was invited to deliver the Kale Memorial Lecture at the Gokhale Institute of Politics and Economics, Poona (now Pune), where he spoke on the structure of federalism and the GOI Act 1935. He critiqued the Act, as it did not allow the legislature to amend the Act in any way. He noted:

> Under the Government of India Act neither the Federal Legislature, nor the Provincial Legislature have any powers of altering or amending the Constitution. The only thing, which the Act by virtue of Section 308 does is to permit the Federal Legislature and Provincial Legislature to pass a resolution recommending any change in the Constitution, and make it obligatory upon the Secretary of State to place it before both Houses of Parliament. This is contrary to the provisions contained in the constitutions of the United States, Australia, the German Federation and Switzerland. There is no reason why constituent power should not have been given within certain defined limits to the Legislatures in India when they were fully representative of all sections and of all interests.[15]

Dr Ambedkar stated that he was not against the provincial autonomy of the States, but did not support the federal scheme in the 1935 Act, which in effect provided that the Princely States have 'a right to walk out of the [Indian] Federation'.[16]

He noted, 'I also realize that a Federal Form of Government is inevitable if there is to be Provincial Autonomy.'[17] However, he added that 'there is no use hugging to Provincial Autonomy and leaving responsibility in the Centre hanging in the air', and that 'without real responsibility at the Centre, Provincial Autonomy is an empty shell'.[18] Dr Ambedkar once noted that he favoured a strong Centre in the sense that it would enact laws for the protection of minorities and prevent the States from perpetuating violence against the oppressed castes.[19] He relied on the example of the US and spoke of Lincoln and the Civil War against the American States.[20] His views on the Centre were in the context of the global history of social oppression.

Furthermore, in most of Dr Ambedkar's writings, he would analyse the constitutional systems and practices of other countries. He would also discuss constitutional history and the mistakes committed in other countries to talk about evolved constitutional solutions for Indian society and not limit himself to the analysis of dominant countries such as the USA or the UK whose constitutions were most discussed, but bring in examples from the constitutions of countries such as Burma (Myanmar) that were not discussed so often.

Vast Drafting Experience: Concern for the Underdog

Apart from being involved in the drafting of GOI Acts, Dr Ambedkar spent several years doing legislative work— firstly, in the Bombay Legislative Council in the 1920s and 1930s, and later as the Labour member in the Viceroy's Council in the 1940s. Several of his interventions need to be highlighted, as they not only show his legal expertise but also demonstrate how he clubbed it with progressive ideas. Dr Ambedkar would also comment, discuss and debate the legislations brought in by his colleagues in the Legislative Council. For a contextual understanding, it is necessary to mention a few such instances.

Dr Ambedkar passionately supported the Maternity Benefit Bill introduced in the Bombay Legislative Council (27–28 July 1928) by R.S. Asavale, a labour leader,[21] applicable

to factories in the Bombay Presidency. Some members raised
concerns about its practicality to which Dr Ambedkar's reply
was, 'It is in the interests of the nation that the mother ought to
get a certain amount of rest during the pre-natal period.' While
he believed that the government should manage maternity
benefits, he forcefully argued that the employer cannot be
totally exempted from any liability or responsibility towards
the women employees working under them.[22] The Bombay
Maternity Benefit Act was eventually passed in May 1929.

Dr Ambedkar was also one of the earliest proponents of
reproductive rights and birth control. On 10 November 1938,
P.J. Roham, a member of the Bombay Legislative Assembly and
a legislator from the independent Labour Party, presented a
speech on behalf of Dr Ambedkar, who prepared the speech but
was not available that day.[23] Roham, representing Dr Ambedkar,
tabled a resolution recommending that the government 'carry
on an intensive propaganda in favour of birth control among
the masses' and to 'provide adequate facilities for the practice
of birth control'.[24] Dr Ambedkar argued that the issue of birth
control was linked with infant mortality, public health and
the overall development of society.[25] He also highlighted how
untimely marriage and childbirth affected the daily life and
health of women.[26] Dr Ambedkar recognized the freedom of
women to decide on their reproductive health. He believed
that women should have supreme control over their bodily
integrity.[27] As he noted: 'Whenever a woman is disinclined to
bear a child for any reason whatsoever, she must be in a position
to prevent conception and bringing forth progeny which
should be entirely dependent on the choice of women.' He
unequivocally rebutted those who were critical of birth control
as follows: 'If men had to bear the pangs which women have to
undergo during child-birth, none of them would ever consent
to bear more than a single child in his life.' Dr Ambedkar was

a proponent of sex education[28] and was in favour of modern contraceptives for family planning.[29]

In 1937, Dr Ambedkar introduced a Bill to abolish the Khoti system. This system 'was a revenue system controlled by Khots (landlords) in which they used to collect revenue from the tenants'.[30] Furthermore, these 'Khots acted as the agent of the British and were engaged in exploitative and oppressive practices against the tenants such as "Begar" or unpaid labour'.[31] Dr Ambedkar stated:

> The system of Khoti Tenure while it binds the Khot to pay revenue to the Government leaves him free to do what he likes to the inferior holders [tenants] and this freedom has been so grossly abused by the Khots that the inferior holders are not only subjected to all kinds of exactions but they have been reduced to a state of abject slavery.[32]

Dr Ambedkar strongly opposed an amendment introduced to the Bombay Trade Disputes Conciliation Act, 1934, providing for a mandatory conciliation—instead of voluntary—between the parties of an industrial dispute.[33] The amendment also provided that strikes by industrial workers under certain conditions would be considered illegal and liable for criminal punishment.[34] Dr Ambedkar produced statistics to argue that there had not been so many strikes, which would require mandatory conciliation.[35] He further explained that in terms of law, 'strike' can only mean a breach of contract of service, which was not a crime. He strongly contended that making strikes criminal amounted to perpetuating slavery.[36] Responding to those who did not consider 'strike' as the right of workers, Dr Ambedkar stated that it was the right to freedom.[37] He therefore dubbed the Bill as 'The Workers' Civil Liberties Suspension Act'.[38] Dr Ambedkar believed that there was a strong relationship between the working class and the conception of democracy. According to him, 'A democracy which enslaves the working class, a class which is devoid of education, which is devoid of the means of life, which is devoid of any power of organization . . . is no democracy but a mockery of democracy.'[39] This also explains his emphasis on the importance of independent trade unions.[40]

As a member representing the labour class in the Viceroy's Council from 1942 to 1946, Dr Ambedkar advocated for many labour reforms like minimum wage, equal pay, paid leave, fixed number of working hours, etc.,[41] and tried to improve the quality of life of the working class through the legislations he proposed. In his address from the Bombay station of All India Radio in 1943, he said: '. . . labour is not content with securing merely fair conditions of work. What labour wants is fair conditions of life.'[42] Dr Ambedkar was also concerned about the discriminatory treatment meted out to workers from the Untouchable community.[43]

In March 1943, Dr Ambedkar introduced the War Injuries (Compensation Insurance) Bill, which sought to give compensation to workmen who had suffered war injuries and compel employers to provide insurance against the liabilities imposed upon them.[44] After a few rounds of discussion, it came into effect as the War Injuries (Compensation Insurance) Act, 1943, in September 1943. Dr Ambedkar also presided over the Standing Labour Committee meetings. In a meeting on 7 and 8 May 1943, the Standing Committee discussed several questions 'relating to labour welfare, war production, the employment of skilled and semi-skilled personnel, industrial disputes and the collection of statistical information on labour Problems'.[45] The Committee favoured 'the scheme for establishing employment exchanges for skilled and semi-skilled personnel, the scheme being conducted on a voluntary basis'.

Dr Ambedkar also sought to expand the scope of the Indian Boilers Act 1923 with the objective of providing mainly for the safety of life and property of persons from the danger of explosions of steam boilers and for achieving uniformity in registration and inspection during the operation and maintenance of boilers in India.[46] The amendment was adopted. Dr Ambedkar also moved amendments to the Mines Maternity Benefit Act to enlarge the scope of maternity benefits by extending the benefits to women working in underground mines.[47] The Indian Trade Union (Amendment) Bill, introduced by Dr Ambedkar in November 1943, sought to 'compel an employer to recognize a trade union'.[48] Furthermore, he emphasized 'converting unskilled men by giving them technical training and establishing numerous training schools.'[49]

The proposals and legislations introduced by Dr Ambedkar were not just theoretical; they were based on his field visits. Towards the end of 1943, Dr Ambedkar made a visit to Dhanbad (now in Jharkhand state) to study the working conditions of labourers in the coalfields, especially those of women. He went 400 feet underground by ladder to check the conditions of workers cutting coal.[50] During this inspection, Dr Ambedkar had friendly chats with workers regarding their wages and earnings and visited the workers' quarters to check their living conditions. Before entering the house of the resident, he politely asked for permission in Hindustani: '*Hum andar aa sakte hain?*' (Can I come in?). After permission was readily granted, he walked around to inspect the condition of the house and see the facility for ensuring ventilation. He also acquainted himself with the quantity and quality of food available and consumed by workers. Such was his humanist approach.

Speaking in the Central Legislative Assembly on 8 February 1944, Dr Ambedkar presented the Government of India's stand on the employment of women in coal mines. He stated: 'We have also taken care to see, and this is an important point, that women shall be paid the same wages as men. It is for the first time that I think in any industry the principle has been established of equal pay for equal work irrespective of the sex.'[51] Dr Ambedkar was himself involved in formulating the regulations for the coal industry. He also advocated the use of modern technology and argued for the technical and scientific training of workers. This, he believed, would lead towards 'maintaining decent standards of living for their people'.[52]

Dr Ambedkar also suggested a fair wage clause in government contracts[53] and introduced a Bill in November 1944 providing for a compensatory holiday to workers, if a compulsory holiday was cancelled. He said: 'Health and efficiency of the worker requires that he should have the requisite number of holidays which are prescribed by law.'[54] Presiding over the Seventh Labour Conference in November 1945, Dr Ambedkar presented a balance sheet of the State's obligations to labour and urged legislation to raise Indian labour standards to the international level.[55] This was also evident from the Indian Mines (Amendment) Bill 1946 introduced by him to impose an obligation upon the mine owners to provide pit-head baths

> equipped with shower baths and locker rooms for the use of men employed in mines and of similar and separate places and rooms for the use of women in mines where women are employed and for prescribing either generally or with particular reference to, the numbers of men and women ordinarily employed in a mine, the number and standards of such places and rooms.[56]

Dr Ambedkar also introduced a Bill that reduced the number of working hours per week in factories and also provided for payment for overtime—these changes were later accepted.[57]

As a Labour Member, he stated that the Government/State's responsibility and duty towards the betterment of the labour class also provides it with the power to regulate the private sector, which employs a large amount of labour.[58]

Facilitating the Unification of India

Sardar Patel is popularly credited with the unification of Indian princely states. But Dr Ambedkar must also be credited for creating a legal basis for the unification of these princely states into India. As noted in an earlier chapter, Dr Ambedkar had appealed to the members of the Constituent Assembly during the discussion of the Objectives Resolution to wait for the princely states to join the Constituent Assembly. He had on occasion also expressed his hope for a united India. Before Independence, he shared a press release making constitutional arguments that the princely states had no other option than to join the Indian Union. The press release was titled 'Paramountcy and the Claim of The Indian States to be Independent'.[59]

This press release was prepared in the context of the announcement made by two princely states, Travancore and Hyderabad, declaring themselves independent sovereign states on 15 August 1947 when India was initially promised dominion status. Other states also showed an inclination to follow the example of Travancore and Hyderabad.[60] The basis of this declaration was the statement (12 May 1946) issued by the Cabinet Mission that

> the British Government could not and will not in any circumstances transfer paramountcy to an Indian Government which means that the rights of the States which follow from their relationship to the Crown will no longer exist and that all the rights surrendered by the States to the paramount power will return to the States.[61]

Dr Ambedkar called this statement an incorrect understanding of law[62] and critiqued the then Congress Working Committee, which was negotiating with the Cabinet Mission for a settlement, for not calling out this statement.

As per the principle of Paramountcy, Dr Ambedkar argued, the British Parliament had supreme powers—not the agreements entered into with the Indian princely states. In other words, the sovereignty of the British Crown was supreme in India. In his press release, Dr Ambedkar demolished all claims of the princely states to declare independence on their own.

The press release was carried in several newspapers on 18 June 1947.[63] The newspaper *National Standard* reported this with the heading 'Princes Must Join Indian Union: Ambedkar Pooh-Poohs Alleged UNO Support'. The full front page of *National Standard,* which carried Dr Ambedkar's arguments, was then couriered by him to Sardar Patel on 19 June 1947, as the latter was negotiating with the princely rulers. The newspaper copy sent by Dr Ambedkar is still present in the private papers of Sardar Patel at the National Archives of India.[64]

Dr Ambedkar argued that the British Crown would function on the advice of India, if it became a Dominion. This constitutional position would be similar to how the British Crown functioned on the advice of other Dominions such as Canada, Australia, South Africa and Ireland in their respective regions. He noted,

> According to the principle of the Constitutional Law, while the prerogative vests in the King, the King has no discretion in the exercise of his prerogative but can exercise it only in accordance with the advice given to him by his Ministers. The King cannot exercise it independently of the advice of his Ministers . . . It follows that when India becomes a Dominion, the Crown will be bound to act in the exercise of

its prerogative rights, *i.e.,* Paramountcy on the advice of the Indian Cabinet.[65]

That is, the paramountcy enjoyed by the British Empire would be transferred to the Indian Parliament. He added, 'The moment India gets the Status of a Dominion it automatically acquires the capacity to advise the Crown on Paramountcy.'[66]

Dr Ambedkar also dismissed the statement of the Cabinet Mission, that Paramountcy would lapse. He argued:

> This is a most astounding statement and runs contrary to another well-established principle of the Constitutional Law. According to this principle, the King cannot surrender or abandon his prerogative rights. If the Crown cannot transfer Paramountcy the Crown cannot also abandon it . . . It would not be legal for the simple reason that after India becomes a Dominion, the Statute abrogating Paramountcy can be passed by the Dominion Parliament of India and the British Parliament would have no jurisdiction in this matter at all.[67]

Dr Ambedkar then examined the scenario if India became completely independent, and not a Dominion under the British Crown. He made a clear statement: 'Independent India can [. . .] make a valid claim for the inheritance of Paramountcy.' He clarified that when India became independent, the rule of the British Crown would end, and 'Independent India will be a succession State'. He argued that being a succeeding State in terms of international law, India would inherit the rights of the British Crown arising out of treaties, etc. Because of this phenomenon, he concluded that:

> [T]he Indian States will continue to be in the same position when India becomes Independent as they are now. They will

be sovereign States to the extent they are, but they cannot be independent States so long as they remain under the suzerainty, as they must be, either of the Crown, if India remains a Dominion and under the suzerainty of the succession State, if India becomes independent. While the suzerainty remains they can never be independent.[68]

He submitted that the only option before the princely states was, therefore, to join the Indian Union. He noted:

The States may declare themselves independent. But they must realize that while the suzerainty lasts and it must continue even when India becomes independent, India will not recognize their independence nor can a foreign State accord them the status of an independent State. The only way by which the Indian States can be free from Paramountcy would be to bring about a merger of sovereignty and suzerainty. That can happen only when the States join the Indian Union as constituent units thereof. The States' spokesmen ought to know this.[69]

He added that joining the Indian Union would only benefit the States. He stated:

The joining of the Federation will no doubt involve the introduction of responsible government but it has this advantage, viz., that the Union will guarantee to the Princes the rights relating to dynastic succession which is the most that a Prince can expect. To be independent and to hope to get recognition and protection from the UNO is to live in one's own paradise. It is doubtful if the UNO will give recognition to Indian States ignoring the claim by India of suzerainty over them. But even if that happens, the UNO will never grant any assistance to an Indian State from external aggression or internal commotion.[70]

Clearly, this intervention would have meant that Dr Ambedkar would have been seen as a person in favour of a united India, who had all the credentials, expertise and experience (more than anyone else) to lead the Constitution-drafting process.

When Dr Ambedkar lost his seat (from undivided Bengal) in the Constituent Assembly as a result of the Partition, Dr Rajendra Prasad, as president of the Constituent Assembly, wrote a letter on 30 June 1947 to B.G. Kher, the then prime minister of Bombay, requesting him to elect Dr Ambedkar back to the Constituent Assembly immediately. He wrote that Dr Ambedkar's work is 'of such an order' that 'we should not be deprived of his services'.[71]

Interestingly, Ashok Gopal narrates in Dr Ambedkar's biography:

> An undated letter of Edwina Mountbatten to Ambedkar sent soon after he was elected chairman of the Drafting Committee suggests that his name had been 'recommended' to Viceroy Mountbatten or Nehru by Eamon De Valera, the Irish statesmen who supported the Indian freedom movement and had played a leading role in the framing of the Constitution of Ireland in 1937. Edwina told Ambedkar she was 'personally glad' he was 'supervising' the constitution making, as he was the 'only genius who can give equal justice to every class and creed.[72]

Dr Ambedkar's presence as the head of the drafting process provided legitimacy to the process as well as to the Constitution.[73]

16

Constitution-Making

During the framing of India's Constitution, the Constituent Assembly, through a resolution on 24 January 1947, had appointed an Advisory Committee of fifty members (with Sardar Patel as chairman, and other members[1] from the Assembly, including Dr Ambedkar) to assist the assembly by drawing upon a 'list of fundamental rights, clauses for protecting minorities, and a scheme for the administration of Tribal and Excluded Areas'. The Advisory Committee, consisting of the members of the assembly, divided its work between three sub-committees: Fundamental Rights, Minorities, Tribal and Excluded Areas.[2]

While various aspects of the Constitution were being discussed, Dr Ambedkar's views on several provisions were foresighted and impactful. Some of the points and concerns raised by him, though not accepted by other members, later became true. Though this chapter does not contain all the details regarding the drafting of all provisions, the selected provisions and ideas, I believe, highlight Dr Ambedkar's vision. His role during the proceedings of the drafting of the Constitution is the subject for a separate book.

Right to Vote as a Fundamental Right

In the first meeting of the Fundamental Rights Sub-Committee on 27 February 1947, K.M. Munshi, a member of the sub-committee, raised the issue of the nature of fundamental rights to be embodied in the Constitution, i.e., whether and what should be the justiciable rights, and whether the Constitution should provide for writs to be issued by the courts.[3] Dr Ambedkar agreed with him. He informed the sub-committee that he had already prepared a long list of fundamental rights which he proposed to lay before the sub-committee and suggested that prerogative writs should be provided for in the Constitution.[4] The chairman of the sub-committee (Acharya J.B. Kriplani) then asked various members of the Fundamental Rights Sub-Committee to submit their notes, memorandums and drafts of constitutional provisions to be discussed and adopted by the sub-committee.[5] Three weeks were given to the members to prepare their drafts. As mentioned in the last chapter, Dr Ambedkar had already prepared 'States and Minorites', which was submitted for the consideration of other members.

As has been highlighted in various chapters of the book, equal voting rights or franchise was one of the main demands in Dr Ambedkar's proposed constitutional framework. He found the idea of voting rights to be non-negotiable. The provision of voting as a fundamental right was suggested by the Fundamental Rights Sub-Committee. However, when the Advisory Committee was considering the provision, there was resistance against the idea of making universal franchise and free and fair elections a fundamental right, even by Sardar Patel. Dr Ambedkar appealed to save the provision.

On 21–22 April 1947, when the provision of franchise came up for consideration, Shyama Prasad Mukherjee asked, 'Shall we make it a fundamental right or shall we leave it to the Franchise Regulations to be made?' The provisions on franchise also considered 'free' and 'periodical' elections. Dr Ambedkar responded to Mukherjee in clear terms: 'Let it be a fundamental right.'[6] However, Sardar Patel disagreed, and said, 'This clause about adult franchise is dropped for the present. It will be decided in the Constituent Assembly. It is kept over for future consideration and it is considered that that should be considered in the whole Constituent Assembly.'[7] However, Dr Ambedkar could not accept Patel's view. He argued, 'The Constituent Assembly will consider matters which are sent up to it by the different committees. The main thing will be franchise. This is a fundamental right. Franchise is the principal thing of the constitution.'[8] Babu Jagjivan Ram echoed Dr Ambedkar and noted: 'Franchise is a fundamental right. We may leave details about voting to the Constituent Assembly, but we may decide the right of the citizens to vote here.' Sardar Patel interjected, 'That is not what is mentioned here [in the provision].' Dr Ambedkar had endorsed the whole provision, arguing, 'We cannot leave it to party governments. They might manipulate elections and therefore it is much better that a self-contained provision is contained in the clause.'[9] Alladi Krishnaswamy Ayyar did not agree with this view and argued that the details of electoral rules ought to be left to the provincial constitution (being drafted for provinces at that time). C. Rajagopalachari also did not agree with Dr Ambedkar's suggestion, as he noted: 'I do not think in a list of fundamental rights we could go into such details as we have gone into.'[10]

But Dr Ambedkar was not willing to give up his core demand so easily. He argued,

I must say I attach a very great deal of importance to this clause on adult suffrage, and I do not think we can allow any exception to this . . . There must be adult franchise. In no other way can we be in a position to exert such influence as we have and we ought to exercise in the formation of the government, executive and the legislature, and I am sure about it that our elections cannot be independent unless and until the question of election is taken out from the hands of the Government of the day.[11]

He further noted, 'When we pass this, it does not mean that we have stopped the Constituent Assembly from reconsidering the question. But so far as this committee is concerned my point is that we should support the proposition that the committee is in favour of adult suffrage.'

C. Rajagopalachari still argued that this provision on franchise should be considered directly by the Constituent Assembly.[12] He further asked Dr Ambedkar if there were any examples where franchise is included as a fundamental right. Dr Ambedkar responded, 'The American Constitution provides this. The right of the citizens of the United States to vote shall not be denied or abridged by the United States or any other State on account of race, colour or previous conditions of servitude.' Rajagopalachari and Sardar Patel did not agree. Sardar Patel said in clear terms: 'Such a provision cannot be a fundamental right.'[13] That is, it could be a legal right, but not a fundamental right. Dr Ambedkar responded, 'My fear is this. If the report of this committee goes to the Constituent Assembly without including in it this fundamental right, it may be later on argued that this particular right either was condemned or was not approved of by this committee.'

After this, Govind Ballabh Pant made a proposition that the clause on voting rights and elections may be 'sent to the Constituent Assembly, not as part of these fundamental rights, but included in the letter of the Chairman to the effect that we recommend to the Constituent Assembly the following principles in regard to the framing of the constitution.' Sardar Patel agreed.[14] But Dr Ambedkar said: 'The clause should go as it is . . . I want the whole clause as it is to be sent by the Chairman.'[15] He could foresee the consequences of not having the right to vote as a fundamental right, as he argued: 'If it is a fundamental right, then the legislature and the executive cannot alter it. If it is not a fundamental right, it may be liable to alteration. This sort of position could be easily safeguarded by a clause in the Constitution.' But his pleas were not heeded. Sardar Patel noted that he would recommend the provision in a letter to the Constituent Assembly 'that this clause should find a place in the Constitution'.[16] The minutes of the meeting reflected this accordingly.[17] Unfortunately, Dr Ambedkar did not get support in the Constituent Assembly, as the provision on adult franchise was not included as a fundamental right.[18]

Dr Ambedkar's fear came true in 2015, when a significant population of voters in Haryana were denied the right to contest elections, as a law prohibited their right on the grounds of educational requirements, electricity arrears, etc.[19] Interestingly, in April 2023, in his dissenting opinion on the issue, Justice Ajay Rastogi declared that the right to vote should be considered a fundamental right.[20]

Reservations for Backward Classes in Services[21]

When the Sub-Committee on Fundamental Rights prepared a clause on the right to 'equality of opportunity,' the Minorities Sub-Committee recommended the addition of a proviso to this initial clause, to enable the government to reserve a certain proportion of posts in the public services for the 'minorities' (including Backward Classes, as the term 'minorities' was then understood). This was suggested to meet the claims of minorities for special representation in the services.[22]

Dr Ambedkar was a member of both these sub-committees. A redrafted version of the clause, which then came before the Advisory Committee on 22 April 1947, provided for the state to make 'provision for reservations in favour of classes not adequately represented in the public services'.[23]

In the Advisory Committee proceedings, Dr Ambedkar supported this clause. He, however, suggested deleting the words 'not adequately represented', and that the clause be rephrased to provide reservations 'in public services in favour of classes as may be prescribed by the State'.[24] He argued that if the words 'not adequately represented' were retained, any reservations made by the state 'would be open to challenge in the court of law on the ground that the classes in whose favour reservation was made happened to be in fact already adequately represented'.[25] He further added,

> I do not want this matter to be litigated in a court of law. Once the legislature or the constitution or whatever authority you authorize has made a reservation, that reservation should continue without being challenged in a court of law. It will be quite impossible for a minority community for the matter of that to face a litigation in a court of law if somebody took up the matter stating here is a community for which reservation is made, which in fact is adequately represented. I do not want that to be a matter of litigation.[26]

When a member, M. Ruthnaswamy, pointed out, 'You have placed it among justiciable rights', Dr Ambedkar replied in the affirmative by explaining,

> In the sense that the executive *shall not override* . . . I am going to insist on some provision in the Constitution itself that this shall not be a matter which will be left to the sweet

will of the legislature or the executive. It will be part of the
Constitution.[27]

Thus, Dr Ambedkar made it clear that the provisions on
reservations in services were in the form of a justiciable
fundamental right. K.M. Munshi suggested the phrase
'classes which in the opinion of the State are not adequately
represented'.[28] Dr Ambedkar wanted to have 'as may be
prescribed by the State', but when Rajagopalachari stated that
both the phrases convey the same meaning, Dr Ambedkar
agreed to accept the phrase 'classes which in the opinion of the
State are not adequately represented,' as suggested by Munshi.[29]
In the Constituent Assembly, it was also clarified that the term
'adequate' in the reservation provision may mean more than
proportionate representation if the situation so demanded.[30]

The clause (numbered 5) was included in the Interim
Report on Fundamental Rights, which was tabled by Sardar
Vallabhbhai Patel (as chairman of the Advisory Committee)
before the Constituent Assembly on 29 April 1947. The clause,
listed in the 'justiciable fundamental rights' section of the
Interim Report, was discussed, and adopted by the assembly
on 30 April 1947. It was later reassigned as Article 10(3) of the
draft Constitution prepared by the Dr Ambedkar-led Drafting
Committee with one modification: instead of the words 'in
favour of any particular class of citizens,' the words 'in favour of
any backward class of citizens' were inserted.[31] On 30 November
1948, Dr Ambedkar explained on the floor of the Constituent
Assembly that the addition of the word 'backward' before 'class
of citizens' reflects the larger purpose of equality by granting
the overriding provision of reservation in their favour.[32] It was
adopted as Article 16(4) of the Constitution.

Unfortunately, even though Dr Ambedkar emphasized that
Article 16(4) is a justiciable fundamental right, it was treated

as merely an enabling provision in the hands of the State, i.e., that the executive/legislature could decide whether it wanted to give reservations to Backward Class citizens or not.[33]

Non-discrimination and Access to Resources

One of the most powerful provisions under the Indian Constitution is Article 15(2), which prohibits discrimination even by private citizens. This provision initially appeared in the draft of Dr Ambedkar, who had been highlighting it previously as well.

During the Round Table Conference, he had proposed the insertion of a clause, which would create the 'Offence of Infringement of Citizenship'. The clause was phrased by him as follows: 'Whoever denies to any person except for reasons by law applicable to persons of all classes and regardless of any previous condition of untouchability *the full enjoyment of any of the accommodations, advantages, facilities, privileges of inns, educational institutions, roads, paths, streets, tanks, wells and other watering places, public conveyances on land, air or water, theatres or other places of public amusement, resort or convenience* whether they are dedicated to or maintained or licensed for the use of the public shall be punished with imprisonment of either description for a term which may extend to five years and shall also be liable to fine.'[34] The above clause was also reproduced by him in 'States and Minorities'.[35]

It has also been rightly pointed out that the language contained in the constitutional provisions of equality and non-discrimination did not 'emerge out of [Dr] Ambedkar's imagination, but constituted the culmination of decades of political struggle'.[36] Furthermore, Dr Ambedkar argued that the liberty of an individual must be protected from 'invasion by other individuals',[37] and therefore demanded active State protection for Dalits.

The final text of Article 15(2) provides prohibition of discrimination in access to 'shops', among other services and entities. When asked about the scope of this term, Dr Ambedkar clarified in the Constituent Assembly[38] (29 November 1948) that the term 'shops' had been included in the Constitution 'in a generic sense' and would 'include anybody who offers his services'. He added, 'I should like to point out therefore that the word "shop" used here is not used in the limited sense of permitting entry. It is used in the larger sense of requiring the services if the terms of service are agreed to.' Thus, Dr Ambedkar was suggesting a broader reading of the non-discrimination provisions under the Constitution to protect the interests of the marginalized communities.

Qualified Joint Electorates

As mentioned in the chapter on power sharing, Dr Ambedkar wanted to have an electoral system through which the real representatives of the marginalized communities could be elected. He had suggested the system of qualified joint electorates, where electoral candidates from reserved seats need to secure a designated minimum percentage of votes from their community. Dr Ambedkar suggested this proposal to the Minorities Sub-Committee, but no other member supported him.[39] He tried again to bring such a provision in the text of the Constitution by suggesting an amendment before the Constituent Assembly when it was discussing the provisions related to reserved seats. In this endeavour, Dr Ambedkar found support in Sardar Nagappa, a Congress leader who became his ally in protecting the rights of the Untouchables. On 28 August 1947, Sardar Nagappa presented an amendment, in the name of Dr Ambedkar and himself, that 'Provided that in the case of the Scheduled Castes the candidate before he is declared elected to the seat reserved for the Scheduled Castes, shall have secured not less than 35 per cent of the votes polled by the Scheduled Castes in the election to the reserved seat.'[40] Nagappa argued that such a system would ensure the election of real representatives for the Scheduled Castes. However, the proposal was not liked by other members of the Constituent Assembly. Not only was Sardar Nagappa forced to withdraw this proposal, but a few members of the Constituent Assembly, including Sardar Patel, made personal attacks on Dr Ambedkar for suggesting such a proposal.[41]

The current system of reserved seats in joint electorates remains contentious, as the constituencies for reserved candidates do not allow them to win elections by appealing to the Scheduled Caste voters alone. It has been argued that candidates on reserved constituencies are dependent on the votes of oppressor castes, as a result of which it has been argued that they are not able to push an agenda for the welfare of the Scheduled Castes.[42] Dr Ambedkar's proposal is relevant in the light of such criticism of the system of joint electorates with reserved seats.

Independence of the Judiciary

The process and procedure for selecting judges for the higher judiciary has been a point of contestation between the executive and the judiciary. Dr Ambedkar's views are relevant to discuss the issue. He emphasized representation in every institution. Accordingly, there have been demands that the judiciary also needs to be representative.[43] On 28 November 1998, then President K.R. Narayanan wrote on an official file:

I would like to record my views that while recommending the appointment of Supreme Court judges, it would be consonant with constitutional principles and the nation's social objectives if persons belonging to weaker sections of society like SCs and STs, who comprise 25 per cent of the population, and women are given due consideration.[44]

It has been demanded that the selection process has to account for this principle of representation.[45] The collegium resolutions of 2023 have indicated that diversity and representation are some of the criteria in considering judges for appointment to the Supreme Court.[46] Making suggestions as the leader of Scheduled Castes, Dr Ambedkar had demanded in the Minorities Sub-Committee that on every selection committee, the Scheduled Castes should have at least one representative.[47] This needs to be ensured for different marginalized communities.

Furthermore, the issue of whether the executive through the President or the Chief Justice of India should have a primacy in appointments was discussed in the Constituent Assembly. Dr Ambedkar addressed various amendments made in this regard respectively. Whether the power for judicial appointments should vest in the President, Dr Ambedkar stated:

There can be no difference of opinion in the House that our judiciary must both be independent of the executive and must also be competent in itself . . . it would be dangerous to leave the appointments to be made by the President, without any kind of reservation or limitation, that is to say, merely on the advice of the executive of the day. Similarly, it seems to me that to make every appointment which the executive wishes to make subject to the concurrence of the Legislature is also not a very suitable provision. Apart from its being cumbrous, it also involves the possibility of the appointment being influenced by political pressure and political considerations.

On the primacy of the opinion of the Chief Justice of India alone, Dr Ambedkar stated:

> With regard to the question of the concurrence of the Chief Justice, it seems to me that those who advocate that proposition seem to rely implicitly both on the impartiality of the Chief Justice and the soundness of his judgment. I personally feel no doubt that the Chief Justice is a very eminent person. But after all the Chief Justice is a man with all the failings, all the sentiments and all the prejudices which we as common people have; and I think, to allow the Chief Justice practically a veto upon the appointment of judges is really to transfer the authority to the Chief Justice which we are not prepared to vest in the President or the Government of the day. I therefore think that is also a dangerous proposition.

Thus, Dr Ambedkar did not agree with the primacy of either the President or the Chief Justice alone in their individual capacity. He called for a deliberative process for the selection of judges—'there should be consultation of persons who are *ex hypothesi,* well qualified to give proper advice in matters of this sort'.[48] After the judgment of the Supreme Court of India in the *Third Judges* case,[49] the process of appointment of judges became more consultative than it was before.

President of India

What is the scope of the President's role under the Indian Constitution? Various judgments have relied upon the statement of Dr Ambedkar made in the Constituent Assembly on this issue.[50]

On 4 November 1948, Dr Ambedkar explained:

In the Draft Constitution there is placed at the head of the Indian Union a functionary who is called the President of the Union. The title of this functionary reminds one of the President of the United States. But beyond identity of names there is nothing in common between the forms of government prevalent in America and the form of government proposed under the Draft Constitution . . . Under the Presidential system of America, the President is the chief head of the Executive. The administration is vested in him. Under the Draft Constitution the President occupies the same position as the King under the English Constitution. He is the head of the State but not of the Executive. He represents the Nation but does not rule the Nation. He is the symbol of the nation. His place in the administration is that of a ceremonial device on a seal by which the nation's decisions are made known. Under the American Constitution the President has under him Secretaries in charge of different Departments. In like manner the President of the Indian Union will have under him Ministers in charge of different Departments of administration. Here again there is a fundamental difference between the two. The President of the United States is not bound to accept any advice tendered to him by any of his Secretaries. *The President of the Indian Union will be generally bound by the advice of his Ministers*. He can do nothing contrary to their advice nor can he do anything without their advice.'

Thus, under the Indian Constitution, the President is bound by the advice of the Council of Ministers.

Furthermore, Dr Ambedkar was of the view that the conduct of the President as well as that of the governors should be guided by what was called the 'Instrument of Instructions', similar to what was contained in the GOI 1935 Act.[51]

That would prevent any arbitrary decision-making by the president or the governor. But this proposal was not accepted.

Sequencing of Articles in Fundamental Rights Chapter

It was a constant demand of Dr Ambedkar that the Constitution should provide certain safeguards to protect the rights of the socially oppressed. It is for this reason that the constitutional provision prohibiting untouchability (Article 17) was intentionally placed in the fundamental rights chapter of the Constitution, which guarantees enforceable rights. This was done so that the right against untouchability could be enforced by the socially oppressed against their oppressor castes. It could also be enforced against government officials. Interestingly, it must be seen that Article 17 was kept in a sequence along with the provisions guaranteeing equality before the law and equal protection of the law (Article 14), non-discrimination (Article 15), and equality of opportunity to all citizens including a clause guaranteeing affirmative action in the form of quotas for the socially backward (Article 16). This shows the larger constitutional project of guaranteeing substantive equality. The combination of Articles 14–17 shows that equality cannot be achieved without its components: equality before the law, equal protection of law, non-discrimination, equal opportunity and affirmative action, and abolition of untouchability, i.e., all aspects are interlinked and cannot be considered in isolation. Equality cannot be attained without affirmative action and the prohibition of caste-based discrimination and untouchability. This was Dr Ambedkar's contribution to the concept of equality in a constitutional framework.

Liberty, Equality, Fraternity

In his last address in the Constituent Assembly, Dr Ambedkar reiterated the core constitutional values of 'liberty, equality, fraternity', which he had been consistently advocating in his public career. He noted, 'We must make our political democracy a social democracy as well. Political democracy cannot last unless there lies at the base of it, social democracy. What does social democracy mean? It means a way of life which recognizes liberty, equality and fraternity as the principles of life.'[52]

For Dr Ambedkar, these three features are not separate but are an interconnected trinity. He stated:

> These principles of liberty, equality and fraternity are not to be treated as separate items in a trinity. They form a union of trinity in the sense that to divorce one from the other is to defeat the very purpose of democracy. Liberty cannot be divorced from equality, equality cannot be divorced from liberty. Nor can liberty and equality be divorced from fraternity. Without equality, liberty would produce the supremacy of the few over the many. Equality without liberty would kill individual initiative. Without fraternity, liberty, [and] equality could not become a natural course of things. It would require a constable to enforce them.[53]

He said that the ideas of equality and fraternity are completely missing from Indian soil. Emphasizing equality, he stated:

> On the 26th of January 1950, we are going to enter into a life of contradictions. In politics we will have equality and in social and economic life we will have inequality. In politics we will be recognizing the principle of one man one vote and one vote one value. In our social and economic life, we shall, by reason of our social and economic structure, continue to deny the principle of one man one value. How long shall we continue to live this life of contradictions? How long shall we continue to deny equality in our social and economic

life? If we continue to deny it for long, we will do so only by putting our political democracy in peril.'

He highlighted the importance of fraternity, by noting: 'What does fraternity mean? Fraternity means a sense of common brotherhood of all Indians—if Indians being one people. It is the principle which gives unity and solidarity to social life.'[54]

Dr Ambedkar further added that because of the absence of equality and fraternity in all spheres of life, 'political power in this country has too long been the monopoly of a few'. This monopoly has not merely deprived the oppressed castes of their chance of betterment, it has sapped them of what may be called the significance of life. Connecting the idea of independence with the sharing of power with the oppressed communities, he noted,

> These down-trodden classes are tired of being governed. They are impatient to govern themselves. Therefore, the sooner room is made for the realization of their aspiration, the better for the few, the better for the country, the better for the maintenance for its independence and the better for the continuance of its democratic structure.

Personal Life and Constitution Framing

Having recovered from his health issues, Dr Ambedkar went through a personal emotional journey while he was involved with the drafting of the Constitution. He had to delay his wedding with Dr Savita because he was too occupied with preparing the first draft of the Constitution in 1948 as the chairperson of the Drafting Committee, and with piloting the Hindu Code Bill as the law minister. He passionately convinced Dr Savita (a Brahmin) to wait for a couple of months for the wedding. He also explained to her about the additional rights that she could get as the wife, if the Hindu Code Bill was passed before their marriage. The letters demonstrate Dr Ambedkar's investment in the drafting of the Indian Constitution and legal reforms even at a personal level. In a letter dated 19 February 1948 to his then-to-be wife, he wrote: 'Our marriage should be legal in your own interest. I shall never agree to place you in a false position. The Hindu Marriage Law is being amended and as amended, it will permit inter-caste marriages among Hindus.'[55] In another letter, he expressed his concern about his to-be wife's future: 'Raja's (referring to himself romantically) mind has no peace when he thinks of what will happen to Sharu after Raja passes away.'[56]

After Dr Ambedkar's marriage with Dr Savita, Sardar Patel sent a congratulatory note, stating: 'I am sure, if Bapu were alive, he would have given you his blessings.'[57] Dr Ambedkar responded: 'I agree that Bapu, if he had been alive, would have blessed it.'[58] In fact, Gandhi's views on caste evolved in later years due to the influence of Dr Ambedkar.[59] Socialist leader Dr Lohia once wrote, 'From his belief that the caste system was a part of religion, [Gandhi] went on to say that it was a sin.'[60]

Selection of National Symbols

Along with his letter dated 21 February 1948 to Dr Savita, Dr Ambedkar had sent a courier, which carried the image of Ashoka's pillar. He wrote: 'This image will be printed on the cover page of the Constitution volume that we have prepared. I have selected this.'[61] Dr Savita Ambedkar later noted:

This national emblem adopted by India is the lions atop the Ashoka Pillar. The above letter [of his] gives evidence that this emblem was chosen by Dr Ambedkar. The selection of the national flag and the national emblem along with drafting the Constitution—these were but a few of his services to the nation.[62]

Ashok Gopal also mentions Dr Ambedkar's influence in the selection of the national flag. He notes:

On 23 June 1947, Dr Ambedkar was appointed as one of the members of an ad hoc committee set up by the Constituent Assembly under the chairmanship of Rajendra Prasad to decide on the design of the flag to be adopted for free India. On the basis of its recommendation, Nehru moved a resolution in the Assembly on 22 July stating that the National Flag of India would be a 'horizontal tricolour of deep saffron, white and dark green in equal proportion', with a 'wheel in navy blue to represent that charkha (spinning wheel) in the centre of the white band', but the design of the wheel would be that of the 'wheel which appears on the abacus of the Sarnath Lion Capital of Asoka'.[63]

The Last Warning

Dr Ambedkar had once remarked in the Constituent Assembly:

If we agree that our Constitution must not be a dictatorship but must be a Constitution in which there is parliamentary democracy where government is all the time on the anvil, so to say, on its trial, responsible to the people, responsible to the judiciary, then I have no hesitation in saying that the principles embodied in this Constitution are as good as if not better than, the principles embodied in any other parliamentary constitution.[64]

In his last address to the Constituent Assembly, he sounded off a warning to the members of the Constituent Assembly and Indian society: 'Independence is no doubt a matter of joy. But let us not forget that this independence has thrown on us great responsibilities. By independence, we have lost the excuse of blaming the British for anything going wrong. If hereafter things go wrong, we will have nobody to blame except ourselves.'[65] Dr Ambedkar wished that the people of India would preserve the Constitution by recognizing the evils of inequality that lie across our path.

17

Father of the Indian Constitution

Not only did Dr Ambedkar shape the direction of the Indian constitutional discourse but he also expended extraordinary energy in preparing the final draft of the Constitution. His efforts were acknowledged almost unanimously by all the members of the Constituent Assembly. Even though there were a few other members in the drafting committee, it was Dr Ambedkar who single-handedly managed most of its affairs. This fact was acknowledged and highlighted by many members of the Constituent Assembly in their speeches.

After Dr Ambedkar presented the initial draft of the Constitution in the Constituent Assembly on 4 November 1948, there was much appreciation for his speech and his efforts in piloting the process. As the proceedings continued on the next day (5 November 1948), Sardar Nagappa said that Dr Ambedkar represented the lowest rung of the social ladder and that it was 'our fortune that the task of framing the Constitution has been entrusted to the representative—the real representative—of the lowest rung of the ladder'.[1] Frank Anthony congratulated Dr Ambedkar 'for the symmetrical and lucid analysis which he gave us of the principles underlying our Draft Constitution'.[2] Krishna Chandra Sharma from the then United Provinces stated, 'I join in the pleasant task to compliment Dr. Ambedkar for the well worked out scheme he has placed before the House, the hard work he was put in, and his yesterday's able and lucid speech'.[3]

T.T. Krishnamachari, a prominent member of the Constituent Assembly who later held the position of India's finance minister, shared how the process of preparing the draft Constitution was managed solely by Dr Ambedkar. He said:

> I am aware of the amount of work and enthusiasm that he has brought to bear on the work of drafting this Constitution . . . The House is perhaps aware that of the seven members nominated by you, one had resigned from the House and was replaced. One died and was not replaced. One was away in America and his place was not filled up and another person was engaged in State affairs, and there was a void to that extent. One or two people were far away from Delhi and perhaps reasons of health did not permit them to attend. *So it happened ultimately that the burden of drafting this constitution fell on Dr. Ambedkar* and I have no doubt that we are grateful to him for having achieved this task in a manner which is undoubtedly commendable[4] (emphasis supplied).

B. Das from Orissa, while paying his 'tribute to Dr. Ambedkar and his colleagues', objected to the changes done by Dr Ambedkar in the Preamble. He stated that Dr Ambedkar changed the language of the Preamble 'Independent Sovereign Republic' to 'Sovereign Democratic State'.[5] This shows that Dr Ambedkar had a key role in the shaping of the final language of the Preamble as well.[6]

Kazi Syed Karimuddin described Dr Ambedkar as 'a great constitution-maker.'[7] Lakshmi Kanta Maitra appreciated 'the stupendous amount of time and energy' that Dr Ambedkar 'spent in giving the constitutional proposals a definite shape'.[8]

Many other members also shared their belief that Dr Ambedkar was solely responsible for preparing the draft Constitution. In the proceedings of 6 November 1948, Arun Chandra Guha described Dr Ambedkar as 'a learned professor', and shared his belief: 'I think the Draft Constitution is mainly his handicraft.'[9] T. Prakasam from Madras appreciated Dr Ambedkar, highlighting,

> My honourable friend, Mr. T.T. Krishnamachari when he was speaking explained the handicap under which the Honourable Dr. Ambedkar had been labouring on account of as many as five or six members of the Committee having dropped out and their places not having been filled up.' But he also expressed his disagreements with the 'Draft Constitution of Dr. Ambedkar.[10]

Some members referred to specific provisions of the Constitution, which they thought were Dr Ambedkar's brainchild. Thakur Dass Bhargava said, 'I cannot withhold my need of praise for the labour, the industry and the ability with which Dr. Ambedkar has dealt with this Constitution.' Bhargava also expressed his gratitude to Dr Ambedkar 'for having added the word "fraternity" to the Preamble'. It had not been part of the Objectives Resolution.[11] This again shows that Dr Ambedkar had a final say in the words chosen for the Preamble.[12] Later, Dr Ambedkar was also celebrated as the man who 'finally dealt the death blow to [the] custom of untouchability, of which he was himself a victim in his younger days'.[13]

When the draft Constitution was presented for adoption towards the end of 1949, the members of the Constituent Assembly again showered their praise and thanked Dr Ambedkar for managing the entire drafting process, despite his poor health. On 17 November 1949, V.I. Muniswamy Pillay, a member of the Scheduled Caste community and a constant supporter of Dr Ambedkar in the Constituent Assembly, stated: 'I must say a word of praise to the caliber and capacity of the Chairman of the Drafting Committee— Dr. B.R. Ambedkar.' This was followed by loud cheers in the Constituent Assembly. Pillay added, 'Coming as I do from a community that has produced Dr. Ambedkar, I feel proud that his capacity has now been recognized, not only by the Harijans but by all communities that inhabit India.' Expressing personal satisfaction with the presence of Dr Ambedkar, Pillai shared that Dr Ambedkar 'has been able to show to the world that, the Scheduled Castes are no less important but they can rise to heights and give to the world their great services'.[14]

On 21 November 1949, H.J. Khandekar, a Congress leader, expressed how the Constitution framed by Dr Ambedkar would be revolutionary for Indian society. He said:

[W]e are enacting a law of Independent India under the genius of Dr. Ambedkar, the President of the Drafting Committee... I call this Constitution the Mahar law because Dr. Ambedkar is a Mahar and now when we inaugurate this constitution on the 26th of January 1950 we shall have the law of Manu replaced by the law of Mahar and I hope that unlike the law of Manu under which there was never a property in the country the Mahar law will make India virtually a paradise. Well Sir, even the social, political and religious reformers in the country like Gautama Buddha, Ramanuja, Kabir, Sant Tukaram, Raja Ram Mohan Roy, Swami Dayanand Saraswati, Paramahansa, Mahatma Joti Rao Fulley, Vithal Ramji Shinde, Thakkar Bapa and last but not the least, Mahatma Gandhi, found it very difficult to get rid of this ghost of untouchability' (sic). Khandekar said that Dr Ambedkar did 'the greatest service to this country in these three years'.[15]

Mahboob Ali Baig Sahib congratulated Dr Ambedkar 'for the outstanding ability with which he piloted the Draft Constitution'.[16] He said, 'Dr. Ambedkar was unique in his clarity of expression and thought, and his mastery over the Constitutional problems including those of finance has been marvelous, unique, singular and complete.'

Sardar Nagappa was again raising points of full honour for Dr Ambedkar.[17] He said:

Now I call this a Constitution for the benefit and betterment of the common man. It can be called a Common man's Constitution. This assures the right of common people more than that of the landed aristocracy or of industrialists and capitalists. This will go a long way for the betterment of the common people of this country. It is so because though Dr. Ambedkar happens to be a man of high status in society, yet he has been drawn from the lot of common people. He has not forgotten the interest of the common people and he has been good enough to do all that is possible for their betterment.[18]

Jaspat Roy Kapoor observed that Dr Ambedkar was a man of solutions. He said: 'I have always found him to bring to bear upon the subject a very constructive approach. On many an occasion when there seemed to be a deadlock, he came forward with suggestions which resolved those deadlocks.'[19] This sentiment was echoed by R.V. Dhulekar. He said: '[Dr Ambedkar] always tried to understand the opponent's view and he always tried to accommodate him, and he always tried to put his own views in the most clear language. We are very grateful to him.'[20] According to Dhulekar, Dr Ambedkar 'performed the task with clarity of vision, clarity of thought and clarity of language'.[21]

Some writers such as Arundhati Roy and Shashi Tharoor have observed that Dr Ambedkar did not pursue the cause of the Scheduled Tribes.[22] They are clearly mistaken,[23] as they must not have read the proceedings of the Constituent Assembly. Jaipal Singh Munda, the legendary icon from the Adivasi community, had thanked Dr Ambedkar for introducing a clause providing for political representation (reservation) to Scheduled Tribes.[24] On 24 November 1949, Munda paid an 'unqualified tribute' to Dr Ambedkar and his team.[25]

The next day, on 25 November 1949, Pattabhi Sitaramayya had many adjectives of praise for Dr Ambedkar.[26] Mahavir Tyagi described Dr Ambedkar as 'the main artist' who 'laid aside his brush and unveiled the picture for the public to see and comment upon'.[27]

When Dr Ambedkar's turn came to give his final address in the Constituent Assembly, he showed statesmanship and leadership, and expressed his gratitude towards everyone.[28] He even credited the Congress party—to which he was often critical in his previous works—for facilitating a 'smooth sailing of the Draft Constitution in the [Constituent] Assembly'.[29]

The Constitution of India was adopted in the Constituent Assembly on 26 November 1949. In his speech, the president of the Assembly, Dr Rajendra Prasad, acknowledged that the selection of Dr Ambedkar as the chairman of the Drafting Committee was the most apt decision made by the members of the Assembly. He said:

Sitting in the Chair and watching the proceedings from day to day. I have realized as nobody else could have, with what zeal and devotion the members of the Drafting Committee and especially its Chairman, Dr. Ambedkar in spite of his indifferent health, have worked. (Cheers). We could never make a decision which was or could be ever so right as when we put him on the Drafting Committee and made him its Chairman. He has not only justified his selection but has added luster to the work which he has done (sic).[30]

These speeches from the members of the Constituent Assembly show a consensus view that they considered Dr Ambedkar as the 'main artist' behind the Constitution. T.T. Krishnamachari and Dr Rajendra Prasad's speeches most accurately show that the working of the Drafting Committee was mostly managed by Dr Ambedkar alone. Even Constitutional Adviser B.N. Rau was not available later, as he left India after being appointed as permanent representative to the United Nations in the fall of 1948, 'even as the process of constitution-making was underway'.[31] No doubt that the contributions of others, including Rau's, were significant.[32] Dr Ambedkar himself acknowledged these contributions in his last address to the Constituent Assembly.[33] However, the process of managing the entire affairs with reference to preparing the draft of the Constitution from scratch to its final form over a period of three years was done by Dr Ambedkar, despite his deteriorating health. It is for these reasons he is popularly known as the *Father of the Indian Constitution*.

18

Conditions Precedent for the Successful Working of Democracy

After the Constitution came into force, Dr Ambedkar was active in building a constitutional culture in the practice of democracy. In line with these efforts, he gave a speech before an audience in the Poona District Law Library on 22 December 1952 on the topic 'Conditions Precedent for the Successful Working of Democracy'. Dr Savita Ambedkar accompanied Dr Ambedkar for the lecture.[1]

Importantly, Dr Ambedkar defined what a democracy meant and what its purpose was. Tracing the evolution of the conception of democracy, he stated that '[t]he purpose of modern democracy is not so much to put a curb on an autocratic King [ruling establishment] but to bring about the welfare of the people'.[2] He then defined democracy as 'a form and a method of government whereby revolutionary changes in the economic and social life of the people are brought about without bloodshed'.[3] He added, 'If democracy can enable those who are running it to bring about fundamental changes in the social and economic life of the people and the people accept those changes without resorting to bloodshed, then I say that there is democracy.'[4] This definition was important in the light of how the oppressor castes and communities resorted to violence, boycott and bloodshed whenever there were efforts to bring about social change. He then laid down conditions that needed to be followed, if the people of India wanted to retain the new democracy set up through the Constitution.

No Glaring Inequalities

The first and foremost condition, according to Dr Ambedkar, was that 'there must be no glaring inequalities in the society'. There should not be any 'oppressed class' and 'suppressed class'. All had to be equal. He added, 'There must not be a class which has got all the privileges and a class which has got all the burdens to carry.'[5] This division can lead to 'a bloody revolution'. In Dr Ambedkar's view, 'the deep cleavages between class and class are going to be one of the greatest hindrances in the success of democracy'.[6] He argued that if the 'privileged few' do not 'willingly and voluntarily surrender their privileges, then the distance between them and the lower orders will destroy democracy and bring into existence something quite different'. He stated examples from global history, where 'one of the causes for the breakdown of democracy is the existence of these social cleavages'.[7]

Opposition Rights

Dr Ambedkar demonstrated that the second condition necessary for a democracy is the 'existence of opposition' in a political system. He stated, 'Democracy requires not only that the Government should be subject to the veto, long-term veto of five years, at the hands of the people, but there must be an immediate veto.' That immediate checks and balances can take place only with the entrenchment of political opposition in a constitutional system. Dr Ambedkar argued:

> There must be people in the parliament immediately ready there and then to challenge the Government . . . [D]emocracy means that nobody has any perpetual authority to rule, but that rule is subject to sanction by the people and can be challenged in the house itself. You will see how important it is to have an opposition.

According to Dr Ambedkar, 'Opposition means that the Government is always on the anvil. The Government must justify every act that it does to those of the people who do not belong to its party . . . *The opposition is a condition precedent for democracy.*'[8]

Dr Ambedkar expressed displeasure that 'in our country all our newspapers, for one reason or other, I believe, it is the revenue from advertisements, have given far more publicity to the Government than to the opposition, because you cannot get any revenue from the opposition.'[9] He therefore wanted the recognition of opposition rights in the constitutional system. He gave the example of English and Canada, where opposition rights are protected. He noted:

> [In England, not] only is the opposition recognized, but the leader of the opposition is paid a salary by the government in order to run the opposition. He gets a secretary, he gets a small staff of stenographers and writers, he has a room in the House of Commons where he does his business. In the same way, you will find that in Canada the leader of the opposition gets a salary in the way as a Prime Minister does, because in both these countries democracy feels that there must be someone to show whether the government is

going wrong. And this must be done incessantly and perpetually and that is why they do not mind spending money on the leader of the opposition.[10]

Equality in Law and Administration

Dr Ambedkar said that the third condition for the success of democracy is that of 'equality in law and administration'. This is larger than the equality before law principle, which means that everyone is equal in the eyes of the law. He stated that there needs to be 'equality of treatment in administration'. That is, those in charge of administration should not discriminate. That they should treat members of socially oppressed and minority communities equally—something which Dr Ambedkar emphasized in his different writings. That those in administration should not be biased towards vulnerable groups. He noted, 'It is quite possible for good many of you to imagine or to recall cases where a party Government is carrying on the administration for the benefit of the members of the party.'[11]

Constitutional Morality

In the Constituent Assembly, Dr Ambedkar had noted that the people of India do not have something called 'constitutional morality'. The observance of constitutional morality is the fourth condition for preserving democratic ideas. According to Dr Ambedkar, the Constitution was not going to work on its own and would depend on how people practise it. According to him: '[We] have a Constitution which contains legal provisions, only a skeleton. The flesh of that skeleton is to be found in what we call constitutional morality. However, in England, it is called the conventions of the constitution and people must be ready to observe the rules of the game.'[12] Constitutional morality requires certain conduct—which is the following of constitutional conventions and practices—from those in power as well as citizens. He gave examples from the US as to how the President stayed in power only for two tenures to prevent abuse of power and the creation of a cult.

Protection of Minorities

Dr Ambedkar emphasized that democracy must protect the minorities. In his words, 'in the name of democracy there must be no tyranny of the majority over the minority'. That is to say, democracy should not confused with majoritarian rule. Dr Ambedkar stated, 'The minority must always feel safe that although the majority is carrying on the Government, the minority is not being hurt, or the minority is not being hit below the belt.'[13]

Social Moral Order

Dr Ambedkar was clear that 'democracy does require the functioning of moral order in society'.[14] According to him, democracy, politics and ethics went together. He expressed his dissatisfaction that political scientists do not focus on this relation, as he noted: 'You may learn politics and you may know nothing about ethics as though politics can work without ethics. To my mind it is an astounding proposition.' He said that the law will only be successful when society has the morality to support it. That is, laws bringing social changes need to be supported by society. He argued:

> Free Government means that in vast aspects of social life people are left free to carry on without interference of law, or if law has to be made, then the law maker expects that society will have enough morality in it to make the law a success . . .

If there is no moral order, democracy will go to pieces as it is going now probably in our own country.[15]

Public Conscience

Dr Ambedkar noted that a society needs a public conscience. If there is injustice anywhere, then it should shock the public conscience.[16] He gave examples of other countries where people of the oppressor group had joined the struggle of the oppressed.

Referring to the discriminatory society in South Africa, he noted:

> I have been wondering within myself whether we who are talking so much against segregation and so on do not have South Africa in every village. There is; we have only to go and see. There is South Africa everywhere in the village and yet I have very seldom found anybody not belonging to the Scheduled Caste taking up the cause of the Scheduled Caste . . . and why? Because there is no 'public conscience'.

He stated that 'the minority which is suffering from injustice gets no help from others for the purpose of getting rid of this injustice'.[17] He argued that citizens, especially those having privileges, ought to have a conscience and shed their privileges.

Democracy is a Constant Process

Lastly, Dr Ambedkar believed that democracy is a constant and evolving process. He said that the task of maintaining democracy is not limited to mere adoption of the Constitution. He said:

> The Britishers have gone. We have got a constitution which provides for democracy. Well, what more do we want? . . . Let me warn you against this kind of smug feeling that with

the making of the constitution our task is done. It is not done. It has only begun.[18]

He stated that if one looks at the political histories of the world, then it can be seen that democracy has not survived in every country. He said, 'Democracy is not a plant which grows everywhere.' It survives only when the conditions precedent for democracy are fulfilled, only when it is cherished. Therefore, Dr Ambedkar appealed to the citizens to 'be very cautious and very considerate regarding our own future'.[19]

19

A Constitutional Vision for Political Democracy

Dr Ambedkar was concerned that the politics of independent India should focus on improving the conditions of the marginalized communities. He therefore emphasized a vision of a politics that ought to emerge to bring into practice the protection of marginalized groups given under the Constitution. He reiterated this vision after the adoption of the Constitution.

Dr Ambedkar tendered his resignation on 27 September 1951 from his position as independent India's first law minister, to register his protest on a number of issues, including the apathy of the government towards protecting the interests of the Scheduled Castes, Backward Classes and women. In his explanatory note on his resignation, he stated that he was dissatisfied with the government's 'treatment accorded to the Backward Classes and the Scheduled Castes'.[1] He expressed his regret that the Constitution did not embody a mandatory safeguard for the Backward Classes. The process of safeguards 'was left to be done by the Executive Government on the basis of the recommendations of a Commission [under Article 340] to be appointed by the President'. Dr Ambedkar was unhappy that the government had not even appointed the Backward

Classes Commission, though more than a year had passed since the enactment of the Constitution. He said that he wanted to provide more safeguards to the Scheduled Castes in the Constitution but could not do so due to the lack of support from other members of the Constituent Assembly. The most disturbing fact, Dr Ambedkar noted, was that the government was not showing any determination to make even those limited provisions effective.[2] He said that the triggering reason for his resignation was the government's lack of will to pass the Hindu Code Bill—a legal code advanced by Dr Ambedkar to give property rights to women and which 'sought to alter the order of succession and designed new laws on maintenance, marriage, inter-caste marriages, divorce, adoption, and minors and their guardianship'.[3]

At that time, Dr Ambedkar was running his political party—the Scheduled Castes Federation. On 3 October 1951, the Federation released its manifesto under Dr Ambedkar's leadership.[4] Among its principles, vision and strategies, the manifesto emphasized political cooperation between the Scheduled Castes and Backward Classes. It was noted in the manifesto that 'the Scheduled Castes Federation would like to work in co-operation with the Backward Classes and the Scheduled Tribes'.[5] It further added: 'These classes unfortunately have not developed that degree of political consciousness which the Scheduled Castes have by reason of political and social activity of the Scheduled Castes Federation during the last twenty years.' The manifesto emphasized: 'The Constitution of Free India has made the Backward Classes, the Scheduled Tribes and the Scheduled Castes virtually the masters of the country. Hitherto the minority of Caste Hindus have made themselves the rulers of the country.' The goal of the Scheduled Castes Federation was to help the Backward Classes and Scheduled Tribes 'to get on their feet'. Dr Ambedkar's party was also ready to change its name from 'Scheduled Castes Federation' to 'Backward Classes Federation' to create a broader coalition of marginalized social groups.[6]

Besides emphasizing the points in the manifesto, Dr Ambedkar was also making efforts to build political alliances to promote the constitutional vision. One such interesting exchange was between Dr Ambedkar and Dr Ram Manohar Lohia—the socialist icon of India. In the mid-1950s, both were trying to forge a principled alliance.

Dr Ambedkar gave a speech in Hindi to the office-bearers of the Scheduled Caste Federation in Nagpur on 15 October 1956, where he said:

> We must look around for people who understand our suffering. We must be prepared to bring together all such people and work with them. I am trying to bring together such people. If the effort is successful, we will have to form a new party, and its door will be opened to people other than us.[7]

The 'people who understand our suffering', whom Dr Ambedkar was referring to, included Dr Lohia, with whom he was holding talks.[8]

On 10 December 1955, Dr Lohia wrote a letter to Dr Ambedkar, requesting him to write an article for his new journal *Mankind*, which he said intended to 'reveal the caste problem in its entirety'. Dr Lohia also mentioned the speeches he had made about Dr Ambedkar in a parliamentary campaign in Madhya Pradesh. Dr Lohia was so keen on having a collaboration that he also invited Dr Ambedkar to address a study camp and attend the 'foundation conference' of his Socialist Party as a 'special invitee'. Dr Lohia said he wanted Dr Ambedkar to become 'a leader not alone of the Scheduled Castes, but also of the Indian people'.

A few months later, Dr Lohia's colleagues met Dr Ambedkar in Delhi, after which they told Lohia (in a letter dated 27 September 1956) that Dr Ambedkar would meet him during his next visit. The letter also conveys that Dr Ambedkar wanted a strong Opposition in a democracy and was in 'favour of a new political party with strong roots'. In a letter to his colleagues dated 1 October 1956, Dr Lohia highlighted the importance of his proposed meeting with Dr Ambedkar: 'My meeting with Dr Ambedkar will be as much a tribute to the fact that the backward and the Scheduled Castes can produce an intellect like him as for its political consequences.' On the same date, Dr Lohia also wrote to Dr Ambedkar, asking him to take proper care of his health. On 5 October 1956, Dr Ambedkar wrote to Dr Lohia regarding the proposed timing of their meeting.

Before the meeting could take place, Dr Ambedkar passed away on 6 December 1956. The sudden demise of Dr Ambedkar was a 'personal loss' for Dr Lohia. In a letter dated 1 July 1957, Dr Lohia wrote to his close associate, Madhu Limaye, about his grief: 'You can well understand that my sorrow at Dr Ambedkar's sudden death has been, and is, somewhat personal. It had always been my ambition to draw him into our fold, not only organizationally but also in full ideological sense, and that moment seemed to be approaching.' Dr Lohia added: 'Dr Ambedkar was to me, a great man in Indian politics, and apart from Gandhiji, as great as the greatest of caste Hindus. This fact had always given me solace and confidence that the caste system of Hinduism could one day be destroyed.' Dr Ambedkar, for him, was 'learned, a man of integrity, courage and independence', who could be shown to the outside world as a 'symbol of upright India'.

Furthermore, Dr Ambedkar had argued that elected candidates should have 'knowledge (*Pradnya*) and Character (*Sheel*)'.[9] He stated:

[E]ducation can hardly be the sole qualification for membership of this House. If I may use the words of Buddha, he said that man requires two things. One is Gyan and the other is Sheel. Gyan without Sheel is very dangerous: it must be accompanied by Sheel, by which we mean character, moral courage, ability to be independent of any kind of temptation, truthful to one's ideals.[10]

Dr Ambedkar was also 'aware that although the elected candidates may have knowledge and character, but still, they need to possess a training of parliamentary legislative procedures'.[11]

With these thoughts to 'invigorate the democratic forces in India', he established the Training School for Entrance to Politics in July 1956. Dr Ambedkar was its director, and S.S. Rege was the registrar. As the editors of his collected works note:

The school was meant for those who cherished the ambition of joining the legislature and it was the first of its kind in the country. He insisted that the new comers must develop oratory in order to put forth their views on various subjects like Economics, Political, Social and Parliamentary procedural matters. He was in search of a principal with a good personality, well-versed in the subject, having a good delivery on an attractive personality. He was convinced that the reputation of the school greatly depends upon the ability and speaking capacity of the teacher. The school started with 15 students and worked from July, 1, 1956 to March 1957. Dr. Ambedkar planned to deliver lectures on oratory in the month of December 1956 for the students of this school. But due to untimely demise he could not visit the school.[12]

The Constitution was not merely a legal framework for Dr Ambedkar. It was the source of democratic politics and constitutional vision to be pursued. It required taking measures to protect and promote the interests of marginalized social groups. As Prof. Sukhadeo Thorat notes:

> Ambedkarite politics is centered on the idea of a nation as a sovereign, socialist, secular, democratic republic and the goals of justice (social, economic, and political); liberty of thought, expression, belief, faith and worship; equality of status and of opportunity to all irrespective of religion, caste, race, colour, ethnicity, gender and region; and finally, fraternity, assuring the dignity of the individual and the unity and the integrity of the nation. However, the major concern for the Dalits relates to the non-inclusion into the governing structure of some remedies proposed by Ambedkar for the political, economic and social empowerment of the Dalits and other deprived groups.[13]

Dr Ambedkar called for constant public engagement towards enhancing the constitutionally recognized rights of marginalized social groups, including women. The Hindu Code Bill, which could not get 'passed as a whole because of bitter opposition', was subsequently passed 'in piecemeal manner'.[14]

Throughout his writings, Dr Ambedkar went beyond the normative aspects of the law and the Constitution, and perceived them as a continuing process of social dialogue which could result in the transformation of the centuries-old social order.

20

Did Dr Ambedkar Want to Burn the Constitution?[*]

Those opposed to the idea of the Indian Constitution as the overarching norm of Indian society often narrate that Dr Ambedkar wanted to burn it. Similarly, those who cannot tolerate Dr Ambedkar's contributions to nation-building and Constitution-framing due to their caste-hatred criticize him by arguing that he had nothing to do with the Indian Constitution, as he himself wanted to burn it. Unfortunately, even scholars cite one line from a speech by Dr Ambedkar in the Rajya Sabha (upper house of the Indian Parliament) in 1953 to make generalized claims about the Constitution and Dr Ambedkar himself. The said line, which is often quoted by writers without giving the full picture, is as follows: 'I shall be the first person to burn it out.' (2 September 1953)[1]

Dr Ambedkar's biographer Dhananjay Keer stated that Dr Ambedkar 'had made the attack [on the Constitution] and volleyed his thunder in a spirit of utter desperation and frustration'.[2] Scholar Gail Omvedt has also cited this excerpt to refer to it as Dr Ambedkar's 'disillusionment . . . with

[*] This is an edited version of a portion of my article. See Anurag Bhaskar, 'Ambedkar's Constitution: A Radical Phenomenon in Anti-Caste Discourse?', CASTE: A Global Journal on Social Exclusion, (2021) 2(1).

the promises of progressiveness' and a 'moment of rage'.[3] In his work on the making of the Indian Constitution, Arvind Elangovan called it 'Ambedkar's public disavowal of the Constitution'.[4] Elangovan is of the view that Dr Ambedkar 'publicly distanced himself from the constitutional document that he helped draft'.[5]

In his book *Caste Matters* (2019), Suraj Yengde refers to the said line of Dr Ambedkar to state that 'the same document [Constitution] that Dr Ambedkar had so laboriously authored, he was now willing to burn to ashes'. In addition to this, Yengde notes, 'The burning of a juridical text was not a foreign act for Dr Ambedkar,' as he had previously burnt the *Manusmriti* (the ancient Hindu caste code) publicly in 1927.[6] Yengde also argues that the 'over-reliance' on the constitutional method 'as a route to Dalit emancipation precludes the call for the total liberation of Dalits'.[7] Furthermore, he states that the 'idea of the Constitution is romantic',[8] and that constitutionalism reflects the 'state's narrative',[9] which has been promoted to create 'Dalit passivism' and deviation from core demands.[10] The author argues that the attribution of the authorship of the Constitution to Dr Ambedkar has been 'clever propaganda'[11] spread by the ruling castes and the State that has thus taken away 'Dalit radicalism'.[12]

However, in my view, all these views have not contextualized or presented the original full source of the said statement made by Dr Ambedkar. The veracity of this line of argument that Dr Ambedkar wanted to burn the Constitution falls flat on the face when the complete context and content of Dr Ambedkar's speech is read. Consequently, the claims made by citing the said statement also ring hollow and untrue.

On 2 September 1953, Dr Ambedkar was making his submissions[13] on the Andhra State Bill, which was tabled in the Rajya Sabha for the formation of Andhra Pradesh state on the principle of linguistic provinces. He was clearly unhappy with the fact that the Indian Government agreed to form the linguistic state of Andhra only after Potti Sriramalu (a leader demanding a linguistic state) sacrificed his life for the sake of creating an Andhra Province.[14] At the same time, he was very critical of the then Home Minister K.N. Katju for not making special provisions for 'granting protection [to minorities, including Dalits as well as linguistic minorities] against tyranny, against oppression, against communalism'[15] in the proposed Andhra State. Dr Ambedkar suggested that the governor of the state may be given special powers to protect the minorities. This suggestion was contrary to the constitutional principle of 'aid and advice' adopted in the Indian Constitution, according to which a governor generally did not have powers of his own and followed the decision of the Council of Ministers of the State. Dr Ambedkar's suggestion was in line with his similar arguments, as stated in the previous section, made in his works, 'Communal Deadlock'[16] and 'States and Minorities',[17] where he made a case for additional special safeguards for minorities.

In response, Katju and another member argued that the existing constitutional provisions were justified by Dr Ambedkar earlier in the Constituent Assembly.[18] It was to justify his own new suggestion that Dr Ambedkar said that he had earlier defended the tradition (of aid and advice) in the Constituent Assembly because the majority of the members had adopted it.[19] That was the statesman in him. His quote mentioned this tradition: 'Now, Sir, we have inherited a tradition. People always keep on saying to me: "Oh, you are the maker of the Constitution." My answer is I was a hack. What I was asked to do, I did much against my will.'[20]

Dr Ambedkar gave examples from the Canadian Constitution, and British constitutional practices, where there was special protection provided to linguistic minorities.

He submitted before the chairman of the Rajya Sabha that 'no harm can be done to democracy and to democratic Constitution, if our Constitution was amended and powers similar to those given to the Governor General under [Canadian Constitution] were given to the Governor [in India]'.[21] It is only then there would be a 'safeguard to certain small linguistic areas or linguistic groups who find that the majority in the State are not doing justice to them'.[22] It was against the argument of not making special provisions for minorities (including Dalits) by the Government that Dr Ambedkar made the rhetorical speech of burning the Constitution, which deserves to be quoted fully:

> It is by placating the sentiments of smaller communities and smaller people who are afraid that the majority may do wrong, that the British Parliament works. Sir, my friends tell me that I have made the Constitution. But I am quite prepared to say that I shall be the first person to burn it out. I do not want it. It does not suit anybody. But, whatever that may be, if our people want to carry on, they must not forget that there are majorities and there are minorities, and they simply cannot ignore the minorities by saying, 'Oh, no. To recognize you is to harm democracy.' I should say that the greatest harm will come by injuring the minorities.[23]

In conclusion of his address, Dr Ambedkar made the submission to the home minister to see 'whether he can find any solution to the problem of linguistic provinces, based on the suggestions that [Ambedkar] made'.[24] It is clear from this discussion that the rhetorical excerpt of Dr Ambedkar's speech was made in the specific context of linguistic states and adopting a provision, which would be different from the already adopted tradition of governors having no power of their own. Even after the said quote, Dr Ambedkar wanted the home minister to consider his constitutional proposal. This entire context is not mentioned in any book or article, which cites Dr Ambedkar's rhetorical quote on burning the Constitution. Contrary to these assumptions, Dr Ambedkar was not asking for the entire Constitution to be burnt down as a matter of principle.

Dr Ambedkar made his position clear in a subsequent discussion, which took place in the Rajya Sabha two years later (19 March 1955).[25] In a discussion on the Constitution (Fourth Amendment) Bill, 1954, Dr Ambedkar was speaking on the relevance of fundamental rights. He summed up his views on the Constitution as follows:

> If I may say so, and *I say it with a certain amount of pride* [that] *the Constitution which has been given to this country is a wonderful document.* It has been said so not by myself, but by many people, many other students of the Constitution. It is the simplest and the easiest. Many, many publishers have written to me asking me to write a commentary on the Constitution, promising a good sum. But I have always told them that to write a commentary on this Constitution is to admit that the Constitution is a bad one and an understandable one. It is not so. Anyone who can follow English can understand the Constitution. No commentary is necessary[26] [emphasis added].

To this statement, a fellow Rajya Sabha member, Anup Singh, reminded Dr Ambedkar of his speech to burn the Constitution. Dr Ambedkar responded rhetorically again:

> We built a temple for a god to come in and reside, but before the god could be installed, if the devil had taken possession of it, what else could we do except destroy the temple? We did not intend that it should be occupied by the Asuras (evil). We intended it to be occupied by the devas (good). That is the reason why I said I would rather like to burn it.[27]

When another member, B.K.P. Sinha, passed a remark to

> destroy the devil rather than the temple'[28] Dr Ambedkar
> initially tried to explain a bit, but then pointed out to the
> Rajya Sabha chairperson that his attempts to make his
> submissions on the Constitution Amendment Bill were being
> interrupted. He clearly said that he was being drawn 'into all
> sorts of things into which [he did] not wish to enter.[29]

He continued with his submissions on 'why the Constitution
[especially fundamental rights] should not be amended and
tampered with so easily'.[30] Thus, Dr Ambedkar himself
clarified that he did not want to discuss his previous rhetorical
statement.

It is clear therefore that this entire context cannot be
compared with the earlier burning of the *Manusmriti* by
Dr Ambedkar, as certain individuals keep 'repeating'.[31] There is
no similarity between *Manusmriti* and the Indian Constitution.
The *Manusmriti* denied any basic human rights to Dalits, women
and other oppressed, while the Constitution not only provides
equal rights but also includes provisions for their special
protection. The *Manusmriti* recommended cruel and inhuman
punishment for the oppressed, while the Constitution, in the
chapter on fundamental rights, criminalizes the practice of
untouchability against Dalits. Dr Ambedkar recognized the
importance of fundamental rights. In the same speech in the
Rajya Sabha (19 March 1955), Dr Ambedkar was defensive
of the fundamental rights enshrined in the Constitution. He
noted: 'Caste system is a sword of political and administrative
discrimination. The result was that the fundamental rights
became inevitable.'[32] In effect, the Constitution rejected
the *Manusmriti* in its essence and content and diluted the
caste system.

Furthermore, the entire context shows that Dr Ambedkar's frustration was with the people entrusted with the responsibility of enforcing the Constitution, and not with the idea of the Constitution itself. He had also previously expressed this sentiment in his letter explaining his reasons for resigning as independent India's law minister in 1951. As discussed in a previous chapter, one of the main reasons was that the Hindu Code Bill, a social reform measure introduced by Dr Ambedkar to provide property inheritance rights to women, was dropped from Parliament.[33] Expressing his dissatisfaction, Dr Ambedkar noted: 'To leave inequality between class and class, between sex and sex which is the soul of Hindu Society untouched and to go on passing legislation relating to economic problems *is to make a farce of our Constitution and to build a palace on a dung heap.*'[34]

In his consistent efforts, Dr Ambedkar argued for codification of rights and procedures, as he believed (discussed in a previous chapter) that the people were yet to learn constitutional morality—'a paramount reverence for the forms of the Constitution'.[35] Even in his most radical demands, as reflected in his works 'Communal Deadlock' and 'States and Minorities', Dr Ambedkar wanted a constitutionally encoded solution. His emphasis on the enforcement of the Constitution also reflects the same. In the Constituent Assembly (4 November 1948), he noted thus: 'if things go wrong under the new Constitution . . . the reason will not be that we had a bad Constitution. What we will have to say is that Man was vile.'

Thus, it is not Dr Ambedkar (as few writers have claimed), but the oppressor castes who have always wanted to attack the Constitution through different means. Years later, Dr Ambedkar's image as the chief architect of the Constitution was popularized by Dalit activists and politicians as a part of the strategy to revive his legacy and to inculcate a sense of empowerment among Dalits.[36]

21

The Myth of the Ten-Year Limit on Reservations and Dr Ambedkar's Stance[*]

In recent years, it has been an oft-repeated argument by many, including constitutional officeholders, that 'Ambedkar wanted reservations only for a decade'.[1] In this chapter, I demonstrate that the argument of Dr Ambedkar wanting reservations for only a period of ten years is a falsehood. The temporary time limit was imposed only on political reservations, subject to a few conditions, and not on reservations in services and education.

To clearly develop a perspective on this matter, one needs to deeply examine India's constitutional history from the Poona Pact (1932), as this event marked a significant moment for the discourse around special rights for oppressed castes in political office and time limits upon it.[2]

The Poona Pact

Dr Ambedkar clashed with Mahatma Gandhi during the second RTC in London in 1931 over the issue of separate electorates

---

[*] A version of this chapter was previously published as an article. Anurag Bhaskar, 'The Myth of the Ten-Year Limit on Reservations and Dr Ambedkar's Stance', *Contemporary Voice of Dalit* (2022), https://doi.org/10.1177/2455328X221101674.

for the Depressed Classes. Gandhi was completely opposed to separate electorates for the Depressed Classes.[3] In 1932, the British government adjudicated on the issue and announced a communal award providing separate electorates for the Depressed Classes for a period of twenty years.[4] In protest, Gandhi went on a fast unto death. After this, Dr Ambedkar had to negotiate with him and other caste Hindu leaders on the issue of separate electorates.

Raja Sekhar Vundru (2017) has documented all the details of the negotiations that took place between 19 and 24 September 1932 in the Yerawada prison (in Poona), where Gandhi was fasting. On 23 September, it 'was agreed that 18 per cent of the seats allotted to the general electorate for British India should be reserved for the Depressed Classes in the central legislature'.[5] In replacement of the communal award, Dr Ambedkar demanded that the system of reservation should continue for a period of twenty-five years, after which there would be a referendum of the voters of the Depressed Classes, through which they 'could decide the course of action on their method of election by choosing either separate electorate or *joint electorate and reservation of seats*'.[6]

While Hindu leaders refused to accept Dr Ambedkar's position on the time limit for holding a referendum, Gandhi agreed to this proposal.[7] But he proposed that the referendum should be held after a period of five years.[8] While Gandhi was 'adamant on this point',[9] Dr Ambedkar also took a strong stand that the referendum be held not before ten years.[10] Vundru notes: 'For [Dr Ambedkar], the referendum was a strong political weapon in the hands of the Depressed Classes and at any cost, he was not ready to lose it.'[11]

The time period for holding the referendum became a non-negotiable point for each of the parties. It was at this juncture that a proposal by C. Rajagopalachari resolved the imbroglio on 24 September 1932. The condition of the referendum 'was replaced by a clause which [mentioned] that the system of representation of Depressed Classes by reserved seats in the provincial and central legislatures shall continue *until determined by mutual agreement* between both the communities concerned in the settlement'. The two communities in this instance were the Untouchables and caste Hindus.[12] This proposal was agreed to by both Dr Ambedkar and Gandhi, after which it was accepted by the British government on 26 September 1932.[13]

Thus, the time period, which was being discussed during the Poona negotiations, was not for the end of reservations, but for the referendum in which the Depressed Classes got to decide the future method of choosing their own representatives. The Poona Pact was later incorporated into the GOI Act 1935. Elections to provincial assemblies were held in 1937 on the basis of this electoral arrangement. The issue of the time period later raised its head again during the drafting of the Indian Constitution.

Constituent Assembly Debates

Special rights for minorities were a matter of concern for the Constitution framers. As mentioned before, to assist the Constituent Assembly, an Advisory Committee on fundamental rights, minorities and tribal and excluded areas was created under the chairmanship of Sardar Patel.[14] The Committee was further subdivided, and the Minorities sub-committee dealt with minority rights and safeguards.[15] When the Minorities sub-committee met for the first time on 27 February 1947, '[Dr.] Ambedkar (a member of the sub-committee) submitted an exhaustive note on the subject of minorities and fundamental rights'.[16] He proposed that the SCs should have a minimum share of representation according to their population share in the legislature, ministries, municipalities, local boards and public services.[17] Other suggestions of safeguards for the SCs were made by leaders such as Jagjivan Ram and H.J. Khandekar, and organizations such as All India Adi Hindu Depressed Classes Association.[18] The proposed safeguards 'provided that all concessions in privileges given to minority communities should be effective for a period of thirty years, after which the communities should be consulted as regards their modification'.[19] These suggestions, among others, were considered in later meetings of the sub-committee.

After discussions between 21 and 27 July 1947, the Minorities sub-committee decided, by a large majority of 26–3, against a separate communal electorate for elections to the legislature.[20] It was also decided by a large majority of 26–3 that there should be reservation of seats for 'different recognized minorities in the various legislatures; and such reservation would initially be for a period of ten years, the position to be reconsidered at the end of the period'.[21] The SCs were included in this list of minorities.[22] This period of ten years was similar to the demand of Dr Ambedkar during the last days of Poona Pact negotiations. Again, this limit was not a fixed time limit to end reservations in joint electorates. It was an initial limit after which the position of joint electorates with reservations would be reconsidered.

The decisions of the Minorities sub-committee were then included in the recommendations of the Advisory Committee Report on minority rights.[23] These recommendations were then considered by the Constituent Assembly on 27 and 28 August 1947,[24] where they were accepted by the Assembly 'without any modification'.[25] The decision of the Assembly was later incorporated into the Draft Constitution by the constitutional adviser.[26] The various provisions related to minority safeguards were then rearranged by the Drafting Committee under the title 'Special Provisions Relating to Minorities' and were published as part of the Draft Constitution in February 1948.[27]

Political Reservation Removed: Except for SCs

After the Partition, some leaders in the Constituent Assembly became sceptical about reserved seats for all minorities, given the change in the sociopolitical situation. A meeting of the Advisory Committee was held on 24 February 1948 to reconsider the reservation of seats in the legislature for Sikhs in Punjab and minorities in Bengal.[28] On Dr Ambedkar's suggestion, a five-member special committee was constituted to look into the matter. This committee consisted of Vallabhbhai Patel (as chairman), Jawaharlal Nehru, Rajendra Prasad, K.M. Munshi and Dr Ambedkar.[29]

In its report dated 23 November 1948, the special committee made a fundamental departure from the position in favour of political safeguards for minorities adopted by the Constituent Assembly and decided against reservation for Sikhs in Punjab and minorities in West Bengal.[30] This decision was then placed before the Advisory Committee, in a meeting called by Sardar Patel on 30 December 1948.[31] However, at this meeting, suggestions were made by a few members to completely do away with political reservation for all minorities.[32] This would have changed the entire nature of reservation provisions for seats in legislatures. Three members submitted motions of resolution to this effect.[33]

Muniswami Pillai sought an amendment to the proposed resolution and demanded that the Scheduled Castes should be retained for the benefit of political reservations.[34] The meeting was then adjourned to a later date.[35] At this stage, Dr Ambedkar decided to walk out of the proceedings of Constitution framing, as the other members were in discussions to remove political reservations completely, even for SCs.[36] Dr Ambedkar's stand made the members of the Advisory Committee, especially Sardar Patel, reconsider their position on doing away with political reservations for SCs.[37]

In its Report dated 11 May 1949, the Advisory Committee, by a large majority, then adopted the resolution 'That the system of reservation for minorities other than Scheduled Castes in Legislatures be abolished'.[38] It also noted: '(T)he peculiar position of the Scheduled Castes would make it necessary to give them reservation for a period of ten years as originally decided.'[39] It must be noted here that the decision to keep the political reservations for SCs for a period of ten years was made by the Advisory Committee and not by Dr Ambedkar.

On 25 May 1949, Sardar Patel, on behalf of the Advisory Committee, explained the updated scenario to the Constituent Assembly, and stated that 'the time has come' when 'the reservations should be dropped'.[40] He moved the resolution that the Constituent Assembly should recall its early decision of providing political reservations to all minorities, except for SCs.[41] Thakur Das Bhargava then moved an amendment to the resolution that reservation of seats in legislatures would 'last for a period of ten years from the commencement of this Constitution'.[42] Jawaharlal Nehru noted that even though he wanted an end to all reservations 'a backward group (Scheduled Castes) ought to be helped'.[43] Though he added, 'I am glad that this reservation also will be limited to ten years.'[44] The proposal of the Advisory Committee and Bhargava's amendment were adopted by the Constituent Assembly on 26 May 1949, with the effect that no political reservation would be operative for more than ten years.[45]

ST Political Reservation

The Advisory Committee Report (11 May 1949) also noted that its decision to abolish reservations for all minorities, except for SCs, would not affect the representation of STs in legislatures.[46] This was, however, not discussed during the 25–26 May 1949 deliberations in the Constituent Assembly on political reservations. Previously, the draft Constitution published in February 1948 had included reservations for STs in a limited number of states.[47]

In a significant change from this position, on 23 August 1949, Dr Ambedkar moved a motion[48] providing for 'Reservation of seats for Scheduled Castes and Scheduled Tribes in the House of the People' in the proportion of their population to the total population of the State (current Article 330). This new motion thus extended the benefit of political reservations to Scheduled Tribes in all states, as opposed to what was earlier limited to only a few areas. According to Shiva Rao, this 'much further' change, brought by Dr Ambedkar, from the previous position went unnoticed by the Constituent Assembly.[49]

Furthermore, since there was no substantial discussion on the issue of ST reservations earlier, Dr Ambedkar's proposal was a progressive development in terms of the fundamental rights of STs. Jaipal Singh Munda, a leader from the Adivasi community, pointed this out. On 24 August 1949, he stated:

. . . it is most unfortunate that this House has not had an opportunity to discuss the recommendations made by the two Tribal Sub-Committees. I know we had a debate of two days to consider the report of the Minorities Committee in regard to whether the Scheduled Castes and the Muslims were to get any reservation of seats or not. At that time all the discussion was confined to the Muslim problem only . . . Having said that, Sir, I would like to congratulate Dr. Ambedkar for his new amendment which he has presented to us today . . . Sir, we are not begging anything. I do not come here to beg. It is for the majority community to atone for their sins of the last six thousand odd years.[50]

He further explained the importance of reservations for STs, as follows:

> One honourable Member said that he was glad that the Muslims and the Christians had given up something, given up the reservation of seats. Sir, the Adivasis are not giving up anything because they never had anything. It seems very surprising that people should talk of democracy when their whole conduct has been anti-democratic in the past.[51]

Jaipal Singh Munda also expressed his dissatisfaction with the ten-year limit on political reservations and stated:

> I am not at all optimistic that in the short space of ten years, which means two general elections, *Adibasis* will have come to the level of the rest of India and therefore at the end of ten years reservation of seats should be done away with. I am not one who will be so bold as to believe in such a miracle. Things are not going to move as fast as we would like them to move. I would have preferred that this matter should have been reviewed at the end of ten years to find out whether *Adibasis* and Scheduled Castes in the two general elections that will take place during the ten years had made good, whether they had been able to assert themselves in the Councils and take their share in the national life of the country. When that had been made, then *I think the Parliament could decide whether or not these reservations should be done away with or continued for a further period of say ten or fifteen or twenty-five years.* I would have preferred it that way but if there is any suspicion in the minds of non-Scheduled Caste people or non-*Adibasis*, I would not insist on it. The generous thing would have been to give them ample scope to come into all the Councils in the provinces and at the Centre and not to limit them only to two general elections.[52]

Dr Ambedkar's motion was adopted by the Constituent Assembly on 24 August 1949. On the same day, he then moved a new article (current Article 334)[53] providing 'the reservation of seats for the Scheduled Castes and the Scheduled Tribes either in House of the people or in the Legislative Assembly of a State shall cease to have effect on the expiration of a period of ten years from the commencement of this Constitution'.[54] He reiterated that this newly proposed article is 'also in accordance with the decision of the House (referring to 25-26 May 1949)'.[55] The proposed article was not a personal decision of Dr Ambedkar, as he would explain later. In fact, Jaipal Singh and Dr Ambedkar shared similar views on the time limit debate on reservations.

Dr Ambedkar's Position on Ten-Year Limit

The debate on the ten-year time limit on political reservations then continued on 25 August 1949. Several members from the SC community expressed anxiety that 'the period of ten years would be quite an insufficient period and that reservations might be necessary even thereafter'.[56] Sardar Nagappa wanted an amendment that 'reservation should last for ten years, provided the Government takes this actually into its head and sees that these people are brought to the level of the advanced classes'.[57] Referring to future governments, he said:

> You must realize that greater responsibility is now lying on your shoulders. You have to bring us to that level by which we will be able to say that we do not want reservations. We cannot go on begging for a favour. As it is, we are making the Government to commit itself for the future advancement of this country and of this community.[58]

Muniswami Pillai declared the ten-year limit 'a premature
one'.[59] Monomohan Das sought an amendment that

> . . . these safeguards will come to an end at the end of ten
> years, but if the Parliament, after consideration of the
> situation then of the Scheduled Castes, and the Scheduled
> Tribes, thinks that these provisions for reservation of seats
> should be continued, for some further period, then these
> reservations of seats, these political concessions granted
> to the Scheduled Castes and the Scheduled Tribes will
> continue and not come to an end.[60]

None of these suggestions were accepted in the Assembly.

As Dr Ambedkar, being the chairman of the Drafting
Committee, was bound by the earlier mandate of the
Constituent Assembly, he clarified that any change in the time
limit may be made 'by the amendment of the Constitution
itself'.[61] The motion on the ten-year time limit on political
reservations was then adopted by the Constituent Assembly
on 25 August 1949.

Dr Ambedkar also shared his opinion that he preferred
a longer time for political reservation for SCs and STs, as
he noted:[62]

> *I personally was prepared to press for a larger time, because I do feel that
> so far as the Scheduled Castes are concerned, they are not treated on the
> same footing as the other minorities* . . . it would have been quite
> proper I think, and generous on the part of this House to
> have given the Scheduled Castes a longer term with regard
> to these reservations . . . *For the Scheduled Tribes I am prepared to
> give far longer time.* But all those who have spoken about the
> reservations to the Scheduled Castes or to the Scheduled
> Tribes have been so meticulous that the thing should end by

ten years. All I want to say to them in the words of Edmund Burke, is '*Large Empires and small minds go ill together.*'

Dr Ambedkar, however, also suggested a way out of extending political reservations further, by adding:[63]

> If at the end of the ten years, the Scheduled Castes find that their position has not improved or that they want further extension of this period, *it will not be beyond their capacity or their intelligence to invent new ways of getting the same protection which they are promised here.*

In a later election campaign at Ludhiana, Punjab, on 28 October 1951, he delivered a speech stating that he wanted reservation of seats in the Assemblies and Parliament as long as 'untouchability was prevalent in India'.[64] He even confronted the first elected government on 2 September 1953 in the Rajya Sabha, as he asked: 'I want to know for myself, especially in view of the fact whether the reservation, which was so blissfully granted to us by the Congress Party for ten years, is going to disappear.'[65]

Thus, it becomes clear that Dr Ambedkar was never in favour of a fixed time limit of ten years for political reservations for SCs and STs. He wanted a much 'larger time'. Therefore, all those who have been saying that Dr Ambedkar wanted the end of reservations after ten years either have not read history or are deliberately propagating a falsehood.

No Time Limit for Reservations in Services and Educational Institutions

Unlike the deliberations on the time limit of ten years on political reservations, there was no such discussion on the

time limit on reservations in public services. This is clear
from the proceedings of the Constituent Assembly related to
the drafting of Article 16(4), which provides for reservations
in public services for backward classes.[66] The reservation
in educational institutions was introduced, by way of the
first constitutional amendment, in 1951, i.e., one year after
the Constitution came into force. The debates during the
passing of the first constitutional amendment (insertion of
Article 15(4)) show that there was no discussion on the time
limit.[67] The amendment was brought to undo the decision of
the Supreme Court in *State of Madras v. Champakam Dorairajan*
(1951),[68] which had declared reservations in educational
institutions as unconstitutional. Dr Ambedkar, as the then
law minister, used harsh words to criticize the Champakam
Dorairajan judgment, and termed it 'utterly unsatisfactory'.[69]

Conclusion

Dr Ambedkar was not in favour of a fixed time limit of
ten years, even for political reservations for SCs and STs.
His demand during the Poona Pact was that after ten years,
there should be a reconsideration of the position of reserved
constituencies in joint electorates and that the SCs should
decide by referendum if they wanted to continue with the
system. This would mean deciding whether to adopt another
method of electing candidates from SCs. Even though this
demand was not included in the final text of the Constitution,
Dr Ambedkar had left it to the SCs to '*invent new ways of getting the
same protection*'.[70] In effect, without the consent of SCs and STs,
political reservations cannot be done away with. The political
reservations were a result of a '*mutual agreement*'[71] between
SCs and caste Hindus. When it was incorporated into the
Constitution, it became akin to a *constitutional promise*. Though

the Constituent Assembly fixed a time limit of ten years on political reservations, Dr Ambedkar himself had prescribed the method of constitutional amendment to extend this time limit, if the situation of SCs and STs did not improve.[72] The extension of this time limit since 1960 is in consonance with the spirit of Dr Ambedkar's demands. No time limit was ever set on reservations for Backward Classes in public services and educational institutions.

Epilogue*

While presenting the Constitution for independent India, Dr B.R. Ambedkar, as chairman of the Constitution drafting committee, had said:

> . . . however good a Constitution may be, it is sure to turn out bad because those who are called to work it, happen to be a bad lot. However bad a Constitution may be, it may turn out to be good if those who are called to work it, happen to be a good lot . . . The factors on which the working of those organs of the State depend are the people and the political parties they will set up as their instruments to carry out their wishes and their politics.[1]

He added: 'By independence, we have lost the excuse of blaming the British for anything going wrong. If hereafter things go wrong, we will have nobody to blame except ourselves.'[2]

But, instead of self-reflecting, the caste elites in India began blaming and villainizing Dr Ambedkar. As Bhagwan Das notes:

---

* A few paragraphs of this epilogue appeared in a portion of my previously published article—Anurag Bhaskar, 'Ambedkar's Constitution: A Radical Phenomenon in Anti-Caste Discourse?', *CASTE: A Global Journal on Social Exclusion*, (2021) 2(1).

'His virtues in the eyes of the oppressors became vices. His well-intentioned moves were branded the tricks of politics . . . There is scarcely an epithet of abuse to be found in Indian languages that was not heard at him.'[3] The reasons were many, and so were the methods. After all, Dr Ambedkar had constantly questioned the oppression practised by the ruling castes, which he once termed as 'the system of graded inequality'.[4] In a public career of four decades, he had shown a mirror to Indian society and was able to succeed in changing the social dynamics to a significant extent towards the establishment of an egalitarian social order.

The fear of lynching was real for Dr Ambedkar. He would receive numerous threat letters for the work that he was doing to safeguard the rights of the oppressed communities. Once a letter said, 'If you do not give up your vehemence, you will be killed'. A plot to kill Dr Ambedkar made by some youth from the oppressor castes of Poona was reported by a newspaper.[5]

After his death, the sharp attacks against Dr Ambedkar became vitriolic, as he was no longer around to respond. He was called a British stooge, who compromised the cause of Indian independence.[6] His credentials were questioned, as it was rumoured that he had almost no role to play in the drafting of the Indian Constitution.[7] Some even erased his identity as a Dalit by declaring him 'a Brahmin', arguing that it is 'nothing wrong to call a learned person a Brahmin.'[8] The Indian Constitution, with which Dr Ambedkar's name is attached, has been consistently criticized on the basis of certain myths.

It has been said that the Constitution was merely a copy of the GOI Act 1935 and other constitutions in the world.[9] It was also propagated that B.N. Rau, and not Dr Ambedkar, had the main role in the drafting. Dr Ambedkar has been misquoted and the canard spread that he wanted to burn the Constitution or wanted reservations (affirmative action) to end after ten years. The fact that a Dalit has been popularly regarded as 'the father of the Indian Constitution' or appreciated for drafting the supreme law of the land is difficult for casteist people to digest. Therefore, remarks have been consistently made either to denigrate the originality and credentials of the Constitution or to take away the credit from Dr Ambedkar.[10] This book rejects all the myths and rumours spread against Dr Ambedkar and is an attempt to highlight his extraordinary influence in the Indian constitutional discourse. As this book demonstrates, Dr Ambedkar shaped Indian constitutionalism in so many ways.

It is unfortunate that most of the scholarly works on the Indian Constitution shy away from discussing Dr Ambedkar as a central figure in Indian constitutionalism, despite his influence during several decades of constitutional reforms. Dr Ambedkar has resurged in the public sphere,[11] but credit must be given to the anti-caste movement, which has kept the memories of Dr Ambedkar and his contribution to the Constitution alive.

Dr Ambedkar's image as the chief architect of the Constitution was popularized by the anti-caste movement as part of a strategy to revive his legacy and inculcate a sense of empowerment among Dalits. Dr Ambedkar further became a powerful symbol to radicalize Dalits about the importance of education.[12] The countless number of statues and photos of Dr Ambedkar holding the Constitution in his hand, which were installed in different parts of the country by social activists and political leaders, had a deep effect. Dr Ambedkar had once called Indian villages a 'den of localism',[13] where the oppressor castes called all the shots. In such places, when Dalits started installing statues of Dr Ambedkar with the Constitution,[14] it was a kind of radical assertion of claiming social space. The Constitution of independent India was the biggest achievement which they could have highlighted about their icon. Taking pride in Dr Ambedkar and his Constitution became a method of asserting self-identity and claiming dignity in both rural and urban spaces.

Dr Ambedkar's statues have also been installed in institutional spaces. On 26 November 2023, the President of India unveiled a statue of Dr Ambedkar on the premises of the Supreme Court of India.[15] As Justice B.R. Gavai, a judge of the Supreme Court of India noted on the occasion:

> Dr. Ambedkar had famously called Article 32, which provides the right to Indian citizens to approach the Supreme Court, as "heart and soul" of the Constitution. The statue of Dr Ambedkar is facing the Court No. 1, i.e. Chief Justice's Court. By placing the statue in front of Court No. 1, we have paid homage to Dr Ambedkar as well as reaffirmed his idea that the right to approach the Supreme Court is indeed the "heart and soul" of the Constitution.[16]

However, in finality, it is necessary to highlight that the core of Dr Ambedkar's constitutional ideas lies in his emphasis on constitutional culture among the citizens. He had once pointed out in his classic essay 'Ranade, Jinnah, and Gandhi', that the fundamental rights provided by the Constitution ought to be protected by the 'social conscience' of the citizens, because 'if the fundamental rights are opposed by the community, no Law, no Parliament, no Judiciary can guarantee them in the real sense of the word'.[17] Dr Ambedkar was thus anxious about the fate of the Indian Constitution when he said: 'What would happen to her democratic Constitution? Will she be able to maintain it, or will she lose it?'[18] While declaring the caste system to be 'anti-national', Dr Ambedkar remarked: 'If we wish to preserve the Constitution . . . let us resolve not to be tardy in the recognition of the evils that lie across our path . . . nor to be weak in our initiative to remove them.'[19] He was laying emphasis on the responsibility of citizens and the governing class.

In the above sense, the iconography of Dr Ambedkar's statues and portraits has several messages. One aspect is that Dr Ambedkar is referring to the responsibility of constitutional institutions and their access by the citizens. The other aspect is that, as scholar Aishwary Kumar notes, 'perhaps the image, in all its revolutionary and messianic intensity, captures an Ambedkar who must remind the citizens of the republic that the virtues of true gift—here, the constitution that a people gives itself—remain incomplete without a shared love of truth'.[20]

Before his death, Dr Ambedkar had proposed to write a detailed treatise with the title '*Revolution and Counter Revolution in Ancient India*'.[21] He considered the establishment of democratic principles in the Buddhist era as a revolution. According to him, the counter-revolution pioneered by casteist forces resulted in the decline and fall of those democratic principles.[22] This history was pointed out by him even in his last address (25 November 1949) to the Constituent Assembly. If one were to apply that analogy to the modern era, then the adoption of the Constitution of India must be seen as a form of revolution. If that revolution has to be preserved, then it has to be consistently supported by constitutional values and culture, which the citizens must follow.

Lastly, Dr Ambedkar had warned that it is 'perfectly possible to pervert the Constitution . . . by merely changing the form of the administration and to make it inconsistent and opposed to the spirit of the Constitution'.[23] The discourse on constitutionalism will be enriched by continuously engaging with the constitutional ideas of Dr Ambedkar.

Afterword

This book, *The Foresighted Ambedkar: Ideas That Shaped Indian Constitutional Discourse*, deals with the vision of Dr B.R. Ambedkar and his influence on Indian constitutional discourse. Within its pages, the book reveals Dr Ambedkar as a towering figure who has left an indelible mark on the contours of Indian constitutionalism. Through a detailed study of several documents and literature, the author captures and brings insight into the unique contribution made by Dr Ambedkar. Through a nuanced exploration of Dr Ambedkar's vision, this book sheds light on his multifaceted role as a scholar, leader and social reformer. It serves as a beacon, illuminating the transformative ideas that have sculpted the constitutional discourse in India.

The book commences by tracing Dr Ambedkar's ascent on to the Indian public stage and his evolution into a prominent figure in Indian public affairs. Before delving into Dr Ambedkar's early endeavours, it sheds light on the constitutional discourse preceding his emergence in the public domain. It meticulously chronicles Dr Ambedkar's initial involvement with the Southborough Committee in 1919, during his tenure as a young faculty member at Sydenham College in Bombay. It illustrates how Dr Ambedkar's understanding of citizenship surpassed mere franchise considerations, embracing a notion of universal rights.

Subsequent sections delve into Dr Ambedkar's endeavours to shape discussions on rights through various initiatives and the examination of social, economic and political inequalities, particularly focusing on the plight of the Untouchables. The author recounts the history of the Mahad Satyagraha, portraying it as a pivotal moment in Indian constitutional discourse. He contends that the provision of non-discrimination in the Indian Constitution can be traced back to Dr Ambedkar's struggles, including the Mahad Satyagraha for access to public water tanks and the Nasik Temple entry satyagraha in the 1930s.

Moreover, the author elucidates Dr Ambedkar's conception of equal voting rights, demonstrating how he connected universal franchise with adequate representation for oppressed groups and other civil liberties. The discussion delves into Dr Ambedkar's responses to the critics of constitutional reservations for Backward Classes. The book offers a detailed narrative of Dr Ambedkar's negotiations during the Round Table Conferences in the early 1930s and the formulation of the Government of India Act 1935. It underscores Dr Ambedkar's substantial role in shaping this Act.

The chapter on the annihilation of caste from a constitutional perspective is unique in its presentation. It entails examining the ideas put forth by Dr Ambedkar in his seminal work as well as understanding how these ideas resonate with the principles and provisions enshrined in the Indian Constitution. From a constitutional perspective, Dr Ambedkar's call for the annihilation of caste aligns with the foundational values of the Indian Constitution.

An equally important issue, which is discussed with great clarity, is Dr Ambedkar's proposal to deal with the communal problem. The author highlights the less-known fact about Dr Ambedkar's statesmanship during the initial days of the establishment of the Constituent Assembly. In this line of historical events, the author discusses Dr Ambedkar's original draft Constitution, which he prepared as a document called 'States and Minorities', and points to the interconnection between the enjoyment of fundamental rights, and the structure and pattern of the economy and society.

Besides highlighting the significance which Dr Ambedkar attached to a truly participative form of rights and government in the Constitution, the author, in fact, articulates Dr Ambedkar's direct role in framing several provisions of the Constitution, including how his qualifications and experience made Dr Ambedkar an appropriate candidate for the position of chairman of the Drafting Committee. To substantiate this, the later discussion compiles how Dr Ambedkar's colleagues from the Drafting Committee considered his contributions towards the Constitution indispensable and praiseworthy.

Another insightful feature of the book is the discussion about the meaning and purpose of Dr Ambedkar's vision of democracy. The author, through careful analysis, contextualizes Dr Ambedkar's comments on 'burning the Constitution' by refocusing historical truths surrounding his statement and rejects the claim that he wanted to burn the Constitution in a literal sense or as a matter of principle. In the end, the author, with clear evidence, debunks the myth that Dr Ambedkar intended reservations to be protected for ten years and proves that he was not in favour of any time limit on reservations.

In my view, the book brings a new insight into issues under exploration by the author and throws a new light and fresh understanding. This will be immensely useful for the scholars of Dr Ambedkar and the Constitution.

Professor Sukhadeo Thorat
Professor Emeritus and former chairman,
University Grants Commission

Acknowledgements

Any work by a writer is never his sole contribution. There exist several individuals behind the final product which a writer brings before the world. This book is a result of such collective endeavour. I was able to write the first draft of this book during Fall 2022. However, the book is a result of several years of my engagement with Dr Ambedkar's ideas on a personal and professional level, which I would like to mention.

This book is a tribute to Dr Ambedkar, whose *continued presence* transformed the lives of several generations, like mine. He laid down the path on which those who see humanity as a way of life, could walk. I am indebted to the social movements, and people who were part of these movements, who kept alive the memory of Dr Ambedkar after his death. Social and political activists, as well as members from marginalized communities who benefited from affirmative action and came to academia, have played a significant role in documenting Dr Ambedkar's struggle and his vision. This book traces its intellectual origins to numerous previous writings on Dr Ambedkar. For instance, the collected works of Dr Ambedkar (BAWS) was a result of a long social movement in Maharashtra. Numerous archival sources have been included in BAWS, thus making them easily accessible for researchers.

I am grateful to my family, who used to participate in public celebrations on the birth anniversary of Dr Ambedkar when I was a child, thereby creating a spark in my mind to learn more about the man whose life we celebrated. My family has supported me in my life decisions. I am indebted to my mother Shashi Kiran, my father Angan Prasad, my sister Shweta, my brother Aniket, my lovely cousins, and well-wishing relatives.

Dr Ambedkar's life inspired me to pursue a career in law. I must acknowledge the names of all those persons who contributed to my journey in the legal fraternity, which has now led to the culmination of this book.

For the lovely five years at Dr Ram Manohar Lohia National Law University (RMLNLU, Lucknow) and beyond, I am thankful to the following people (in no specific order): Amit Bandhu, Bhupendra Singh Bisht, Himanshu Chaudhary, Vijay Priya, Tarun Kumar, Jyoti Gautam, Shashankraj Singh, Kaushalendra Singh, Devendra, Anil Maurya, Neeraj Singh, Naveen Gautam, Deepak Kumar, Sandhya, Aditya Shrivastava, Shubham Kumar, Anchal Singh, Deesha Dalmia, Divyank Yadav, Saurabh Yadav, Vishal Sharma, Dr K.A. Pandey, Dr. Sanjay Singh, Dr Poonam Jayant Singh, Dr Sandeep Pandey, Ms Puja Awasthi, Surbhi Karwa, Malik Fahd, Neil Modi and many more. I also fondly remember the conversations with the faculty and support staff, including security guards, attendants, mess contractor, etc. of the University.

In his classes, Prof. C.M. Jariwala, dean, RMLNLU, would encourage students to explore the contributions of Dr Ambedkar in Constitution-making. I am thankful to Prof. Jariwala, as his words then motivated me to start reading on topics that now form the subject of this book. Mr Arjun Prasad, now deputy registrar at the Lucknow High Court, had arranged my first entry pass to the high court building. In the years that followed, I interned with several judges of the high court in Lucknow, which helped me hone my research skills. Therefore, I am indebted to Mr Arjun Prasad for his help. At the high court, in particular, I affectionately remember interning with Justice Devendra Kumar Upadhyaya (now Chief Justice, Bombay High Court) and Justice Rajan Roy.

Justice Upadhyaya has been a great source of support since my law school days.

During my LLM at Harvard Law School, I could draw parallels between Dr Ambedkar's writings and American civil rights history. Divya Tripathi, Shree Agnihotri, Apurva Vishwanath, Puja Awasthi, Poonam Jayant Singh, Ankit Yadav, Hari Krishnan and others helped me a lot in my application to Harvard Law School. Apurva and Savita also helped arrange financial support for my education at Harvard, for which I shall always be grateful. At Harvard Law School, I am glad that I could meet the following amazing people (in no specific order): Prof. David Wilkins and Prof. Michael Klarman, who believed in my endeavours, and my classmates, Vatsal Vasudev, Preeti Dash, Kumar Shanu, Ashutosh Salil, Sheela Sail, Jhalak Kakkar, Pragya Surana, Jay Lopez, Binendri Perera, Shawn Rajanayagam, Emily Negus, Nona Tamale, Chikondi Mandala, Nerissa Naidoo, Zariya Mushtaq, Gichora Githaiga, Ndunge and others.

I would like to specifically mention the role of my close friend, Mahtab Alam, who has always supported me and has been one of my expert advisers in life, whenever I have been in doubt about anything. Mahtab had read one of my articles and came out of his way to meet me in Lucknow when I was a student. Since then, we have had many conversations. Mahtab had once introduced me to Karthik Venkatesh, who is my commissioning editor at Penguin. After I came back from Harvard, Karthik approached me to submit a book proposal. I am grateful that he trusted me to bring out this book. Since the time of the book contract, he has always been available to answer even the smallest queries.

Some of the ideas in the book are a result of my previous writings on Dr Ambedkar. I thank the editors at different platforms, M.A. Rashid, P.V. Dinesh, Rama, Siddharth, Anand and Alex, who pushed me to think innovatively on the subject. Laurence Simon, Vinod Mishra, and Ashok Gurung have also supported my writing and academic assignments. I am also grateful to Mr Siddharth Luthra and the late Mr Amarendra Sharan for believing in me in the early years of my career.

Several ideas of the book developed while I was teaching an elective course on Dr Ambedkar at Jindal Global Law School (JGLS), Sonipat. I benefited from the discussions with the students, in particular, Achintya, Amulya, Ravi Parmar, Anahita and others. Achintya later worked as a research assistant on this book and provided valuable inputs and research. I also acknowledge the student interns who worked with me at different moments and assisted me with research, in particular Arsalan, Spandana, Sudipti and Aman. I am grateful to all of them. My time at JGLS was made much easier by the presence of my friend and colleague, Surendra Kumar, with whom I often used to have conversations about Dr Ambedkar's ideas.

A few ideas in the book are a result of my month-long stay at the University of Oxford in October 2022. I could spend time at Oxford only because of the Indian Equality Law Fellowship established by Prof. Tarunabh Khaitan, now a professor at the London School of Economics. I enjoyed my time at Oxford, due to the company of wonderful people like Shireen Azam, Suraj Thube, Pritam Singh, Abdullah Azzam and others.

Most importantly, the thoughts in various chapters in this book came out of my frequent conversations with three individuals: Prof. Sukhadeo Thorat, Dr Raja Sekhar Vundru and Disha Wadekar—Prof. Thorat being a legendary academic and mentor; Dr Vundru, a leading bureaucrat and author; and Disha, an extraordinary lawyer and scholar, now studying LLM at Columbia Law School on the Fulbright fellowship.

Prof. Thorat has done a tremendous amount of scholarly work on the ideas of Dr Ambedkar. I could think of writing this book because people like Prof. Thorat, Dr Vundru and many more had already opened the door on this subject through their various writings. Prof. Thorat, Dr Vundru and Disha gave me references to many academic sources relevant for this book. I am heavily indebted to them.

In particular, for the last three and a half years, I have been having conversations with Disha on the vision of Dr Ambedkar almost on a daily basis. In fact, she and I co-taught an elective course at JGLS titled 'Caste, Courts, and Constitution', which she had designed, and co-founded an initiative CEDE[1] (along with Avinash Mathews). Through these daily exchanges, I have had the opportunity to explore and gain a deeper understanding of Dr Ambedkar's vision, which spans a wide spectrum of socio-economic aspects. The richness of these conversations with Disha has played a pivotal role in refining and formulating my thoughts on various critical issues. In essence, these conversations have been a valuable journey of intellectual growth and self-discovery.

My friends Pritam Singh, Rajesh Ranjan and Rashmi proofread some of the draft chapters of this book. I thank them for taking out time. I am grateful to Prof. Shailaja Paik for pointing out a few factual mistakes/typos in the draft. I am inspired by people like Mahendra Ram Meghwal and Lehari Devi, who continue to fight for justice for their daughter, despite all odds. This book would not have been complete without Malti didi, Shahida didi and Usha didi, who were domestic workers in places I lived. With their contribution, I was able to focus on writing this book.

I am also grateful to everyone who agreed to write a blurb for this book. I also acknowledge the assistance of the copy editors of Penguin. I thank Malvika Raj, the amazing artist, whose painting is being used on the cover of the book.

Lastly, I would like to acknowledge the support of Chief Justice Dr D.Y. Chandrachud. I first met him in July 2014, when he was Chief Justice of Allahabad High Court. I was interning with Justice Upadhyaya in Lucknow, and out of his kindness, he introduced me to Justice Chandrachud. For a law student like me, that 'twenty-minute' conversation with Justice Chandrachud was a key highlight of the initial law school journey. Later, when he got elevated to the Supreme Court in May 2016, I applied to his office and was his first intern. One year later, Justice Chandrachud shortlisted me for a judicial clerkship in his office. After my tenure was over, we stayed in touch, and I came back to work with him, after he took oath as Chief Justice of India.

The year of clerkship with Justice Chandrachud was a pivotal period in my personal and professional development, particularly in honing my writing skills. His mentorship not only refined my legal acumen but also imparted invaluable lessons on effective communication through the written word. Over these years, he and Kalpana ma'am have supported me like no one else. Their encouragement and belief in my capabilities have been instrumental in shaping my professional journey. I am also grateful to several judges of the Supreme Court under whose guidance I continue to learn.

I present this book with a profound sense of gratitude to everyone, even if I have somehow missed mentioning their name here.

Notes

Chapter 1. Introduction

1. B.R. Ambedkar, 'Ranade, Gandhi and Jinnah', in *Dr. Babasaheb Ambedkar: Writings and Speeches*, ed. Vasant Moon, Ministry of Social Justice and Empowerment 2019, Vol. 1, p. 240.
2. Anurag Bhaskar, 'If Ambedkar and Lohia Met: How History Missed a Crucial Moment in Social Justice Politics', ThePrint, 20 April 2018, https://theprint.in/opinion/dalit-history-month/if-ambedkar-lohia-had-met-how-history-missed-a-crucial-moment-in-social-justice-politics/51047/.
3. *Indian Young Lawyers Association v. Union of India*, 2018 SC 1690.
4. For instance, speaking in the Rajya Sabha in 1954, Dr Ambedkar had presented a carefully considered view on the strong possibility of violent aggression from China. This eventually happened in 1962, six years after his death. See B.R. Ambedkar, 'On Chinese Aggression and Foreign Policy', Rajya Sabha, 26 August 1954, as reproduced in *A Stake in the Nation: Selected Speeches*, ed. Bhagwan Das (Navayana 2020), p. 171.
5. B.R. Ambedkar, 'Revolution and Counter-Revolution in Ancient India', in *Dr. Babasaheb Ambedkar: Writings and Speeches*, ed. Vasant Moon, Ministry of Social Justice and Empowerment 2019, Vol. 3, p. 149.

6. Critical race theorist Devon Carbado notes: 'One might start by saying that CRT rejects the standard racial progress narrative that characterizes mainstream civil rights discourse—namely, that the history of race relations in the United States is a history of linear uplift and improvement. Of course, America's racial landscape has improved over time, and CRT scholars should be ready to point this out. The problem with the racial progress narrative, however, is that it elides what I would call the "reform/retrenchment dialectic" that has constituted America's legal and political history. Consider the following three examples: (1) the end of legalized slavery and the promulgation of the Reconstruction Amendments (the reform) inaugurated legalized Jim Crow and the promulgation of Black Codes (the retrenchment); (2) Brown v. Board of Education's dismantling of separate but equal in the context of K-12 education (the reform) was followed by Brown II's weak "with all deliberate speed" mandate (the retrenchment); (3) Martin Luther King, Jr's vision of racial cooperation and responsibility, which helped to secure the passage of the Civil Rights Act of 1964 (the reform), was re-deployed to produce a political and legal discourse that severely restricts racial remediation efforts: colorblindness (the retrenchment). A linear narrative about American racial progress obscures this reform/retrenchment dynamic.' See Devon W. Carbado, 'Critical What What Commentary: Critical Race Theory: A Commemoration: Afterword', *Connecticut Law Review* (2011). Vol. 43, No. 5, pp. 1607–08, available online at https://opencommons.uconn.edu/law_review/127.

7. B.R. Ambedkar, 'Evidence before the Southborough Committee on Franchise', in *Dr. Babasaheb Ambedkar: Writings*

and Speeches, ed. Vasant Moon, Ministry of Social Justice and Empowerment 2019, Vol. I, p. 251.

8. 'The Capability Approach', *Stanford Encyclopaedia of Philosophy*, https://plato.stanford.edu/entries/capability-approach/.

9. A version of the last two sentences previously appeared in Anurag Bhaskar, 'Introduction: The Resurgent Icon' in *A Stake in the Nation: Selected Speeches*, ed. Bhagwan Das, (Navayana 2020), p. 8.

Chapter 2. The Rise of Dr Ambedkar

1. Christophe Jaffrelot, *Dr. Ambedkar and Untouchability* (New York: Columbia University Press, 2005), p. 6.

2. Ibid. See also Narendra Jadhav, *Ambedkar: Awakening India's Social Conscience* (Konark Publisher India, 2014).

3. *Indian Young Lawyers Association v. State of Kerala* (judgment dated 28 September 2018).

4. Christophe Jaffrelot, *Dr. Ambedkar and Untouchability*.

5. Ibid.

6. Ibid.

7. G.P. Deshpande, *Selected Writings of Jotirao Phule* (New Delhi: Leftword Books).

8. Christophe Jaffrelot, *Dr. Ambedkar and Untouchability*.

9. Shailaja Paik, 'Forging a New Dalit Womanhood in Colonial Western India: Discourse on Modernity, Rights, Education, and Emancipation', *Journal of Women's History* (2016), Volume 28, Number 4, Winter 2016, pp. 14–40, at p. 16.

10. Christophe Jaffrelot, *Dr. Ambedkar and Untouchability*.

11. Ibid.

12. Ibid., p. 30.

13. Eleanor Zelliot, 'Dr. Ambedkar and America', *Columbia University Ambedkar Centenary* (1991), http://www.columbia.edu/itc/mealac/pritchett/00ambedkar/timeline/graphics/txt_zelliot1991.html.

14. Anupama Rao, 'Ambedkar in America: An Archive for Our Times', *South Asia: Journal of South Asian Studies*, Vol. 45, Issue 2, pp. 350–71, at pp. 361, 362.

15. Scott R. Stroud, 'Creative Democracy, Communication, and the Uncharted Sources of Bhimrao Ambedkar's Deweyan Pragmatism', *Education and Culture*, 34 (1) (2018): 61–80.

16. Scott R. Stroud, *The Evolution of Pragmatism in India: An Intellectual Biography of B.R. Ambedkar* (HarperCollins, 2023), p. 21.

17. 'Dr. B.R. Ambedkar: His Life and Work—Ambedkar Timeline—in the 1910s', http://www.columbia.edu/itc/mealac/pritchett/00ambedkar/timeline/1910s.html.

18. Eleanor Zelliot 'Dr. Ambedkar and America', *Columbia University Ambedkar Centenary* (1991).

19. Kaoukab Chebaro, 'Dr. Ambedkar and Columbia University: A Legacy to Celebrate', *Columbia University Libraries* (15 April 2019), available at https://blogs.cul.columbia.edu/global-studies/2019/04/15/speaking-truth-to-power-dr-ambedkar-and-columbia-university/.

20. Daniel Payne, 'Educate. Agitate. Organise.: Ambedkar and LSE exhibition', LSE Blog, 7 July 2021, https://www.lse.ac.uk/library/whats-on/exhibitions/educate-agitate-organise.

21. Daniel Payne, 'Educate. Agitate. Organise.: Ambedkar and LSE exhibition'.

22. Ibid.

23. Ibid.

24. For a list of courses taken by Dr Ambedkar at LSE, see Sue Donnelly and Daniel Payne, 'A Student in London: Ambedkar at the London School of Economics and Political Science', in *Ambedkar in London,* ed. William Gould et al. (London: Hurst & Company, 2022), pp. 44–45.

25. Dhananjay Keer, *Dr. Ambedkar: Life and Mission,* (1990) 3rd ed. (Bombay: Popular Prakashan Private Limited), p. 51.

26. Dr Ambedkar, addressing a Session of Political Scientists Parliament at Jalandhar, 15 October 1956, as cited in *Reminiscences and Remembrances of Dr Ambedkar*, ed. Nanak Chand Rattu (New Delhi: Samyak Prakash, 2017), p. 79.

27. Rohit De, 'Lawyering as Politics: The Legal Practice of Dr. Ambedkar, Bar-at-Law', in *The Radical in Ambedkar*, eds. Suraj Yengde and Anand Teltumbde (Penguin, 2019), p. 98.

28. Dr Ambedkar, Addressing a Session of Political Scientists Parliament at Jalandhar, 15 October 1956, *Reminiscences and Remembrances of Dr Ambedkar*, ed. Nanak Chand Rattu (New Delhi: Samyak Prakash, 2017), p. 79.

29. Urmila Pawar and Meenakshi Moon, *We Also Made History: Women in the Ambedkarite Movement*, Wandana Sonalkar, trans., (Zubaan, 2008).

30. Sue Donnelly and Daniel Payne, 'A Student in London: Ambedkar at the London School of Economics and Political Science', *Ambedkar in London,* ed. William Gould et al. (London: Hurst & Company, 2022), p. 59.

31. Urmila Pawar and Meenakshi Moon, *We Also Made History: Women in the Ambedkarite Movement,* Wandana Sonalkar, trans., pp. 166–67.

32. B.R. Ambedkar, 'Waiting for a Visa', in *Dr. Babasaheb Ambedkar: Writings and Speeches*, ed. Vasant Moon, Ministry of Social Justice and Empowerment 2019, Vol. 12, p. 667.

33. Ibid.

34. Ibid., p. 670.

35. Ibid., p. 673.

36. Ibid., p. 678.

37. Ibid., p. 681.

38. Salim Yusufji, *Ambedkar: The Attendant Details* (Navayana, 2017), p. 95.

39. Ibid., p. 100.

40. Ibid.

41. Scott R. Stroud, 'How Do We Know What Ambedkar Read?', *Round Table India,* 21 September 2023, https://www.roundtableindia.co.in/how-do-we-know-what-ambedkar-read/.

42. Ibid.

43. V. Geetha, 'Unpacking a Library: Babasaheb Ambedkar and His World of Books', *The Wire,* 29 October 2017, https://thewire.in/caste/unpacking-library-babasaheb-ambedkar-world-books.

44. Savita Ambedkar, *Babasaheb: My Life with Dr Ambedkar,* translated from the Marathi by Nadeem Khan, (Penguin Random House, 2022), p. 75.

45. Ashok Gopal, *A Part Apart: The Life and Thought of B.R. Ambedkar* (Navayana Publishing, 2023), p. 239.

46. Rohit De, 'Lawyering as Politics: The Legal Practice of Dr. Ambedkar, Bar-at-Law', in *125 Years of Babasaheb Ambedkar: Looking Back, Moving Forward,* eds. Anand Teltumbde and Suraj Yengde, 2018, p. 143.

47. Steven Gasztowicz KC, 'Ambedkar as Lawyer: From London to India in the 1920s', in *Ambedkar in London,* ed. William Gould et al. (London: Hurst & Company, London, 2022), p. 79.

48. 'Centenary of Dr. B.R. Ambedkar's enrolment as an advocate', https://main.sci.gov.in/AMB/.

Chapter 3. Constitutional Discourse before Dr Ambedkar and in Subsequent Years

1. P. Sanal Mohan, *Modernity of Slavery: Struggles against Caste Inequality in Colonial Kerala* (Oxford University Press, 2015).

2. Ibid., p. 16.

3. Ibid.

4. Sumit Bhattacharjee 'The Forgotten Warriors against British Rule', *The Hindu*, 18 September 2019, https://www.thehindu.com/news/cities/Visakhapatnam/the-forgotten-warriors-against-british-rule/article29446455.ece.

5. Ibid.

6. Nolina S. Minj and Rahi Soren, 'Remembering Santal Hul, a 19th Century Struggle Against Imperialism', Wire.in, 30 June 2021, https://thewire.in/history/santal-hul-revolution.

7. Ibid.

8. Harsh Vardhan and Shivam Mogha, 'Santhal Hul Wasn't Just the First Anti-British Revolt, It Was Against All Exploitation', Wire.in, 30 June 2022, https://thewire.in/history/santhal-hul-wasnt-just-the-first-anti-british-revolt-it-was-against-all-exploitation.

9. Rohit De, 'Constitutional Antecedents', in *The Oxford Handbook of the Indian Constitution,* ed. Sujit Choudhry, Madhav Khosla and Pratap Bhanu Mehta (Oxford Academic, 2016).

10. Ibid., p. 25.

11. Ibid., p. 23.

12. Michael J. Klarman, *Unfinished Business: Racial Equality in American History* (Oxford: Oxford University Press, 2007).

13. Ibid.

14. James Baldwin, *Four Great Americans* (Werner School Book Company, 1896).

15. Abraham Lincoln, Speech at Peoria, Illinois, 16 October 1854.

16. Mukulika Banerjee, 'Vote', *South Asia: Journal of South Asian Studies*, (2017) 40:2, 410–12, DOI: 10.1080/00856401.2017.1302673.

17. B.R. Ambedkar, 'Education of Depressed Classes', in *Dr. Babasaheb Ambedkar: Writings and Speeches*, ed. Vasant

Moon, Ministry of Social Justice and Empowerment 2019, Vol. 2, p. 409.

18. Y.C. Simhadri, 'Denotified Tribes, a Sociological Analysis' (Classical Publishing Company, 1991), https://ccnmtl. columbia.edu/projects/mmt/ambedkar/web/readings/ Simhadri.pdf.

19. Stewart N. Gordon, 'Bhils and the Idea of a Criminal Tribe in Nineteenth-Century India', in *Crime and Criminality in British India,* ed. Anand Yang (Tucson: University of Arizona Press, 1986), pp. 129–39; Anastasia Piliavsky, 'The "Criminal Tribe" in India before the British', Comparative Studies in Society and History, Vol. 57, No. 2 (April 2015), pp. 323–54; Ramnarayan Rawat, *Reconsidering Untouchability: Chamars and Dalit History in North India* (Bloomington: Indiana University Press, 2011), p. 187; Disha Wadekar, 'Understanding Civil Liberties from an Ambedkarite Perspective', *The Leaflet,* 14 April 2022, https://theleaflet. in/understanding-civil-liberties-from-an-ambedkarite- perspective/.

20. Ramnarayan Rawat, *Reconsidering Untouchability: Chamars and Dalit History in North India* (Bloomington: Indiana University Press, 2011), p. 187.

21. Meena Radhakrishna, *Dishonoured by History: 'Criminal Tribes' and British Colonial Policy* (Orient Blackswan 2001).

22. Stewart N. Gordon, 'Bhils and the Idea of a Criminal Tribe in Nineteenth-Century India', in *Crime and Criminality in British India,* ed. Anand Yang, p. 139.

23. Ramnarayan Rawat, *Reconsidering Untouchability: Chamars and Dalit History in North India*, p. 26.

24. Arun Kumar, 'Amidst UK Heatwave, a Reminder of How British Colonials Exploited "Punkah-Walas" in India's Summers', Scroll.in, 21 July 2022, https://scroll. in/article/1028513/amidst-uk-heatwave-a-reminder-of-

how-british-colonials-exploited-punkah-walas-in-indias-summers; Ritam Sengupta, 'Keeping the Master Cool, Every Day, All Day: Punkah-Pulling in Colonial India', the *Indian Economic & Social History Review*, Vol. 59(1), 2022, pp. 37–73, https://doi.org/10.1177/00194646211064592.

25. Rohit De, *A People's Constitution: The Everyday Life of Law in the Indian Republic* (Princeton University Press. 2018), p. 20.

26. Ibid.

27. Radhey Shyam Verma, 'Gopal Krishna Gokhale and His Presentation before the Welby Commission', *Proceedings of the Indian History Congress*, 68 (2007): 745–59. http://www.jstor.org/stable/44147884.

28. Part Five of the Presidential address of Rahimatulla Sayani to the Indian National Congress, 1896, http://www.columbia.edu/itc/mealac/pritchett/00litlinks/sayani_congress_1896/sayani2435.html.

29. B.R. Ambedkar, 'Public Services', in *Dr. Babasaheb Ambedkar: Writings and Speeches*, ed. Vasant Moon, Ministry of Social Justice and Empowerment 2019, Vol. 2, p. 397.

30. Ibid., p. 398.

31. Rohit De, 'Constitutional Antecedents', in *The Oxford Handbook of the Indian Constitution*, eds. Sujit Choudhry, Madhav Khosla and Pratap Bhanu Mehta (Oxford Academic, 2016), Constitution of India Bill 1895 Constitutionofindia.net, https://www.constitutionofindia.net/historical_constitutions/the_constitution_of_india_bill__unknown__1895__1st%20January%201895.

32. Constitution of India Bill 1895, Constitutionofindia.net, https://www.constitutionofindia.net/historical_constitutions/the_constitution_of_india_bill__unknown__1895__1st%20January%201895.

33. 'In 1895, when the Congress met in Poona, this Anti-Social Reform section rebelled and threatened to burn

the Congress pandal if the Congress allowed it to be used by the Social Conference. This opposition to the Social Conference was headed by no other person than the late Mr Tilak, one of those social Tories and political radicals with which India abounds and who was the father of the slogan "Swaraj is my birthright" which is now seen blazoned on Congress banners. Justice M.G. Ranade's faction which was initially emphasizing social reforms were forced to back off.' See B.R. Ambedkar, *What Congress and Gandhi Have Done to the Untouchables: A Strange Event*, in *Dr. Babasaheb Ambedkar: Writings and Speeches*, ed. Vasant Moon, Ministry of Social Justice and Empowerment 2019, Vol. 9, p. 13.

34. Charles H. Heimsath, 'The Origin and Enactment of the Indian Age of Consent Bill, 1891', the *Journal of Asian Studies* 21, No. 4 (1962): pp. 491–504, at p. 499, https://doi.org/10.2307/2050879.

35. 'Letter to the Editor by "an observer from within"', *Mahratta*, 5 May 1901, p. 9, as cited in Gaurav Somwanshi, 'The Granddaddy of all Hindutvavadis', *Round Table India*, 19 May 2015, https://www.roundtableindia.co.in/tilak-the-granddaddy-of-all-hindutvavadis/. Several of such views are highlighted in the following article: Parimala V. Rao, 'Educating Women and Non-Brahmins as "Loss of Nationality": Bal Gangadhar Tilak and the Nationalist Agenda in Maharashtra', *Centre for Women Development Studies* (2016).

36. Ibid.

37. B.G. Tilak, *Mahratta*, p. 1., 24 August 1884, as cited in Parimala V. Rao, 'Educating Women and Non-Brahmins as "Loss of Nationality": Bal Gangadhar Tilak and the Nationalist Agenda in Maharashtra', *Centre for Women Development Studies* (2016), p. 5.

38. Shri Prakash Singh. 'Tilak's Concept of Nationalism,' the *Indian Journal of Political Science*, vol. 75, no. 2, 2014,

pp. 255–64. JSTOR, http://www.jstor.org/stable/24701133, accessed 3 August 2022.

39. B.G. Tilak, '"What Shall We Do Next?", Editorial', Mahratta, pp. 2–3, 22 March 1891, as cited in Parimala V. Rao, 'Educating Women and Non-Brahmins as "Loss of Nationality": Bal Gangadhar Tilak and the Nationalist Agenda in Maharashtra', Centre for Women Development Studies (2016), p. 24.

40. B.G. Tilak, 'Letter to the Editor by "an observer from within"' Mahratta, 5 May 1901, p. 9, as cited in Parimala V. Rao, 'Educating Women and Non-Brahmins as "Loss of Nationality": Bal Gangadhar Tilak and the Nationalist Agenda in Maharashtra', Centre for Women Development Studies, p. 6.

41. Ibid.

42. Abhinav Chandrachud, These Seats Are Reserved: Caste, Quotas and the Constitution of India (Penguin. 2023), p. 23.

43. B.R. Ambedkar, What Congress and Gandhi Have Done to the Untouchables: A Plea to the Foreigners, in Dr. Babasaheb Ambedkar: Writings and Speeches, ed. Vasant Moon, Ministry of Social Justice and Empowerment 2019, Vol. 9, p. 209.

44. Ibid.

45. Ibid., p. 208.

46. Indra Sawhney v. Union of India, 1992 Supp (3) SCC 217, see paras 766–71 (plurality opinion of Justice BP Jeevan Reddy).

47. Ibid.

48. Bhagwan Das, 'Moments in a History of Reservations', Economic & Political Weekly, Vol. 35, Issue No. 43–44, 21 October 2000, p. 3831.

49. Courtenay Ilbert, 'The Indian Councils Act, 1909', Journal of the Society of Comparative Legislation 11, no. 2 (1911): pp. 243–54. http://www.jstor.org/stable/752520.

50. Rohit De, A People's Constitution: The Everyday Life of Law in the Indian Republic (Princeton University Press. 2018), p. 25.

51. Mukulika Banerjee, 'Vote', *South Asia: Journal of South Asian Studies*, 40:2, pp. 410–12, 2017, DOI: 10.1080/00856401.2017.1302673; Courtenay Ilbert, 'The Indian Councils Act, 1909', *Journal of the Society of Comparative Legislation 11*.

52. Marc Galanter, 'Law and Caste in Modern India,' *Asian Survey*, Vol. 3, No. 11, 1963, pp. 544–59, JSTOR, https://doi.org/10.2307/3023430, accessed 17 August 2022.

53. Ibid.

54. Ibid.

55. Marc Galanter, 'Untouchability and the Law', *Economic and Political Weekly* (1969), Vol. 4, No. 1/2, pp. 133–70.

56. Ibid.

57. Ibid.

58. Bernard S. Cohn, 'Anthropological Notes on Disputes and Law in India,' *American Anthropologist*, Vol. 67, No. 6, 1965, pp. 82–122, JSTOR, http://www.jstor.org/stable/668841, accessed 17 August 2022.

59. Ibid.

60. Bharat Patankar and Gail Omvedt, 'The Dalit Liberation Movement in Colonial Period,' *Economic and Political Weekly* 14, no. 7/8, 1979: pp. 409–24, http://www.jstor.org/stable/4367359.

61. Ibid.

62. Ibid., p. 411.

63. Disha Wadekar, 'Understanding Civil Liberties from an Ambedkarite Perspective', *The Leaflet*, 14 April 2022, https://theleaflet.in/understanding-civil-liberties-from-an-ambedkarite-perspective/

64. Ibid.

65. For a general account, see *B.R. Ambedkar: Perspectives on Social Exclusion and Inclusive Policies*, eds. Sukhadeo Thorat and Narender Kumar (Oxford University Press, 2008), pp. 11–40.

66. Rohit De, 'Between Midnight and Republic: Theory and Practice of India's Dominion Status', *International Journal of Constitutional Law*, Volume 17, Issue 4, October 2019, pp. 1213–34, https://doi.org/10.1093/icon/moz081.

67. The Montagu–Chelmsford Report, the *Round Table*, 1918, pp. 778–802, DOI: 10.1080/00358531809412568.

68. Letter from Lord Southborough to the Governor-General, Delhi, dated 26 February 1919, https://dspace.gipe.ac.in/xmlui/bitstream/handle/10973/19912/GIPE-213368-Contents.pdf?sequence=2&isAllowed=y.

69. B.R. Ambedkar, *What Congress and Gandhi Have Done to the Untouchables: A Strange Event,* in *Dr. Babasaheb Ambedkar: Writings and Speeches*, ed. Vasant Moon, p. 1.

70. Ibid., Vol. 18.

71. Chinnaiah Jangam, *Dalits and the Making of Modern India* (Oxford University Press, 2019), p. 139.

72. The Montagu–Chelmsford Report, the *Round Table*, 1918, pp. 778–802, DOI: 10.1080/00358531809412568.

73. Suhail Shahzad, Fayyaz-ur-Rehman and Misal Zada, 'Evolution of Federalism in the Pre-Independence Sub-Continent', 34 J.L. and Soc'y 139, 2006.

74. *Babasaheb Ambedkar: Writings and Speeches*, Vol. 2, p. 364.

75. 'Its non-Indian character posed an affront to almost all Indian parties. The Congress party decided to boycott the Commission at every stage and in every form. So, on its arrival, the Simon Commission was greeted with black flags, curses and placards with the slogan "Go back, Simon!" Congressmen staged hostile demonstrations on a nation-wide scale, and the police had to open fire at some places. This black welcome was also extended later to the Commission during its second visit in the winter of 1928–29.' Taken from *Dr. Babasaheb Ambedkar: Writings and Speeches*, ed. Vasant Moon, Ministry of Social Justice and Empowerment 2019, Vol. 17(1), p. 64.

76. Ibid.

77. 'The Planning of the Nehru Committee and the Future of India', 18 January 1929, as translated in *Bahiskrit Bharat—Part III,* ed. B.R. Kamble, Dr Babasaheb Ambedkar Research Institute in Social Growth, Kolhapur, pp. 94–95.

78. B.R. Ambedkar, 'Role of Dr. B.R. Ambedkar in Bringing the Untouchables on the Political Horizon of India and Laying a Foundation of Indian Democracy', in *Dr. Babasaheb Ambedkar: Writings and Speeches,* ed. Vasant Moon, Ministry of Social Justice and Empowerment 2019, Vol. 17(1), p. 65.

79. Ibid.

80. Ibid.

81. Rohit De, 'Constitutional Antecedents', in *The Oxford Handbook of the Indian Constitution,* eds. Sujit Choudhry, Madhav Khosla and Pratap Bhanu Mehta (Oxford Academic, 2016).

82. B.R. Ambedkar, *What Congress and Gandhi Have Done to the Untouchables: A Mean Deal,* in *Dr. Babasaheb Ambedkar: Writings and Speeches,* ed. Vasant Moon, Ministry of Social Justice and Empowerment 2019, Vol. 9, p. 28.

83. Ibid.

84. Sukhadeo Thorat. 'Ambedkar's Proposal to Safeguard Minorities Against Communal Majority in Democracy', *Journal of Social Inclusion Studies*, 5(2), 2019, pp. 113–128, https://doi.org/10.1177/2394481120913779.

Chapter 4. Ideas on Popular Government and Citizenship

1. Vijay Prashad, 'The Untouchable Question,' *Economic and Political Weekly,* 1996, pp. 551–59.

2. Dhananjay Keer, *Dr. Ambedkar: Life and Mission,* 3rd ed. (Bombay: Popular Prakashan Private Limited, 1990).

3. Mukulika Banerjee, 'Vote', *South Asia: Journal of South Asian Studies*, 40:2, 2017, 410–12.

4. Ibid.

5. As documented by Dr Ambedkar in his submissions— B.R. Ambedkar, 'Evidence before the Southborough Committee on Franchise', in *Dr. Babasaheb Ambedkar: Writings and Speeches*, ed. Vasant Moon, Ministry of Social Justice and Empowerment 2019, Vol. I.

6. Raja Sekhar Vundru, *Ambedkar, Gandhi and Patel: The Making of India's Electoral System* (Bloomsbury India, 2018).

7. Sukhadeo Thorat and Narender Kumar, *B.R. Ambedkar: Perspectives on Social Exclusion and Inclusive Policies* (Oxford University Press, 2008), p. 15.

8. B.R. Ambedkar, 'Evidence before the Southborough Committee on Franchise', in *Dr. Babasaheb Ambedkar: Writings and Speeches*, ed. Vasant Moon, Vol. I, p. 251.

9. Ibid.

10. Ibid., p. 247.

11. Ibid.

12. Ibid.

13. B.R. Ambedkar, 'Evidence before the Southborough Committee on Franchise', in *Dr. Babasaheb Ambedkar: Writings and Speeches*, ed. Vasant Moon, Ministry of Social Justice and Empowerment 2019, Vol. I, p. 255.

14. Ibid.

15. Ibid.

16. Ibid.

17. Ibid., p. 256.

18. Ibid.

19. Ibid.

20. Ibid., p. 261.

21. Ibid.

22. Ibid.

23. Ibid., p. 262.

24. Ibid., p. 265.

25. Ibid., p. 268.

26. Ibid.

27. Ibid.

28. Ibid., p. 275.

29. Ibid.

30. Manoj Mitta, *Caste Pride: Battles for Equality in Hindu India* (Context [Westland], 2023), p. 238; Masao Naito, 'Anti-Untouchability Ideologies and Movements in Maharashtra from the Late Nineteenth Century to the 1930s', in *Caste System, Untouchability and the Depressed,* ed. H. Kotani, (Manohar, 1997), p. 189.

31. Christophe Jaffrelot, *India's Silent Revolution: The Rise of the Lower Castes in North India* (New York: Columbia University Press, 2003).

Chapter 5. Shaping the Language of Rights

1. Narendra Jadhav, *Ambedkar: An Economist Extraordinaire* (Konark Publishers Pvt. Ltd, 2015), p. 38.

2. B.R. Ambedkar, *What Congress and Gandhi Have Done to the Untouchables*, in *Dr. Babasaheb Ambedkar: Writings and Speeches*, ed. Vasant Moon, Ministry of Social Justice and Empowerment 2019, Vol. 9.

3. Dhananjay Keer, *Dr. Ambedkar: Life and Mission*, 1990, 3rd ed. (Bombay: Popular Prakashan Private Limited), p. 40.

4. Prabodhan Pol, '100 Years of Mooknayak, Ambedkar's First Newspaper that Changed Dalit Politics Forever', Wire.in, 31 January 2020, https://thewire.in/media/mooknayak-ambedkar-newspaper.

5. Gail Omvedt, *Seeking Begumpura: The Social Vision of Anticaste Intellectuals* (Navayana, 2009), pp. 106–07.

6. B.R. Kamble translation of B.R. Ambedkar, 'From the pages of Mook Nayak', *Round Table India,* 13 April 2015, https://www.roundtableindia.co.in/from-the-pages-of-mook-nayak/.

7. V. Ratnamala, 'Ambedkar and Media', *Round Table India,* 13 April 2012, https://www.roundtableindia.co.in/ambedkar-and-media/.

8. Prabodhan Pol, '100 Years of Mooknayak, Ambedkar's First Newspaper that Changed Dalit Politics Forever', Wire.in.

9. B.R. Kamble translation of BR Ambedkar, 'From the pages of Mook Nayak', *Round Table India.*

10. Dhananjay Keer, *Dr. Ambedkar: Life and Mission,* 1990, 3rd ed., p. 42.

11. Siddharth, 'Through "Mooknayak", Ambedkar questioned Gandhi's Swaraj', *Forward Press,* 29 January 2020, https://www.forwardpress.in/2020/01/100-years-of-the-launch-of-mooknayak/.

12. Dhananjay Keer. *Dr. Ambedkar: Life and Mission.* (1990) 3rd ed.

13. Prabodhan Pol, '100 Years of Mooknayak, Ambedkar's First Newspaper that Changed Dalit Politics Forever', Wire.in.

14. Yogesh Maitreya, 'Mooknayak Turns 100: How Babasaheb Ambedkar's Marathi Weekly for Dalits Came into Being', First Post, 30 January 2020, https://www.firstpost.com/living/mooknayak-turns-100-how-babasaheb-ambedkars-marathi-weekly-for-dalits-came-into-being-7983101.html.

15. Prabhakar Gajbhiye, *Mooknayak Mein Prakashit Dr. Bhimrao Ambedkar Ke Sampadkiya* (Pushpanjali Prakashan: India, 2019).

16. Narendra Jadhav, *Ambedkar: Awakening India's Social Conscience* (Konark Publisher India, 2014), p. 46.

17. Ibid., p. 47.

18. Ibid.

19. Dhananjay Keer. *Dr. Ambedkar: Life and Mission.* (1990) 3rd ed., p. 42; Narendra Jadhav *Ambedkar: Awakening India's Social Conscience*, p. 48.

20. Dhananjay Keer. *Dr. Ambedkar: Life and Mission.* (1990) 3rd ed., p. 47.

21. Steven Gasztowicz KC, 'Ambedkar as Lawyer: From London to India in the 1920s', in *Ambedkar in London,* ed. William Gould et al. (London: Hurst & Company, 2022), p. 73.

22. Ibid., p. 73.

23. Ibid., p. 74.

24. Dhananjay Keer. *Dr. Ambedkar: Life and Mission.* (1990) 3rd ed., p. 47.

25. Daniel Payne, 'Ambedkar and LSE', LSE Blog, 7 July 2021, https://www.lse.ac.uk/library/whats-on/exhibitions.

26. Ashok Gopal, *A Part Apart: The Life and Thought of B.R. Ambedkar* (Navayana Publishing, 2023), p. 212.

27. Savita Ambedkar, *Babasaheb: My Life with Dr Ambedkar,* translated from the Marathi by Nadeem Khan (Penguin Random House, 2022), p. 36.

28. Dhananjay Keer. *Dr. Ambedkar: Life and Mission.* (1990) 3rd ed., p. 47; Gail Omvedt, *Ambedkar: Towards an Enlightened India,* (Penguin India, 2004).

29. Prabodhan Pol, '100 Years of Mooknayak, Ambedkar's First Newspaper that Changed Dalit Politics Forever', Wire.in.

30. Dhananjay Keer. *Dr. Ambedkar: Life and Mission.* (1990) 3rd ed., p. 52.

31. Gail Omvedt, *Building the Ambedkar Revolution: Sambhaji Tukaram Gaikwad and the Kokan Dalits* (Bhashya Prakashan), p. 49.

32. See photographs on second page in Savita Ambedkar, *Babasaheb: My Life with Dr Ambedkar*, translated by Nadeem Khan, Vintage, 2022.

33. Dhananjay Keer. *Dr. Ambedkar: Life and Mission.* (1990) 3rd ed., p. 53.

34. Ibid.

35. Ibid.

36. Gail Omvedt, *Ambedkar: Towards an Enlightened India* (Penguin India, 2004).

37. Bharat Patankar and Gail Omvedt, 'The Dalit Liberation Movement in Colonial Period,' *Economic and Political Weekly* 14, No. 7/8, 1979, pp. 409–24, http://www.jstor.org/stable/4367359.

38. Dhananjay Keer. *Dr. Ambedkar: Life and Mission.* (1990) 3rd ed., p. 63.

39. Daniel Payne, 'Ambedkar and LSE', LSE Blog, 7 July 2021, https://www.lse.ac.uk/library/whats-on/exhibitions.

40. Nanak Chand Rattu, *Reminiscences and Remembrance of Dr. B.R. Ambedkar* (Samyak Prakashan India, 2017), p. 77.

41. Ibid.

42. Dhananjay Keer. *Dr. Ambedkar: Life and Mission.* (1990) 3rd ed., p. 54.

43. Ibid.

44. Anupama Rao, 'Ambedkar in America: An Archive for Our Times', *South Asia: Journal of South Asian Studies*, Vol. 45, Issue 2, pp. 350–71, at p. 363.

45. B.R. Ambedkar, 'Untouchables or the Children of India's Ghetto', in *Dr. Babasaheb Ambedkar: Writings and Speeches*, ed. Vasant Moon, Ministry of Social Justice and Empowerment 2019, Vol. 5, p. 15.

46. Narendra Jadhav, *Ambedkar: Awakening India's Social Conscience*, p. 65.

47. Ibid., p. 66.

48. B.R. Ambedkar, print version—*Annihilation of Caste* (1935), https://ccnmtl.columbia.edu/projects/mmt/ambedkar/web/readings/aoc_print_2004.pdf.

49. Narendra Jadhav, *Ambedkar: Awakening India's Social Conscience*, p. 67.

50. Ibid., p. 63.

51. Ibid., p. 64; Dhananjay Keer. *Dr. Ambedkar: Life and Mission*. (1990) 3rd ed., p. 62.

52. Rohit De, 'Lawyering as Politics: The Legal Practice of Dr. Ambedkar, Bar-at-Law', in *The Radical in Ambedkar, eds.* Suraj Yengde and Anand Teltumbde, 2019, p. 141.

53. Ibid.

54. Ibid.

Chapter 6. The Mahad Satyagraha— First Walk to Freedom

1. Inspired by the title of the book *Long Walk to Freedom* by former South African President Nelson Mandela.

2. B.R. Ambedkar, 'Untouchables or the Children of India's Ghetto', in *Dr. Babasaheb Ambedkar: Writings and Speeches*, ed. Vasant Moon, Ministry of Social Justice and Empowerment 2019, Vol. 5.

3. Ambika Aiyadurai, 'Even After a Century, Water Is Still the Marker of India's Caste Society', The Wire, 23 August 2022, https://thewire.in/caste/even-after-a-century-water-is-still-the-marker-of-indias-caste-society.

4. Dhananjay Keer, *Dr. Ambedkar: Life and Mission*, 3rd ed. (Bombay: Popular Prakashan Private Limited, 1990), p. 64.

5. Gail Omvedt, *Building the Ambedkar Revolution: Sambhaji Tukaram Gaikwad and the Kokan Dalits* (Bhashya Prakashan, 2011), p. 51.

6. *Memoirs of a Dalit Communist: The Many Worlds of R.B. More*, Satyendra More (Leftword, 2019).

7. Bojja Tharakam, *Mahad: The March That's Launched Every Day* (The Shared Mirror Publishing House India, 2018).

8. Narendra Jadhav, *Ambedkar: Awakening India's Social Conscience* (Konark Publisher India, 2014), p. 79.

9. Ibid, p. 80.

10. Ibid., p. 81.

11. Dhananjay Keer, *Dr. Ambedkar: Life and Mission*, 3rd ed., pp. 71–72.

12. Ibid., pp. 73–77.

13. *Dr. Babasaheb Ambedkar: Writings and Speeches*, ed. Vasant Moon, Ministry of Social Justice and Empowerment 2019, Vol. 17.1, p. 10.

14. Gail Omvedt, *Building the Ambedkar Revolution: Sambhaji Tukaram Gaikwad and the Kokan Dalits*, p. 57.

15. *Browder v. Gayle*, 352 U.S. 903.

16. Anand Teltumbde, *MAHAD: The Making of the First Dalit Revolt* (Routledge London, 2022), pp. 130–40.

17. Ashok Gopal, *A Part Apart: The Life and Thought of B.R. Ambedkar* (Navayana Publishing, 2023), p. 238.

18. Dhananjay Keer, *Dr. Ambedkar: Life and Mission*, 3rd ed., p. 77.

19. Anand Teltumbde, *MAHAD: The Making of the First Dalit Revolt*, p. 141.

20. Ibid.

21. Ibid., pp. 142–44.

22. Ibid., p. 147.

23. Ibid., p. 149.

24. Ibid., p. 150.

25. Ibid., p. 151.

26. Ibid.

27. Ibid., p. 154.

28. Ibid.

29. Ibid., p. 158.

30. Narendra Jadhav, *Ambedkar: Awakening India's Social Conscience*, p. 100.

31. Anand Teltumbde, *MAHAD: The Making of the First Dalit Revolt*, p. 174.

32. Dhananjay Keer, *Dr. Ambedkar: Life and Mission*, 3rd ed., pp. 89–90.

33. Narendra Jadhav, *Ambedkar: Awakening India's Social Conscience*, p. 83.

34. Ibid.

35. Ibid., p. 90.

36. Anand Teltumbde, *MAHAD: The Making of the First Dalit Revolt*, p. 180

37. *Source Material on Dr Babasaheb Ambedkar and the Movement of Untouchables,* Government of Maharashtra, 1982, Vol. I, p. 13.

38. Narendra Jadhav, *Ambedkar: Awakening India's Social Conscience*, p. 84.

39. *Source Material on Dr Babasaheb Ambedkar and the Movement of Untouchables,* Government of Maharashtra.

40. Ibid.

41. Narendra Jadhav, *Ambedkar: Awakening India's Social Conscience*, p. 85.

42. Ibid., pp. 86–87.

43. Ibid., p. 87.

44. Ibid., p. 89.

45. Martin Luther King, Jr, 'Letter from a Birmingham Jail', 1963, https://www.csuchico.edu/iege/_assets/documents/susi-letter-from-birmingham-jail.pdf.

46. Martin Luther King, Jr, 'Letter from a Birmingham Jail'.

47. Dhananjay Keer, *Dr. Ambedkar: Life and Mission*, 3rd ed., pp. 90, 97–98.

48. Narendra Jadhav, *Ambedkar: Awakening India's Social Conscience*, pp. 91–95.

49. Ibid.

50. Ibid.

51. Ibid.

52. Anand Teltumbde, *MAHAD: The Making of the First Dalit Revolt*, pp. 349–52.

53. Ibid.

54. Ibid., p. 351.

55. Ashok Gopal, *A Part Apart: The Life and Thought of B.R. Ambedkar*, p. 280

56. Narendra Jadhav, *Ambedkar: Awakening India's Social Conscience*, p. 100.

57. Rohit De, 'Lawyering as Politics: The Legal Practice of Dr Ambedkar, Bar at Law', in *The Radical in Ambedkar: Critical Reflections*, eds Suraj Yengde and Anand Teltumbde (Penguin, 2018).

58. 'Mahad Satyagraha', *Supreme Court of India,* https://main.sci.gov.in/AMB/mahadsatyagraha.php.

Chapter 7. Equal Voting Rights (Universal Adult Franchise)

1. Some of the notable members of this Committee were Motilal Nehru (Chairman), Sir Ali Imam, Tej Bahadur Sapru and Subhas Chandra Bose. M.R. Jayakar and Annie Besant joined the Committee later. Jawaharlal Nehru, Motilal Nehru's son, was appointed the secretary to the Committee. Nehru Report (Motilal Nehru, 1928), ConstitutionofIndia.net, https://www.constitutionofindia.net/historical_constitutions/nehru_report__motilal_nehru_1928__1st%20January%201928.

2. Dhananjay Keer, *Dr. Ambedkar: Life and Mission.* 3rd ed. (Bombay: Popular Prakashan Private Limited, 1990), p. 115.

3. Ibid., pp. 114–15.

4. B.R. Ambedkar, 'Statement concerning the safeguards for the protection of the interests of the Depressed Classes as a minority in the Bombay Presidency and the changes in the composition of and the guarantees from the Bombay Legislative Council necessary to ensure the same under Provincial Autonomy', in *Dr. Babasaheb Ambedkar: Writings and Speeches*, ed. Vasant Moon, Ministry of Social Justice and Empowerment 2019, Vol. 2, p. 431.

5. Ibid.

6. Ibid.

7. Ibid., p. 441.

8. Ibid., p. 446.

9. Ibid., pp. 429–58.

10. Nehru Report (Motilal Nehru,1928), Constitutionof India.net, https://www.constitutionofindia.net/historical_constitutions/nehru_report__motilal_nehru_1928__1st%20January%201928.

11. Dhananjay Keer, *Dr. Ambedkar: Life and Mission*. 3rd ed., p. 115.

12. B.R. Ambedkar, 'Provincial Legislature—Franchise', in *Dr. Babasaheb Ambedkar: Writings and Speeches*, ed. Vasant Moon, Ministry of Social Justice and Empowerment 2019, Vol. 2, p. 338.

13. 'The Planning of the Nehru Committee and the Future of India', 18 January 1929, as translated in *Bahiskrit Bharat—Part III, ed.* B.R. Kamble, Dr Babasaheb Ambedkar Research Institute in Social Growth, Kolhapur, pp. 94–95.

14. Dhananjay Keer, *Dr. Ambedkar: Life and Mission*. 3rd ed., p. 115.

15. Narendra Jadhav, *Ambedkar: Awakening India's Social Conscience* (Konark Publisher India, 2014), p. 105.

16. Ramnarayan Rawat, *Reconsidering Untouchability: Chamars and Dalit History in North India* (Bloomington: Indiana University Press, 2011), p. 161.

17. Dhananjay Keer, *Dr. Ambedkar: Life and Mission*. 3rd ed., pp. 119–20.

18. B.R. Ambedkar, 'Report on the Constitution of the Government of Bombay Presidency', in *Dr. Babasaheb Ambedkar: Writings and Speeches*, ed. Vasant Moon, Ministry of Social Justice and Empowerment 2019, Vol.2, p. 315.
19. Ibid.
20. Ibid.
21. Ibid., pp. 337–38.
22. Ibid.
23. Ibid., p. 339.
24. Ibid., p. 340.
25. Ibid.
26. Ibid., p. 343.

Chapter 8. Historical Reservation for the Oppressor Castes v. Affirmative Action for Oppressed Castes

1. B.R. Ambedkar, 'Public Services', in *Dr. Babasaheb Ambedkar: Writings and Speeches*, ed. Vasant Moon, Ministry of Social Justice and Empowerment 2019, Vol. 2, p. 393.
2. Ibid.
3. Ibid., p. 394.
4. Ibid.
5. Ibid., p. 395.
6. Ibid., p. 396.
7. Ibid.
8. Ibid.
9. Ibid., p. 397. Ambedkar was referring to the submissions made by Gopal Krishna Gokhale (1866–1915) before the Welby Commission, which was appointed in 1895 by the British government to inquire into the administration and management of the military and civil expenditure incurred under the authority of the secretary of state for India-in-council. Gokhale had submitted: 'The excessive costliness of the foreign agency is not however its only evil.

There is a moral evil, which, if anything, is even greater. A kind of dwarfing or stunting of the Indian race is going on under the present system. We must live all the days of our life in an atmosphere of inferiority and tallest of us must bend in order that the exigencies of the existing system may be satisfied. The upward impulse, if I may use such an expression, which every school-boy at Eton or Harrow may feel that he may one day be a Gladstone, a Nelson, or a Wellington, and which may draw forth the best efforts of which he is capable, is denied to us. The full height to which our manhood is capable of rising can never be reached by us under the present system. The moral elevation which every self-governing people feel cannot be felt by us. Our administrative and military talents must gradually disappear, owing to sheer disuse, till at last our lot, as hewers of wood and drawers of water in our own country, is stereotyped.'

10. Ibid., p. 397–98.
11. B.R. Ambedkar, *What Congress and Gandhi Have Done to the Untouchables,* in *Dr. Babasaheb Ambedkar: Writings and Speeches,* ed. Vasant Moon, Ministry of Social Justice and Empowerment 2019, Vol. 9.
12. Ibid., p. 477.
13. Ibid.
14. Ibid.
15. Ibid., p. 205
16. Ibid.
17. Ibid., p. 478.
18. Ibid., p. 212.
19. Ibid.
20. Ibid., p. 215.
21. Ibid., p. 212.
22. Ibid., pp. 216–17.

23. Ibid., pp. 216–17.
24. Ibid., pp. 472–78.
25. Ibid., p. 226.
26. Ibid., p. 472.
27. Ibid., pp. 226–27.
28. Ibid., pp. 230–31.
29. Ibid., p. 482.
30. Ibid., p. 481.
31. Ibid., p. 480.
32. Ibid., p. 231.
33. B.R. Ambedkar, 'A Peep into the Future', in *Dr. Babasaheb Ambedkar: Writings and Speeches,* ed. Vasant Moon, Ministry of Social Justice and Empowerment 2019, Vol. 12, pp. 723–24.
34. B.R. Ambedkar, 'Public Services', in *Dr. Babasaheb Ambedkar: Writings and Speeches*, ed. Vasant Moon, Ministry of Social Justice and Empowerment 2019, Vol. 2, p. 398.
35. B.R. Ambedkar, 'If Democracy Dies It Will Be Our Doom', in *Dr. Babasaheb Ambedkar: Writings and Speeches,* ed. Vasant Moon, Ministry of Social Justice and Empowerment 2019, Vol. 17.3, pp. 251–52.
36. Ibid.
37. B.R. Ambedkar, 'Provincial Legislature', in *Dr. Babasaheb Ambedkar: Writings and Speeches,* ed. Vasant Moon, Ministry of Social Justice and Empowerment 2019, Vol. 2, pp. 349–50.
38. Ibid.
39. B.R. Ambedkar, *What Congress and Gandhi Have Done to the Untouchables: A False Charge*, in *Dr. Babasaheb Ambedkar: Writings and Speeches*, ed. Vasant Moon, Ministry of Social Justice and Empowerment 2019, Vol. 9, p. 171.
40. Ibid., p. 482.
41. Granville Austin, *The Indian Constitution: Cornerstone of a Nation* (Oxford University Press, 1999), p. 25.

42. Ibid.
43. Constituent Assembly Debates, 24 August 1949. Jaipal Singh Munda said: 'It is most unfortunate that this House has not had an opportunity to discuss the recommendations made by the two Tribal Sub-Committees. I know we had a debate of two days to consider the report of the Minorities Committee in regard to whether the Scheduled Castes and the Muslims were to get any reservation of seats or not. At that time all the discussion was confined to the Muslim problem only . . . Having said that, Sir, *I would like to congratulate Dr. Ambedkar for his new amendment which he has presented to us today* . . . Sir, we are not begging anything. I do not come here to beg. It is for the majority community to atone for their sins of the last six thousand odd years.'
44. Constituent Assembly of India Debates (Proceedings)—Volume I, 17 December 1946, http://164.100.47.194/loksabha/writereaddata/cadebatefiles/C17121946.html.
45. Ibid.

Chapter 9. Drafting of the Government of India Act 1935

1. B.R. Ambedkar, 'Mahad Satyagraha', in *Dr. Babasaheb Ambedkar: Writings and Speeches*, ed. Vasant Moon, Ministry of Social Justice and Empowerment 2019, Vol. 17, p. 71.
2. Ibid., p. 72.
3. Ibid.
4. Daniel Payne, '"Educate. Agitate. Organise." Ambedkar and LSE exhibition', LSE Library, 2020, https://www.lse.ac.uk/library/whats-on/exhibitions.
5. B.R. Ambedkar, 'Mahad Satyagraha', in *Dr. Babasaheb Ambedkar: Writings and Speeches*, ed. Vasant Moon, Vol. 17(I), p. 73.

6. B.R. Ambedkar, 'Dr. Ambedkar at the Round Table Conferences', in *Dr. Babasaheb Ambedkar: Writings and Speeches*, ed. Vasant Moon, Ministry of Social Justice and Empowerment 2019, Vol. 2, pp. 503–04.

7. The next para was initially published as a small portion in 'Introduction: The Resurgent Icon', in *A Stake in the Nation: Selected Speeches*, eds Anurag Bhaskar and Bhagwan Das (Navayana, 2020).

8. 'When we compare our present position with the one which it was our lot to bear in Indian society of the pre-British days, we find that, instead of marching on, we are only marking time.'—B.R. Ambedkar, 'Dr. Ambedkar at the Round Table Conferences', in *Dr. Babasaheb Ambedkar: Writings and Speeches*, ed. Vasant Moon, Ministry of Social Justice and Empowerment 2019, Vol. 2, p. 504.

9. Ibid.

10. Ibid.

11. Ibid., p. 505.

12. Ibid., p. 508.

13. Ibid.

14. Ibid., p. 509.

15. Ibid.

16. Ibid., p. 507.

17. Ibid., p. 506.

18. B.R. Ambedkar, 'Mahad Satyagraha', in *Dr. Babasaheb Ambedkar: Writings and Speeches*, ed. Vasant Moon, Vol. 17.I, pp. 77–78.

19. Ibid., p. 78.

20. B.R. Ambedkar, 'Dr. Ambedkar at the Round Table Conferences', in *Dr. Babasaheb Ambedkar: Writings and Speeches*, ed. Vasant Moon, Vol. 2. p. 514.

21. Ibid., p. 515.

22. Ibid.

23. Ibid.
24. Ibid., p. 523.
25. Attendees—British Library's Round Table Conference records, https://www.nottingham.ac.uk/research/groups/conferencing-the-international/delegates/people.aspx?id=676fb6bf-2202-4a46-a493-4e6a69017dde.
26. B.R. Ambedkar, 'Dr. Ambedkar at the Round Table Conferences', in *Dr. Babasaheb Ambedkar: Writings and Speeches*, ed. Vasant Moon, Vol. 2, p. 511.
27. Ibid.
28. Ibid., p. 546.
29. Ibid., pp. 546–48.
30. Ibid., p. 528.
31. Ibid., p. 533.
32. Ibid., p. 540.
33. Ibid., p. 534.
34. Ibid., p. 535.
35. Ibid., p. 537.
36. Ibid., p. 538.
37. Ibid., p. 554.
38. Ibid., p. 561.
39. Ibid., p. 572.
40. Ibid., p. 574.
41. Ibid., p. 527.
42. *Dr. Babasaheb Ambedkar: Writings and Speeches*, ed. Vasant Moon, Ministry of Social Justice and Empowerment 2019, Vol. 17.I, p. 101.
43. Ibid.
44. Ibid., p. 102.
45. Ibid.
46. Ibid.
47. Ibid., p. 51.
48. Ibid., p. 106.

49. Ibid., p. 52.

50. Ibid., p. 54.

51. Ibid., p. 104.

52. Ibid., p. 110.

53. Ibid.

54. Ibid.

55. Ibid., p. 112.

56. Ibid., p. 111.

57. Ibid., p. 115.

58. Ibid., p. 116.

59. Ibid.

60. Ibid., p. 119.

61. Ibid., p. 121.

62. Ibid., p. 122.

63. Ibid., p. 119.

64. Ibid., p. 124

65. Report of the Indian Franchise Committee 1932, H.M. Stationery Office 1932, p. 1, https://www.nottingham. ac.uk/research/groups/conferencing-the-international/ documents/official-documents/travelling-committee- reports/report-of-the-indian-franchise-committee.pdf.

66. Ibid.

67. Scott R. Stroud, 'What B.R. Ambedkar wrote to Jane Addams', *South Asian American Digital Archive* (3 August 2023), available at https://www.saada.org/tides/article/ambedkar- jane-addams.

68. Ibid.

69. B.R. Ambedkar, 'Mahad Satyagraha', in *Dr. Babasaheb Ambedkar: Writings and Speeches*, ed. Vasant Moon, Vol. 17.I, p. 131.

70. Report of the Indian Franchise Committee 1932, H.M. Stationery Office 1932, p. 21, https://www.nottingham. ac.uk/research/groups/conferencing-the-international/

documents/official-documents/travelling-committee-reports/report-of-the-indian-franchise-committee.pdf.

71. Ibid.

72. Ibid., p. 220.

73. *Dr. Babasaheb Ambedkar: Writings and Speeches,* ed. Vasant Moon, Vol. 17.I, p. 132.

74. Ibid., p. 133.

75. Ibid., p. 136.

76. Marc Galanter, *Competing Equalities: Law and the Backward Classes in India* (Oxford University Press, 1984), p. 32.

77. B.R. Ambedkar, 'Statement by B.R. Ambedkar on Gandhi's Fast', in *Dr. Babasaheb Ambedkar: Writings and Speeches*, ed. Vasant Moon, Ministry of Social Justice and Empowerment 2019, Vol. 9, pp. 311–17.

78. Marc Galanter, *Competing Equalities: Law and the Backward Classes in India*, p. 32.

79. See the chapter on Ten-year limit for details.

80. Indian Round Table Conference (THIRD SESSION) 1932, H.M. Stationery Office 1932, https://www.nottingham.ac.uk/research/groups/conferencing-the-international/documents/official-documents/rtc3/indian-round-table-conference-third-session.pdf.

81. B.R. Ambedkar, 'Mahad Satyagraha', in *Dr. Babasaheb Ambedkar: Writings and Speeches*, ed. Vasant Moon, Vol. 17.I, p. 178.

82. Indian Round Table Conference (THIRD SESSION) 1932, H.M. Stationery Office 1932, p. 9.

83. Ibid., p. 10.

84. Ibid., p. 11.

85. Ibid.

86. Round Table Conferences, 1930–32, https://www.open.ac.uk/researchprojects/makingbritain/content/round-table-conferences-1930-1932.

87. Joint Committee on Indian Constitutional Reform (Session 1932–33), Vol. I, HM Stationery Office 1933,

https://www.indianculture.gov.in/reports-proceedings/
joint-committee-indian-constitutional-reform-session-
1932-33-vol-i.

88. Round Table Conferences, 1930–32, https://www.open.
ac.uk/researchprojects/makingbritain/content/round-
table-conferences-1930-1932.

89. Joint Committee on Indian Constitutional Reform
(Session 1932–33), Vol. I, p. 3, HM Stationery Office 1933,
https://www.indianculture.gov.in/reports-proceedings/
joint-committee-indian-constitutional-reform-session-
1932-33-vol-i.

90. B.R. Ambedkar, 'Evidence Taken before the Joint Committee
on Indian Constitutional Reform', in *Dr. Babasaheb Ambedkar:
Writings and Speeches*, ed. Vasant Moon, Ministry of Social
Justice and Empowerment 2019, Vol. 2, p. 673.

91. Ibid., pp. 675, 692.

92. Ibid., pp. 690, 693.

93. Ibid., p. 694. See also, Narendra Jadhav, *Ambedkar: An
Economist Extraordinaire* (Konark Publishers Pvt. Ltd., 2015),
p. 35, where Jadhav notes: 'Ambedkar's contribution
to Monetary Economics is evident from his Doctor of
Science dissertation 'The Problem of the Rupee: Its
Origin and Its Solution' and his subsequent statement
and evidence before the Royal Commission on Indian
Currency and Finance in 1926 (whose report later led
to the establishment of Reserve Bank of India in 1935.'
Furthermore, Nalin Mehta writes: 'Dr Ambedkar also
helped establish the First Finance Commission, which
delineates funding between the Central government
and the states, in 1951.' See Nalin Mehta, *India's Techade:
Digital Revolution and Change in the World's Largest Democracy*
(Westland, 2023), p. 81; see also Sukhadeo Thorat,
Ambedkar's Role in Economic Planning, Water and Power Policy
(Shipra Publication, 2019 Impression).

94. B.R. Ambedkar, 'Evidence Taken before the Joint Committee on Indian Constitutional Reform', in *Dr. Babasaheb Ambedkar: Writings and Speeches,* Vol. 2, p. 683.

95. Ibid., p. 696.

96. Ibid., p. 686.

97. Ibid., p. 689.

98. Ibid., p. 698.

99. Ibid., p. 701.

100. Nivedita Menon, 'Elusive "Woman": Feminism and Women's Reservation Bill,' *Economic and Political Weekly*, Vol. 35, No. 43/44, 2000, pp. 3835–44, JSTOR, http://www.jstor.org/stable/4409891, accessed 5 November 2022. In September 2023, the Parliament has passed a constitutional amendment providing for 33 per cent reservation for women in the Lok Sabha and State Legislative Assemblies.

101. *Dr. Babasaheb Ambedkar: Writings and Speeches*, ed. Vasant Moon, Ministry of Social Justice and Empowerment 2019, Vol. 2, pp. 708–711.

102. 'Cablegram From Sir Rabindranath Tagore Dated 27th July, 1933', from *Dr. Babasaheb Ambedkar: Writings and Speeches*, ed. Vasant Moon, Ministry of Social Justice and Empowerment 2019, Vol. 2, p. 711.

103. Ibid., p. 728.

104. Ibid., pp. 708–729.

105. Ibid., p. 708.

106. Ibid., p. 730.

107. Ibid., p. 745.

108. Ibid., p. 741. The following exchange happened:
Dr Shafa'at Ahmad Khan: Would not the representatives of the primitive people in the Legislature generally combine with the depressed classes?
Dr B.R. Ambedkar: That is what I am visualizing, and, therefore, they would have many friends.

109. Raja Sekhar Vundru, 'Ambedkar's Representational Politics: Expanding the Possibilities', in *The Dalit Truth: The Battles for Realizing Ambedkar's Vision,* ed. K. Raju (Vintage, 2022), p. 36.
110. B.R. Ambedkar, 'Federation versus Freedom', from *Babasaheb Ambedkar: Writings and Speeches,* ed. Vasant Moon, Vol. 1, p. 346.
111. Ibid., p. 351.
112. Raja Sekhar Vundru, *Ambedkar, Gandhi and Patel: The Making of India's Electoral System* (Bloomsbury, 2018), pp. 99–112.

Chapter 10. Annihilation of Caste: From a Constitutional Perspective

1. Aishwary Kumar, *Radical Equality: Ambedkar, Gandhi and the Risk of Democracy* (Navayana, South Asia, 2019, p. 40.
2. B.R. Ambedkar, 'Annihilation of Caste', in *Dr. Babasaheb Ambedkar: Writings and Speeches*, ed. Vasant Moon, Ministry of Social Justice and Empowerment 2019, Vol. 1, p. 42.
3. Ibid.
4. Ibid.
5. Ibid., p. 43.
6. Ibid., p. 44.
7. Ibid., p. 45.
8. Ibid., pp. 46–47.
9. Ibid., p. 47.
10. Ibid.
11. Ibid., p. 50.
12. Ibid., p. 51.
13. Ibid., p. 52.
14. Ibid., p. 56.
15. Ibid., p. 57.
16. Ibid.

17. Anurag Bhaskar, 'Ambedkar's Ideas on Democracy', The Sixth Annual History for Peace Teaching History conference, Kolkata, 4–6 August 2022.
18. B.R. Ambedkar, 'Annihilation of Caste', in *Dr. Babasaheb Ambedkar: Writings and Speeches*, ed. Vasant Moon, Ministry of Social Justice and Empowerment 2019, Vol. I, p. 57.
19. Ibid.
20. Ibid., p. 58.
21. Ibid.
22. Ibid.
23. Ibid., p. 60.
24. Ibid., p. 61.
25. Ibid., pp. 60–61.
26. Ibid., pp. 62–63.
27. Ibid., p. 67.
28. Ibid., p. 68.
29. Ibid.
30. Ibid., p. 70.
31. Ibid., p. 72.
32. Martin Luther King, Jr, 'Letter from Birmingham Jail', 1963, https://www.csuchico.edu/iege/_assets/documents/susi-letter-from-birmingham-jail.pdf.
33. B.R. Ambedkar, 'Annihilation of Caste', in *Dr. Babasaheb Ambedkar: Writings and Speeches*, ed. Vasant Moon, Ministry of Social Justice and Empowerment 2019, Vol. I, pp. 75–76.
34. Ibid., p. 76.
35. Ibid., pp. 76–77.
36. Ibid., p. 77.
37. Ibid., p. 80.

Chapter 11. An Enhanced Version of Separation of Power

1. Gail Omvedt, *Ambedkar: Towards an Enlightened India* (New Delhi: Penguin 2008).
2. B.R. Ambedkar, 'Communal Deadlock and a Way to Solve It', in *Dr. Babasaheb Ambedkar: Writings and Speeches,* ed. Vasant Moon, Ministry of Social Justice and Empowerment 2019, Vol. 1, pp. 361–64.
3. Ibid. See also Sekhar Bandyopadhyay, 'Transfer of Power and the Crisis of Dalit Politics in India, 1945–47', *Modern Asian Studies*, Vol. 34, No. 4, 2000, pp. 893–942, JSTOR, http://www.jstor.org/stable/313135, accessed 7 October 2022.
4. By the 1940s, the official term was Scheduled Castes. The term 'Scheduled Castes' is a legal term. It was adopted in 1935, when the British listed Hindu castes in a Schedule appended to the Government of India Act. It was required for the purposes of statutory safeguards. Dr Ambedkar rejected moralistic and paternalistic terms like 'Harijan', as used by Gandhi, and relied on terms like Backward Classes or scheduled caste. These terms helped to clearly demonstrate the rights and safeguards that were to be guaranteed to oppressed caste groups. Lelah Dushkin, 'Scheduled Caste Policy in India: History, Problems, Prospects', *Asian Survey 7*, No. 9, 1967, pp. 626–36, https://doi.org/10.2307/2642619.
5. B.R. Ambedkar, 'Communal Deadlock and a Way to Solve It', in *Dr. Babasaheb Ambedkar: Writings and Speeches,* ed. Vasant Moon, Ministry of Social Justice and Empowerment 2019, Vol. 1, p. 358.
6. Ibid., p. 360.
7. Ibid., p. 367.
8. Ibid.
9. Ibid.
10. Ibid., p. 368.

11. Ibid., p. 369.
12. Ibid.
13. Ibid.
14. B.R. Ambedkar, 'States and Minorities', in *Dr. Babasaheb Ambedkar: Writings and Speeches,* ed. Vasant Moon, Ministry of Social Justice and Empowerment 2019, Vol. 1, p. 413.
15. Ibid.
16. Ibid., p. 414.
17. Ibid.
18. B.R. Ambedkar, 'Communal Deadlock and a Way to Solve It', in *Dr. Babasaheb Ambedkar: Writings and Speeches,* ed. Vasant Moon.
19. B.R. Ambedkar, 'Communal Deadlock and a Way to Solve It', in *Dr. Babasaheb Ambedkar: Writings and Speeches,* ed. Vasant Moon, Vol. 1.
20. Ibid., p. 368.
21. Ibid., p. 415.
22. Ibid.
23. B.R. Ambedkar, *What Congress and Gandhi Have Done to the Untouchables: A Mean Deal,* in *Dr. Babasaheb Ambedkar: Writings and Speeches,* ed. Vasant Moon, Ministry of Social Justice and Empowerment 2019, Vol. 9, p. 71.
24. B.R. Ambedkar, 'Communal Deadlock and a Way to Solve It', in *Dr. Babasaheb Ambedkar: Writings and Speeches,* ed. Vasant Moon, Vol. 1, p. 369.
25. Ibid.
26. Ibid.
27. Ibid., p. 376; see also Sukhadeo Thorat, 'Ambedkar's Proposal to Safeguard Minorities Against Communal Majority in Democracy', *Journal of Social Inclusion Studies,* 5(2), 2019, pp. 113–128, https://doi.org/10.1177/2394481120913779.

28. B.R. Ambedkar, 'Communal Deadlock and a Way to Solve It', in *Dr. Babasaheb Ambedkar: Writings and Speeches,* ed. Vasant Moon, Vol. 1, pp. 373–74.

29. Ibid.

30. Sukhadeo Thorat, 'Ambedkar's Proposal to Safeguard Minorities Against Communal Majority in Democracy'. *Journal of Social Inclusion Studies,* 5(2), 2019, pp. 119–20, https://doi.org/10.1177/2394481120913779.

31. B.R. Ambedkar, 'Communal Deadlock and a Way to Solve It', in *Dr. Babasaheb Ambedkar: Writings and Speeches,* ed. Vasant Moon, Vol. 1, pp. 373–74.

32. Ibid.

33. Ibid., p. 376.

34. Ibid., p. 374.

35. Ibid., p. 376.

36. Ibid.

37. B.R. Ambedkar, *What Congress and Gandhi Have Done to the Untouchables: A Mean Deal,* in *Dr. Babasaheb Ambedkar: Writings and Speeches,* ed. Vasant Moon, Vol. 9, p. 171.

Chapter 12. Learning from Global Constitutional Evolution

1. Rohit De, 'Lawyering as Politics: The Legal Practice of Dr Ambedkar, Bar at Law', in *The Radical in Ambedkar: Critical Reflections,* eds Suraj Yengde and Anand Teltumbde (Penguin, 2018), p. 148.

2. B.R. Ambedkar, 'Role of Dr. B.R. Ambedkar in Bringing the Untouchables on the Political Horizon of India and Laying a Foundation of Indian Democracy', in *Dr. Babasaheb Ambedkar: Writings and Speeches,* ed. Vasant Moon, Ministry of Social Justice and Empowerment 2019, Vol. 17(III), p. 82.

3. Ibid.

4. B.R. Ambedkar, 'Slaves and Untouchables', in *Dr. Babasaheb Ambedkar: Writings and Speeches,* ed. Vasant Moon, Ministry of Social Justice and Empowerment 2019, Vol. 5, p. 16.

5. B.R. Ambedkar, *What Congress and Gandhi Have Done to the Untouchables: A False Claim*, in *Babasaheb Ambedkar: Writings and Speeches,* ed. Vasant Moon, Vol.9, 2019, pp. 173–76.

6. Ibid., p. 173.

7. Ibid.

8. Ibid., p. 174.

9. *United States v. Reese*, 92 U.S. 214 (1875).

10. *United States v. Cruikshank et al.*, 92 U.S. 542 (1875).

11. B.R. Ambedkar, *What Congress and Gandhi Have Done to the Untouchables: A False Claim*, in *Babasaheb Ambedkar: Writings and Speeches,* ed. Vasant Moon, Vol.9, p. 174.

12. Ibid., p. 176.

13. 'Letter from B.R. Ambedkar to W.E.B. Du Bois, ca. July 1946', University of Massachusetts Amherst, available at https://credo.library.umass.edu/view/full/mums312-b109-i132.

14. 'Letter from W.E.B. Du Bois to B.R. Ambedkar, 31 July 1946, University of Massachusetts Amherst, available at https://credo.library.umass.edu/view/full/mums312-b109-i133.

15. Michael Klarman, *Unfinished Business: Racial Equality in American History* (Oxford University Press, 2007).

16. A version of the content in this section previously appeared as part of a book introduction I wrote. See Anurag Bhaskar, 'The Resurgent Icon' (Introduction), in *A Stake in the Nation: Selected Speeches (B.R. Ambedkar),* ed. Bhagwan Das (Navayana, 2022), pp. 07–22.

17. Constituent Assembly Debates, 4 November 1948.

18. George Grote, *A History of Greece* (London: Routledge, 2000), p. 93.

19. William D. Guthrie, Constitutional Morality, *The North American Review* 196, 681, 1912, p. 154.

20. B.R. Ambedkar, *What Congress and Gandhi Have Done to the Untouchables: A Plea to the Foreigners*, in *Dr. Babasaheb Ambedkar: Writings and Speeches,* ed. Vasant Moon, Ministry of Social Justice and Empowerment 2019, Vol. 9, p. 203.
21. Constituent Assembly of India Debates (Proceedings)— Volume VII, 4 November 1948, http://164.100.47.194/loksabha/writereaddata/cadebatefiles/C04111948.html.
22. B.R. Ambedkar, 'Constituent Assembly Debates', in *Dr. Babasaheb Ambedkar: Writings and Speeches,* ed. Vasant Moon, Ministry of Social Justice and Empowerment 2019, Vol. 13, p. 63.
23. Ibid., pp. 62–63.
24. Constituent Assembly of India Debates (Proceedings)— Volume XI, 25 November 1949, https://loksabhaph.nic.in/writereaddata/cadebatefiles/C25111949.html.
25. *A Stake in the Nation: Selected Speeches,* ed. Bhagwan Das (Navayana, 2020), p. 119.

Chapter 13. Foundations of Indian Constitution

1. Granville Austin, *The Indian Constitution: Cornerstone of a Nation* (Oxford University Press, 1999), p. 28.
2. CLPR Kruthika R. and Vineeth Krishna E., 'The Legitimacy of the Constituent Assembly #4: Was the Constituent Assembly's Membership Representative?', https://www.constitutionofindia.net/blogs/the_legitimacy_of_the_constituent_assembly__4__was_the_constituent_assembly_s_membership_representative.
3. Granville Austin, *The Indian Constitution: Cornerstone of a Nation*, p. 10.
4. Constituent Assembly of India, 9 December 1946, Vol. 1, http://164.100.47.194/loksabha/writereaddata/cadebatefiles/C09121946.html.

5. Constituent Assembly of India, 13 December 1946, Vol. 1, http://164.100.47.194/loksabha/writereaddata/cadebatefiles/C13121946.html.

6. Granville Austin, *The Indian Constitution: Cornerstone of a Nation*, p. 56.

7. Constituent Assembly of India, 16 December 1946, Vol. 1, http://164.100.47.194/loksabha/writereaddata/cadebatefiles/C16121946.html.

8. Constituent Assembly of India Volume I, 17 December 1946, http://164.100.47.194/loksabha/writereaddata/cadebatefiles/C17121946.html.

9. Ashok Gopal, *A Part Apart: The Life and Thought of B.R. Ambedkar* (Navayana Publishing, 2023), p. 673.

10. Ibid.

11. Ibid.

12. Constituent Assembly of India, Volume II, 22 January 1947, http://164.100.47.194/loksabha/writereaddata/cadebatefiles/C17121946.html.

13. B. Shiva Rao 'The Objectives Resolution—Nehru's Speech' in *The Framing of India's Constitution: Select Documents, Volume 2,* Government of India Press, Nashik 1967.

14. This line initially appeared in my newspaper article, see Anurag Bhaskar, 'Republic at 70: Preamble Embodies Constitution's Vision', *Hindustan Times*, 26 January 2020.

15. Aakash Singh Rathore, *Ambedkar's Preamble: A Secret History of the Constitution of India* (Haryana: Vintage, Penguin Random House, 2020).

Chapter 14. Interrelation between Civil–Political and Socio-Economic Rights

1. B.R. Ambedkar, 'States and Minorities', in *Dr. Babasaheb Ambedkar: Writings and Speeches,* ed. Vasant Moon, Ministry of Social Justice and Empowerment 2019, Vol. 1.

2. Ibid., p. 387.
3. Ibid.
4. Ibid., p. 397.
5. 'The right of the people to be secure in their persons, houses, papers and effects against unreasonable searches and seizures, shall not be violated, and no warrants shall issue, but upon probable cause, supported by oath or affirmation, and particularly describing the place to be searched, and the persons or things to be seized.' Ibid., p. 393.
6. Ibid., p. 406.
7. Ibid., p. 395.
8. Ibid., p. 406.
9. Ibid., pp. 406–08.
10. Ibid., p. 407.
11. Ibid., p. 395.
12. Ibid., p. 408.
13. Ibid., p. 396.
14. Ibid.
15. '(9) Agricultural industry shall be organized on the following basis:
(i) The State shall divide the land acquired into farms of standard size and let out the farms for cultivation to residents of the village as tenants (made up of groups of families) to cultivate on the following conditions:
(a) The farm shall be cultivated as a collective farm;
(b) The farm shall be cultivated in accordance with rules and directions issued by Government;
(c) The tenants shall share among themselves in the manner prescribed the produce of the farm left after the payment of charges properly leviable on the farm;
(ii) The land shall be let out to villagers without distinction of caste or creed and in such manner that there will be no landlord, no tenant and no landless labourer;

(iii) It shall be the obligation of the State to finance the cultivation of the collective farms by the supply of water, draft animals, implements, manure, seeds, etc.;

(iv) The State shall be entitled to—

    (a) to levy the following charges on the produce of the farm: (i) a portion for land revenue; (ii) a portion to pay the debenture-holders; and (iii) a portion to pay for the use of capital goods supplied; and

    (b) to prescribe penalties against tenants who break the conditions of tenancy or wilfully neglect to make the best use of the means of cultivation offered by the State or otherwise act prejudicially to the scheme of collective farming;' Ibid., p. 397.

16. Ibid., p. 408

17. Ibid., p. 409.

18. Ibid.

19. Ibid.

20. Ibid.

21. Ibid., p. 410.

22. bid.

23. Ibid., p. 411.

24. Ibid.

25. Ibid., p. 412.

26. Ibid.

27. Ibid., p. 416.

28. Ibid.

29. Ibid., p. 427.

30. Ibid., p. 404.

31. Ibid., p. 428.

32. *Minerva Mills vs Union of India*, 1980 AIR 1789, *Justice K.S. Puttaswamy v. Union of India*, AIR 2017 SC 4161.

33. *Bandhua Mukti Morcha v. Union of India*, 1984 AIR 802.

Chapter 15. Being Chosen as Chairman of the Drafting Committee

1. As mentioned in a previous chapter of this book.
2. Rau got involved in Indian constitutional discourse only after 1935, and that too, regarding the implementation of the Government of India Act 1935. See Arvind Elangovan, 'Rau's Constitutional Solutions to the Political Conundrum', Norms and Politics: Sir Benegal Narsing Rau in the Making of the Indian Constitution, 1935–50 Oxford Academic (2019).
3. B. Shiva Rao, *Framing of India's Constitution,* Vol. 2, p. 115.
4. B.R. Ambedkar, 'Lectures on the English Constitution', in *Dr. Babasaheb Ambedkar: Writings and Speeches,* ed. Vasant Moon, Ministry of Social Justice and Empowerment 2019, Vol. 12, pp. 157–96.
5. B.R. Ambedkar, *What Congress and Gandhi Have Done to the Untouchables: A Plea to the Foreigners*, in *Dr. Babasaheb Ambedkar: Writings and Speeches,* ed. Vasant Moon, Ministry of Social Justice and Empowerment 2019, Vol. 9, p. 214; B.R. Ambedkar, 'Annihilation of Caste', in *Dr. Babasaheb Ambedkar: Writings and Speeches,* ed. Vasant Moon, Ministry of Social Justice and Empowerment 2019, Vol. 1, p. 70.
6. Dr Ambedkar discussed Dicey's principle of sovereignty in the context of India's caste hierarchy. See B.R. Ambedkar, 'Annihilation of Caste', in *Dr. Babasaheb Ambedkar: Writings and Speeches,* ed. Vasant Moon, Ministry of Social Justice and Empowerment 2019, Vol. 1, pp. 70–71; B.R. Ambedkar, *What Congress and Gandhi Have Done to the Untouchables: What Do the Untouchables Say?*, in *Dr. Babasaheb Ambedkar: Writings and Speeches,* ed. Vasant Moon, Ministry of Social Justice and Empowerment 2019, Vol. 9, p. 480.

7. B.R. Ambedkar, 'Lectures on the English Constitution', in *Dr. Babasaheb Ambedkar: Writings and Speeches,* ed. Vasant Moon, Ministry of Social Justice and Empowerment 2019, Vol. 12, pp. 159–60.

8. Ibid., pp. 163–64.

9. B.R. Ambedkar, 'Common Law', in *Dr. Babasaheb Ambedkar: Writings and Speeches,* ed. Vasant Moon, Ministry of Social Justice and Empowerment 2019, Vol. 12, pp. 209–58.

10. B.R. Ambedkar, 'Notes on the Dominion Status', in *Dr. Babasaheb Ambedkar: Writings and Speeches,* ed. Vasant Moon, Ministry of Social Justice and Empowerment 2019, Vol. 12, pp. 259–74.

11. B.R. Ambedkar, 'The Law of Specific Relief', in *Dr. Babasaheb Ambedkar: Writings and Speeches,* ed. Vasant Moon, Ministry of Social Justice and Empowerment 2019, Vol. 12, pp. 275–314.

12. B.R. Ambedkar, 'Common Law', in *Dr. Babasaheb Ambedkar: Writings and Speeches,* ed. Vasant Moon, Vol. 12, p. 215.

13. Dhananjay Keer, *Dr. Ambedkar: Life and Mission*, 3rd ed. (Bombay: Popular Prakashan Private Limited, 1990), p. 249.

14. B.R. Ambedkar, 'Lectures on the English Constitution', in *Dr. Babasaheb Ambedkar: Writings and Speeches,* ed. Vasant Moon, Vol. 12, p. 151.

15. B.R. Ambedkar, 'Federation Versus Freedom', in *Dr. Babasaheb Ambedkar: Writings and Speeches,* ed. Vasant Moon, Ministry of Social Justice and Empowerment 2019, Vol. 1, p. 335.

16. Ibid., p. 337.

17. Ibid., p. 353.

18. Ibid.

19. B.R. Ambedkar, *What Congress and Gandhi Have Done to the Untouchables: What Do the Untouchables Say?*, in *Dr. Babasaheb*

Ambedkar: Writings and Speeches, ed. Vasant Moon, Ministry of
Social Justice and Empowerment 2019, Vol. 9, p. 270.
20. Ibid.
21. B.L.C. Debates, Vol. XXIII, 28 July 1928.
22. B.R. Ambedkar argued:
'I am not prepared to admit that the employer who
employs a woman, under such circumstances, is
altogether free from the liability of such benefit in the
interests of the woman . . . There is no doubt that an
employer employs women in certain industries because
he finds that there is a greater profit to be gained by him
by the employment of women than he would gain by the
employment of men. He is able to get pro rata larger
benefits out of women than he would get by employing
men. That being so, it is absolutely reasonable to say that
to a certain extent at least the employer will be liable
for this kind of benefit when he gets a special benefit by
employing women instead of men.'
The above statement was crucial on several counts. First,
it demolished the argument that the employers have a loss,
as Ambedkar argues that in entirety, the employer benefits
more by employing a woman. Secondly, it recognized the
economic worth of work done by women. Third, it was given
at a time when there was much opposition to the Maternity
Benefit Bill and society was not advanced enough to accept
such proposals easily. Ambedkar thus stated:
'I think the bill is not altogether wrong if it seeks to
impose the liability under the present circumstances on
the employer. I, therefore, support the bill on that account
. . . the benefits contemplated by this bill ought to be
given by this Legislature to the poor women who toil in
our factories in this Presidency.' See 'B.R. Ambedkar, on
Maternity Benefit Bill', in *Dr. Babasaheb Ambedkar: Writings*

and Speeches, ed. Vasant Moon, Ministry of Social Justice and Empowerment 2019, Vol.2, pp. 166–67.

23. B.R. Ambedkar, 'On Measures for Birth-Control', in *Dr. Babasaheb Ambedkar: Writings and Speeches,* ed. Vasant Moon, Ministry of Social Justice and Empowerment 2019, Vol.2, p. 263.

24. Ibid.

25. Ibid.

26. Ibid., p. 264. As he wrote: 'The present keen struggle of life renders timely marriage impossible for many and thus exposes them to various diseases and habits. Many women become invalid for life and some even lose their lives by the birth of children in their diseased condition or in too great numbers or in too rapid succession. Attempts at abortion, resorted to for the prevention of unwanted progeny, exact a heavy toll of female lives.'

27. Ibid., p. 264.

28. Ibid., p. 265.

29. Ibid.

30. 'Agitation against Khoti System', https://amritmahotsav. nic.in/district-reopsitory-detail.htm?18780.

31. Ibid.

32. B.R. Ambedkar, 'Bill No. xx of 1937 to Abolish the Khoti System', in *Dr. Babasaheb Ambedkar: Writings and Speeches,* ed. Vasant Moon, Ministry of Social Justice and Empowerment 2019, Vol.2, p. 100. The system was later abolished by the Maharashtra Khoti Abolition Act 1950.

33. B.R. Ambedkar, 'On the Industrial Disputes Bill', in *Dr. Babasaheb Ambedkar: Writings and Speeches,* ed. Vasant Moon, Ministry of Social Justice and Empowerment 2019, Vol.2, p. 204.

34. Ibid.

35. Ibid., p. 203.

36. Ibid., p. 207: In his words: 'To make it a crime is to compel a man to serve against his will; [and making him a slave (Hear, hear.)] To penalise a strike, therefore, I contend, is nothing short of making the worker a slave. For what is slavery? As defined in the constitution of the United States, slavery is nothing else but involuntary servitude. And this is involuntary servitude. This is contrary to ethics; this is contrary to jurisprudence.'

37. Ibid., p. 208: He argued: 'A strike is simply another name for the right to freedom; it is nothing else than the right to the freedom of one's services on any terms that one wants to obtain. And once you concede the right to freedom, you necessarily concede the right to strike, because, as I have said, the right to strike is simply another name for the right to freedom.'

38. Ibid., p. 210.

39. Ibid., p. 217.

40. Ibid., p. 218.

41. Arjun Ram Meghwal, 'B.R. Ambedkar Laid the Foundation for Workers' Rights, Social Security in India', *Indian Express*, 1 May 2020, available at https://indianexpress.com/article/opinion/columns/br-ambedkar-migrant-workers-international-labour-day-arjun-ram-meghwal-6387858/, accessed 20 August 2023.

42. *A Stake in the Nation: Selected Speeches (B.R. Ambedkar)*, ed. Bhagwan Das (Navayana, p. 37).

43. *A Stake in the Nation: Selected Speeches (B.R. Ambedkar)*, ed. Bhagwan Das, p. 72.

44. B.R. Ambedkar, 'The War Injuries (Compensation Insurance) Bill', in *Dr. Babasaheb Ambedkar: Writings and Speeches,* ed. Vasant Moon, Ministry of Social Justice and Empowerment 2019, Vol. 10, p. 69.

45. B.R. Ambedkar, 'Employment Exchanges for Skilled and Semi-Skilled Personnel', in *Dr. Babasaheb Ambedkar: Writings and Speeches,* ed. Vasant Moon, Ministry of Social Justice and Empowerment 2019, Vol. 10, p. 78.

46. https://labour.delhi.gov.in/content/indian-boiler-act-1923.

47. B.R. Ambedkar, 'The Mines Maternity Benefit (Amendment) Bill', in *Dr. Babasaheb Ambedkar: Writings and Speeches,* ed. Vasant Moon, Ministry of Social Justice and Empowerment 2019, Vol. 10, pp. 87, 264, 274.

48. B.R. Ambedkar, 'The Indian Trade Unions (Amendment) Bill', in *Dr. Babasaheb Ambedkar: Writings and Speeches,* ed. Vasant Moon, Ministry of Social Justice and Empowerment 2019, Vol. 10, p. 113.

49. B.R. Ambedkar, 'First Session of Plenary Labour Conference', in *Dr. Babasaheb Ambedkar: Writings and Speeches,* ed. Vasant Moon, Ministry of Social Justice and Empowerment 2019, Vol. 10, p. 103.

50. B.R. Ambedkar, 'Labour Member visits Coalmines', in *Dr. Babasaheb Ambedkar: Writings and Speeches,* ed. Vasant Moon, Ministry of Social Justice and Empowerment 2019, Vol. 10, p. 131.

51. B.R. Ambedkar, 'Lifting of Ban on Employment of Women on Underground Work in Coalmines', in *Dr. Babasaheb Ambedkar: Writings and Speeches,* ed. Vasant Moon, Ministry of Social Justice and Empowerment 2019, Vol. 10, p. 143.

52. B.R. Ambedkar, 'Post-war Employment of Skilled Workers', in *Dr. Babasaheb Ambedkar: Writings and Speeches,* Ministry of Social Justice and Empowerment 2019, Vol. 10, p. 181.

53. B.R. Ambedkar, 'Plenary Session of Tripartite Labour Conference', in *Dr. Babasaheb Ambedkar: Writings and Speeches,* ed. Vasant Moon, Ministry of Social Justice and Empowerment 2019, Vol. 10, p. 198.

54. B.R. Ambedkar, 'The Factories (Second Amendment) Bill', in *Dr. Babasaheb Ambedkar: Writings and Speeches,* ed. Vasant Moon, Ministry of Social Justice and Empowerment 2019, Vol. 10, p. 201.

55. B.R. Ambedkar, 'State's Obligations to Labour', in *Dr. Babasaheb Ambedkar: Writings and Speeches,* ed. Vasant Moon, Ministry of Social Justice and Empowerment 2019, Vol. 10, p. 293.

56. B.R. Ambedkar, 'Workmen's Compensation (Amendment) Bill', in *Dr. Babasaheb Ambedkar: Writings and Speeches,* ed. Vasant Moon, Ministry of Social Justice and Empowerment 2019, Vol. 10, p. 323.

57. B.R. Ambedkar, 'Factories (Amendment) Bill', in *Dr. Babasaheb Ambedkar: Writings and Speeches,* ed. Vasant Moon, Ministry of Social Justice and Empowerment 2019, Vol. 10, pp. 326, 376.

58. B.R. Ambedkar, 'Welfare and Social Security of Workers', in *Dr. Babasaheb Ambedkar: Writings and Speeches,* ed. Vasant Moon, Ministry of Social Justice and Empowerment 2019, Vol. 10, p. 339.

59. B.R. Ambedkar, 'Paramountcy and the Claim of the Indian States to be Independent', in *Dr. Babasaheb Ambedkar: Writings and Speeches,* ed. Vasant Moon, Ministry of Social Justice and Empowerment 2019, Vol. 12, p. 197.

60. B.R. Ambedkar, 'Plenary Session of Tripartite Labour Conference', in *Dr. Babasaheb Ambedkar: Writings and Speeches*, ed. Vasant Moon, Ministry of Social Justice and Empowerment 2019, Vol. 10, p. 197.

61. Ibid., p. 198.

62. Ibid.

63. The *Times of India*, dated 18 June 1947, also reproduced in *Dr. Babasaheb Ambedkar: Writings and Speeches*, Vol. 17.2, pp. 350–52.

64. I am grateful to Raja Sekhar Vundru for sharing with me the reference to the private papers of Sardar Patel. Vundru found this while he was researching for his book *Gandhi*

and Patel: The Making of India's Electoral System (Bloomsbury Publishing India, 2018).

65. B.R. Ambedkar, 'Paramountcy of the States', in *Dr. Babasaheb Ambedkar: Writings and Speeches,* Ministry of Social Justice and Empowerment 2019, Vol. 12, p. 201.
66. Ibid.
67. Ibid.
68. Ibid., p. 203.
69. Ibid., p. 204.
70. Ibid.
71. Ashok Gopal, *A Part Apart: The Life and Thought of B.R. Ambedkar* (Navayana Publishing, 2023), p. 675.
72. Ibid., p. 677.
73. Bruce Ackerman, *Revolutionary Constitutions: Charismatic Leadership and the Rule of Law* (Cambridge, Massachusetts, Belknap Press of Harvard University Press, 2019), p. 62.

Chapter 16. Constitution Making

1. The names of the members can be seen here: https://loksabha.nic.in/writereaddata/cadebatefiles/C24011947.html, accessed 13 August 2023.
2. Granville Austin, *The Indian Constitution: Cornerstone of a Nation* (Oxford University Press, 1999), pp. 77–78.
3. B. Shiva Rao. 'Sub-Committee on Fundamental Rights—Item 2', in *The Framing of India's Constitution: Select Documents Volume 2,* Government of India Press, Nashik, 1967, p. 115.
4. Ibid.
5. Ibid., pp. 67–114.
6. B. Shiva Rao, 'Advisory Committee Proceedings', in *The Framing of India's Constitution: Select Documents Volume 2,* Government of India Press, Nashik, 1967, p. 247.
7. Ibid., p. 248.

8. Ibid.

9. Ibid., pp. 250–51.

10. Ibid., p. 251.

11. Ibid., pp. 249–50.

12. Ibid., p. 250.

13. Ibid., p. 251.

14. Ibid.

15. Ibid., pp. 25–52.

16. Ibid., p. 252.

17. Ibid., p. 288.

18. Vineeth Krishna E., 'Democratic Citizenship #3: Not All Constitution Framers Were in Favour of Adult Franchise', *CAD India Blog*, 17 April 2019, https://www.constitutionofindia.net/blogs/democratic_citizenship__3__not_all_constitution_framers_were_in_favour_of_adult_franchise.

19. *Rajbala v. State of Haryana*, (2016) 1 SCC 463; see Indira Jaising, 'A Judgement on Democracy That is Frightening in Its Implications', The Wire, 11 December 2015, https://thewire.in/law/the-supreme-courts-judgement-is-frightening-in-its-implications.

20. https://www.livelaw.in/top-stories/supreme-court-right-to-vote-fundamental-right-constitutional-right-article-326-statutory-right-justice-ajay-rastogi-constitution-bench-223032.

21. The content of this subheading initially appeared as a portion of my article—Anurag Bhaskar, 'Reservations, Efficiency, and the Making of Indian Constitution', *Economic and Political Weekly*, 56(19), 2021, pp. 42–49.

22. B. Shiva Rao, *The Framing of India's Constitution: Select Documents Vol. 5*, Government of India Press, Nashik, 1968, pp. 192–93.

23. Ibid., p. 194.

24. Ibid.
25. Ibid.
26. B. Shiva Rao, *The Framing of India's Constitution: Select Documents Vol. 2*, Government of India Press, Nashik, 1967, p. 258.
27. Ibid., p. 259.
28. Ibid.
29. Ibid., p. 260.
30. Ibid., pp. 261–62.
31. B. Shiva Rao, *The Framing of India's Constitution: Select Documents Vol. 5*, Government of India Press, Nashik, 1968, p. 194.
32. 'If honourable Members understand this position that we have to safeguard two things namely, the principle of equality of opportunity and at the same time satisfy the demand of communities which have not had so far representation in the State, then, I am sure they will agree that unless you use some such qualifying phrase as 'backward' the exception made in favour of reservation will ultimately eat up the rule altogether'.— Constituent Assembly of India Debates (Proceedings)— Volume VII, 30 November 1948, http://164.100.47.194/loksabha/writereaddata/cadebatefiles/C30111948.html.
33. Anurag Bhaskar, 'Reservation as a Fundamental Right: Interpretation of Article 16(4), 10', *Indian Journal of Constitutional Law* 1, 2023.
34. B.R. Ambedkar, 'Dr. Ambedkar at the Round Table Conferences', in *Dr. Babasaheb Ambedkar: Writings and Speeches*, ed. Vasant Moon, Ministry of Social Justice and Empowerment 2019, Vol. 2, p. 547.
35. B.R. Ambedkar, 'States and Minorities', in *Dr. Babasaheb Ambedkar: Writings and Speeches*, ed. Vasant Moon, Ministry of Social Justice and Empowerment 2019, Vol. 1, p. 392.
36. Gautam Bhatia, 'Why the Uniquely Revolutionary Potential of Ambedkar's Constitution Remains Untapped',

Scroll.in, 14 April 2016, https://scroll.in/article/806606/
why-the-uniquely-revolutionary-potential-of-ambedkars-
constitution-remains-untapped.

37. B.R. Ambedkar, 'States and Minorities', in *Dr. Babasaheb Ambedkar: Writings and Speeches,* ed. Vasant Moon, Ministry of Social Justice and Empowerment 2019, Vol. 1, p. 409.

38. Constituent Assembly of India Debates (Proceedings), Vol. VII, 29 November 1948, http://164.100.47.194/loksabha/writereaddata/cadebatefiles/C29111948.html.

39. B. Shiva Rao, *The Framing of India's Constitution: Select Documents Vol. 5,* Government of India Press, Nashik, 1968, pp. 755–56.

40. Constituent Assembly of India Debates (Proceedings), Volume V, 28 August 1947, http://164.100.47.194/loksabha/writereaddata/cadebatefiles/C28081947.html.

41. Ibid.

42. M. Kanshiram, *Chamcha Yug* (Samyak Prakashan India, 2018).

43. https://www.thehindu.com/news/national/parliamentary-panel-says-provision-to-ensure-representation-in-higher-judiciary-should-be-mentioned-in-mop/article67169709.ece.

44. https://www.indiatoday.in/magazine/cover-story/story/19990125-scheduled-caste-representation-in-supreme-court-sours-rashtrapati-bhavan-judiciary-relations-delays-appointment-of-judges-779965-1999-01-24.

45. https://www.thehindu.com/news/national/parliamentary-panel-says-provision-to-ensure-representation-in-higher-judiciary-should-be-mentioned-in-mop/article67169709.ece.

46. https://www.thehindu.com/news/national/sc-collegiums-quiet-transparency-is-driving-a-change/article67087258.ece#:~:text=The%20Supreme%20Court%20Collegium%20

under,which%20involves%20%E2%80%9Cmeaningful%20
discussion%20on.

47. B. Shiva Rao, *The Framing of India's Constitution: Select Documents Vol. 5*, Government of India Press, Nashik, 1968, p. 749.

48. Constituent Assembly Debates (Proceedings), Vol. VIII, 24 May 1949, http://164.100.47.194/loksabha/writereaddata/cadebatefiles/C24051949.html.

49. 1998 Supp 2 SCR 400.

50. *Shamsher Singh v. State of Punjab*, AIR 1974 S C 2192.

51. Constituent Assembly Debates, 31 December 1948.

52. Constituent Assembly of India Debates (Proceedings), Vol. VII, 25 November 1949, http://164.100.47.194/loksabha/writereaddata/cadebatefiles/C29111948.html

53. Ibid.

54. Ibid.

55. Savita Ambedkar, *Babasaheb: My Life with Dr Ambedkar*, translated from the Marathi by Nadeem Khan, (Penguin Random House, 2022).

56. Ibid., p. 69.

57. Ibid., p. 101.

58. Ibid.

59. Anurag Bhaskar, 'This Leader Forced Mahatma Gandhi to Change His Views on Caste', ThePrint, 2 October 2018, https://theprint.in/this-leader-forced-mahatma-gandhi-to-change-his-views-on-caste/128108/.

60. Ram Manohar Lohia, 'Gandhism and Socialism', https://lohiatoday.files.wordpress.com/2018/09/gandhism_socialism.pdf

61. Savita Ambedkar, *Babasaheb: My Life with Dr Ambedkar*, p. 70.

62. Ibid., p. 71.

63. Ashok Gopal, *A Part Apart: The Life and Thought of B.R. Ambedkar* (Navayana Publishing, 2023), p. 674.

64. Constituent Assembly of India Debates (Proceedings), Vol. IX, 17 September 1949, https://loksabhaph.nic.in/writereaddata/cadebatefiles/C17091949.html.

65. Constituent Assembly of India Debates (Proceedings), Volume VII, 25 November 1949, http://164.100.47.194/loksabha/writereaddata/cadebatefiles/C29111948.html

Chapter 17. Father of the Indian Constitution

1. Constituent Assembly of India Debates (Proceedings), Volume VII, 5 November 1948, http://164.100.47.194/loksabha/writereaddata/cadebatefiles/C05111948.html.
2. Ibid.
3. Ibid.
4. Ibid.
5. Ibid.
6. Aakash Singh Rathore, *Ambedkar's Preamble: A Secret History of the Constitution of India* (Haryana: Vintage, Penguin Random House, 2020).
7. Constituent Assembly of India Debates (Proceedings), Volume VII, 5 November 1948, http://164.100.47.194/loksabha/writereaddata/cadebatefiles/C05111948.html.
8. Ibid.
9. Constituent Assembly of India Debates (Proceedings), Volume VII, 6 November 1948, http://164.100.47.194/loksabha/writereaddata/cadebatefiles/C06111948.html.
10. Ibid.
11. Ibid.
12. Aakash Singh Rathore, *Ambedkar's Preamble: A Secret History of the Constitution of India.*
13. Speech by Monomohan Das, Constituent Assembly of India Debates (Proceedings), Vol. VII, 29 November 1948,

http://164.100.47.194/loksabha/writereaddata/cadebatefiles/
C29111948.html.

14. Constituent Assembly of India Debates (Proceedings),
Vol. XI, 17 November 1949, https://loksabhaph.nic.in/
writereaddata/cadebatefiles/C17111949.pdf.

15. Constituent Assembly of India Debates (Proceedings),
Vol. XI, 21 November 1949, https://sansad.in/
uploads/const_Assmbly_Debates_Volume11_21_
November1949_176f0ccc35.pdf?updated_at=2022-09-
15T08:46:47.388Z.

16. Ibid.

17. Ibid. 'From the point of view of the Scheduled Classes,
their point was achieved on the day on which Dr Ambedkar
was elected as Chairman of the Drafting Committee. He
had been one of the stoutest champions of the cause of
the Scheduled Classes. He was elected as the Chairman.
Even since he was elected, the other members of the
Scheduled Classes were very reluctant to cooperate; not
because they did not want to co-operate, but because they
knew Dr. Ambedkar who was a champion of their cause
was there to watch and provide such articles that will be
safeguarding the interests of the Scheduled Classes. Well,
Sir, this has proved to what heights Dr. Ambedkar, though
he is a member of the Scheduled Classes, if an opportunity
was given, can rise. He has proved this by his efficiency
and the stable way in which he has drafted and piloted
this Constitution. Now I think this stigma of inefficiency
attached to the Scheduled Classes will be washed away and
will not be attached hereafter. Only if opportunities are
given, they will prove better than anybody else. Now for
having played such a great part, on behalf of the Scheduled
Classes I congratulate Dr. Ambedkar. It is not the strength
of the Scheduled Classes that made him the President of
the Drafting Committee but it is the generosity of the

majority party and I am very much thankful to them for the same.'

18. Ibid.

19. Ibid.

20. Constituent Assembly of India Debates (Proceedings), Vol. VII, 23 November 1948, http://164.100.47.194/loksabha/writereaddata/cadebatefiles/C23111948.html

21. Ibid.

22. Arundhati Roy, *The Doctor and the Saint* (Navayana Publishing, 2019), p. 66; Shashi Tharoor, *Ambedkar: A Life* (Aleph Book Company, 2022), p. 74.

23. Nishikant Kolge, 'Is Ambedkar's Prejudice against "Tribe" a Settled Matter? A Monument to Academic Carelessness', *Economic and Political Weekly*. LVI, pp. 78–85, 2021.

24. Jaipal Singh Munda in Constituent Assembly of India Debates (Proceedings), Vol. IX, 12 September 1949.

25. Constituent Assembly of India Debates (Proceedings), Vol. VII, 24 November 1948, http://164.100.47.194/loksabha/writereaddata/cadebatefiles/C24111948.html.

26. Constituent Assembly of India Debates (Proceedings), Vol. VII, 25 November 1948, http://164.100.47.194/loksabha/writereaddata/cadebatefiles/C25111948.html.

27. Ibid.

28. Ibid. 'The credit that is given to me does not really belong to me. It belongs partly to Sir B. N. Rau, the Constitutional Adviser to the Constituent Assembly who prepared a rough draft of the Constitution for the consideration of the Drafting Committee. A part of the credit must go to the members of the Drafting Committee who, as I have said, have sat for 141 days and without whose ingenuity of devising new formulae and capacity to tolerate and to accommodate different points of view, the task of framing the Constitution could not have come to so successful a conclusion. Much greater, share of the credit

must go to Mr. S. N. Mukherjee, the Chief Draftsman of the Constitution. His ability to put the most intricate proposals in the simplest and clearest legal form can rarely be equalled, nor his capacity for hard work. He has been an acquisition to the Assembly. Without his help, this Assembly would have taken many more years to finalise the Constitution. I must not omit to mention the members of the staff working under Mr. Mukherjee. For, I know how hard they have worked and how long they have toiled sometimes even beyond midnight. I want to thank them all for their effort and their co-operation.'

29. Ibid. 'The task of the Drafting Committee would have been a very difficult one if this Constituent Assembly has been merely a motley crowd, a tessellated pavement without cement, a black stone here and a white stone there in which each member or each group was a law unto itself. There would have been nothing but chaos. This possibility of chaos was reduced to nil by the existence of the Congress Party inside the Assembly which brought into its proceedings a sense of order and discipline. It is because of the discipline of the Congress Party that the Drafting Committee was able to pilot the Constitution in the Assembly with the sure knowledge as to the fate of each article and each amendment. The Congress Party is, therefore, entitled to all the credit for the smooth sailing of the Draft Constitution in the Assembly.'

30. Constituent Assembly of India Debates (Proceedings), Vol. VII, 26 November 1948. http://164.100.47.194/loksabha/writereaddata/cadebatefiles/C26111948.html.

31. Arvind Elangovan, *Norms and Politics: Sir Benegal Narsing Rau in the Making of the Indian Constitution, 1935-1950* (Oxford University Press, 2019), p. 193.

32. Former Chief Justice of India, Justice E.S. Venkataramiah wrote a monograph of B.N. Rau. He noted: '[Rau] was superb in draftsmanship, endowed with a style which was at once clear, illuminating and precise—qualities which are indispensable in any document of legal or constitutional importance. He was not only deeply learned but careful and circumspect in regard even to the minutest details, so that any problem that he handled received full consideration from every aspect, thus eliminating, as far as possible, mistakes through misunderstanding or misinterpretation. The opinions which he gave on any controversial point that arose in the course of the discussions in the Constituent Assembly were full and judicious and based on a deep study of the subject. His services to the Constituent Assembly were highly appreciated even outside India, and the credit for preparing the framework of the Constitution of Burma goes to him in a large measure.' See Justice E.S. Venkataramiah, *B.N. Rau, Constitutional Adviser* (N.M. Tripathi Pvt. Ltd, 1987), p. 23.

33. Constituent Assembly of India Debates (Proceedings), Vol. VII, 25 November 1948, http://164.100.47.194/loksabha/writereaddata/cadebatefiles/C25111948.html.

Chapter 18. Conditions Precedent for the Successful Working of Democracy

1. B.R. Ambedkar, 'Conditions Precedent for the Successful Working of Democracy', in *Dr. Babasaheb Ambedkar: Writings and Speeches,* ed. Vasant Moon, Ministry of Social Justice and Empowerment 2019, Vol. 17.3, p. 472.

2. Ibid., p. 474.

3. Ibid., p. 475.

4. Ibid.

5. Ibid., pp. 475–76.

6. Here, 'class' refers to social groups.
7. Ibid., p. 476.
8. Ibid., pp. 477–78.
9. Ibid., p. 477.
10. Ibid., p. 478.
11. Ibid.
12. Ibid., p. 480.
13. Ibid., p. 482. It must also be noted that in order to protect the rights of minorities, Dr Ambedkar would envisage novel constitutional safeguards. For instance, when the debates on whether a State should be made on a linguistic basis were happening after Indian Independence, he spoke in the Upper House of the Parliament about the state of linguistic and social minorities in those States, and that there should be safeguards for such minorities. See B.R. Ambedkar, 'Section VII', in *Dr. Babasaheb Ambedkar: Writings and Speeches*, ed. Vasant Moon, Ministry of Social Justice and Empowerment 2019, Vol. 15, pp. 831–983.
14. Ibid., p. 483.
15. Ibid.
16. Ibid., p. 484.
17. Ibid., pp. 484–85.
18. Ibid., p. 485.
19. Ibid.

Chapter 19. A Constitutional Vision for Political Democracy

1. B.R. Ambedkar, 'Statement by Dr. B.R. Ambedkar in Explanation of His Resignation', in *Dr. Babasaheb Ambedkar: Writings and Speeches,* ed. Vasant Moon, Ministry of Social Justice and Empowerment 2019, Vol. 14.2, p. 1319.
2. Ibid., pp. 1319–20. He noted: 'The year 1946 during which I was out of office, was a year of great anxiety to me and to

the leading members of the Scheduled Castes. The British had resiled from the commitments they had made in the matter of constitutional safeguards for the Scheduled Castes and the Scheduled Castes had no knowing as to what the Constituent Assembly would do in that behalf. In this period of anxiety I had prepared a report on the condition of the Scheduled Castes for submission to the United Nations. But I did not submit it. I felt that it would be better to wait until the Constituent Assembly and the future Parliament was given a chance to deal with the matter. The provisions made in the Constitution for safeguarding the position of the Scheduled Castes were not to my satisfaction. However, I accepted them for what they were worth, hoping that the Government will show some determination to make them effective. What is the position of the Scheduled Castes today? So far as I see, it is the same as before. The same old tyranny, the same old oppression, the same old discrimination which existed before, exists now, and perhaps in a worst form.'

3. Poonam Singh, 'The Advent of Ambedkar in the Sphere of Indian Women Question', J-CASTE, Vol. 1, No. 2, October 2020, pp. 17–30.

4. B.R. Ambedkar, 'Scheduled Castes' Emancipation— Draft Manifesto', in *Dr. Babasaheb Ambedkar: Writings and Speeches,* ed. Vasant Moon, Ministry of Social Justice and Empowerment 2019, Vol. 17.1, p. 401.

5. Ibid.

6. Ibid., p. 402.

7. Prabuddha Bharat, 27 October 1956, as cited in Ashok Gopal, *A Part Apart*, p. 702.

8. Ashok Gopal, *A Part Apart*, pp. 702–03. See also D.R. Nagaraj, *The Flaming Feet and Other Essays: The Dalit Movement in India* (Seagull Books London Ltd, 5 April 2011). The next three paragraphs were earlier published as part of an op-ed

in ThePrint. See Anurag Bhaskar, 'If Ambedkar & Lohia
Met: How History Missed a Crucial Moment in Social
Justice Politics', ThePrint, 20 April 2018, https://theprint.
in/opinion/dalit-history-month/if-ambedkar-lohia-had-
met-how-history-missed-a-crucial-moment-in-social-
justice-politics/51047/.

9. *Dr. Babasaheb Ambedkar: Writings and Speeches,* ed. Vasant
Moon, Ministry of Social Justice and Empowerment 2019,
Vol. 17.2, p. 159.

10. Ibid.

11. Ibid., p. 161.

12. Ibid., p. 162.

13. Sukhadeo Thorat, 'The Dalit Idea of the National, Inspired
by Ambedkar', in *The Dalit Truth: The Battles for Realizing
Ambedkar's Vision,* ed. K. Raju (Vintage, 2022), p. 17.

14. Komal Rajak, 'Trajectories of Women's Property Rights
in India: A Reading of the Hindu Code Bill', *Contemporary
Voice of Dalit,* Volume 12, Issue 1, May 2020, pp. 82–88.
Rajak notes: 'In May 1955, the Hindu Marriage Act was
passed, followed by the Hindu Succession Act in May 1956,
the Hindu Adoption and Maintenance Act in December
1956 and the Dowry Prohibition Act in July 1961.'

Chapter 20. Did Dr Ambedkar Want to Burn the Constitution?

1. B.R. Ambedkar, 'Parliamentary Debates', in *Dr. Babasaheb
Ambedkar: Writings and Speeches,* ed. Vasant Moon, Ministry of
Social Justice and Empowerment 2019, Vol. 15, p. 862.

2. Dhananjay Keer, *Dr. Ambedkar: Life and Mission*, 3rd ed.
(Bombay: Popular Prakashan Private Limited, 1990),
pp. 449–50.

3. Gail Omvedt, *Dalits and the Democratic Revolution: Dr. Ambedkar and the Dalit Movement in Colonial India* (New Delhi: Sage Publishing, 1994), p. 325.

4. Arvind Elangovan, 'The Making of the Indian Constitution: A Case for a Non-nationalist Approach', *History Compass*, 12(1), 2014, p. 2.

5. Ibid.

6. Suraj Yengde, *Caste Matters* (Gurgaon: Penguin, 2019), p. 80.

7. Ibid., p. 85.

8. Ibid., p. 76.

9. Ibid.

10. Ibid., p. 79.

11. Ibid.

12. Ibid., p. 78.

13. B.R. Ambedkar, 'Parliamentary Debates', in *Dr. Babasaheb Ambedkar: Writings and Speeches*, ed. Vasant Moon, pp. 851–64.

14. In his address (2 September 1953) in the Rajya Sabha, Dr Ambedkar noted: 'And unless and until one honourable gentleman had sacrificed his life for the sake of creating an Andhra Province, the Government did not think it fit to move in the matter. I have no idea and I do not wish to be harsh on the Government; but I am dead certain in my mind that if in any other country a person had to die in order to invoke a principle which had already been accepted, what would have happened to the Government. It is quite possible that the Government might have been lynched. But here nothing has happened'. See Ambedkar, 2019f, pp. 852–53.

15. Ibid., p. 857.

16. B.R. Ambedkar, 'Communal Deadlock and a Way to Solve It', in *Dr. Babasaheb Ambedkar: Writings and Speeches,* ed. Vasant

Moon, Ministry of Social Justice and Empowerment 2019, Vol. 1.

17. B.R. Ambedkar, 'States and Minorities', in *Dr. Babasaheb Ambedkar: Writings and Speeches,* ed. Vasant Moon, Ministry of Social Justice and Empowerment 2019, Vol. 1.

18. B.R. Ambedkar, 'Parliamentary Debates', in *Dr. Babasaheb Ambedkar: Writings and Speeches,* ed. Vasant Moon, pp. 857–61.

19. Ibid., p. 860.

20. Ibid.

21. Ibid., p. 861.

22. Ibid.

23. Ibid., pp. 862–63.

24. Ibid., p. 864.

25. Ibid., pp. 944–61.

26. Ibid., p. 948.

27. Ibid., p. 949.

28. Ibid.

29. Ibid.

30. Ibid., p. 954.

31. Gail Omvedt, *Dalits and the Democratic Revolution: Dr. Ambedkar and the Dalit Movement in Colonial India,* p. 325.

32. B.R. Ambedkar, 'Parliamentary Debates', in *Dr. Babasaheb Ambedkar: Writings and Speeches,* ed. Vasant Moon, p. 947.

33. B.R. Ambedkar, 'Statement by Dr. B.R. Ambedkar in Explanation of His Resignation', in *Dr. Babasaheb Ambedkar: Writings and Speeches,* ed. Vasant Moon, Ministry of Social Justice and Empowerment 2019, Vol. 14.2, p. 1325.

34. Ibid., p. 1326.

35. Constituent Assembly of India Debates (Proceedings), Vol. VII, 4 November 1948, http://164.100.47.194/loksabha/writereaddata/cadebatefiles/C04111948.html.

36. Anurag Bhaskar, 'Ambedkar's Constitution: A Radical Phenomenon in Anti-Caste Discourse?', *CASTE: A Global Journal on Social Exclusion,* 2(1), 2021.

Chapter 21. The Myth of Ten-Year Limit on Reservations and Dr Ambedkar's Stance

1. '"Ambedkar Wanted Reservations Only for a Decade", Says Lok Sabha Speaker', Scroll, 1 October 2018, https://scroll.in/latest/896502/ambedkar-wanted-reservations-only-for-a-decade-says-lok-sabha-speaker, accessed on 6 October 2022.

2. In this chapter, the terms 'Depressed Classes', 'Untouchables' and 'Scheduled Castes' (SCs) have been used interchangeably, as all these terms appear in Dr B.R. Ambedkar's writings in different phases of history. Similarly, Scheduled Tribes (STs) and Adivasis have been used interchangeably as well.

3. Christophe Jaffrelot, 'Dr Ambedkar and Untouchability: Analysing and Fighting Caste' (Permanent Black, 2005), p. 60.

4. Raja Sekhar Vundru, *Ambedkar, Gandhi and Patel: The Making of India's Electoral System* (Bloomsbury, 2017), p. 53.

5. Ibid.

6. Ibid.

7. Ibid., p. 54.

8. Ibid., p. 55.

9. Ibid.

10. Ibid.

11. Ibid., pp. 55–56.

12. Ibid., p. 57.

13. Ibid., p. 58.

14. Granville Austin, *The Indian Constitution: Cornerstone of a Nation* (Oxford India, 1999), pp. 77–78.

15. Ibid.

16. B. Shiva Rao, 'The Framing of Indian Constitution: A Study', Indian Institute of Public Administration, Vol. V, p. 748.

17. Ibid.

18. Ibid., pp. 749–50.

19. Ibid., p. 750.

20. B. Shiva Rao, 'The Framing of Indian Constitution: A Study', p. 755; Raja Sekhar Vundru, *Ambedkar, Gandhi and Patel: The Making of India's Electoral System*, p. 125; Granville Austin, *The Indian Constitution: Cornerstone of a Nation*, p. 187.

21. B. Shiva Rao, 'The Framing of Indian Constitution: A Study', p. 755; Granville Austin, *The Indian Constitution: Cornerstone of a Nation*, p. 187.

22. B. Shiva Rao, 'The Framing of Indian Constitution: A Study', p. 755.

23. Ibid., p. 758.

24. Ibid., p. 759.

25. Ibid., p. 760.

26. Ibid.

27. Ibid., p. 764.

28. Ibid., p. 766.

29. Ibid.

30. Ibid., pp. 766–68.

31. Ibid.

32. B. Shiva Rao. 'The Framing of Indian Constitution: A Study', pp. 599–601; Granville Austin, *The Indian Constitution: Cornerstone of a Nation*, p. 190; Raja Sekhar Vundru, *Ambedkar, Gandhi and Patel: The Making of India's Electoral System*, p. 136.

33. Ibid.

34. Ibid.

35. B. Shiva Rao, 'The Framing of Indian Constitution: A Study', pp. 599–601.

36. Raja Sekhar Vundru, *Ambedkar, Gandhi and Patel: The Making of India's Electoral System*, p. 138.

37. Ibid.

38. B. Shiva Rao, 'The Framing of Indian Constitution: A Study', p. 601.

39. Ibid.

40. Constituent Assembly Debates, Vol. VIII, 25 May 1949, http://164.100.47.194/Loksabha/Debates/cadebatefiles/ C25051949.html.

41. Ibid.

42. Ibid.

43. Ibid.

44. Ibid.

45. Constituent Assembly Debates, Vol. VIII, 26 May 1949, http://164.100.47.194/Loksabha/Debates/cadebatefiles/ C26051949.html, accessed on 6 October 2022.

46. B. Shiva Rao, 'The Framing of Indian Constitution: A Study', p. 601.

47. B. Shiva Rao, 'The Framing of Indian Constitution: A Study', p. 774.

48. Constituent Assembly Debates, Vol. IX, 23 August 1949, http://164.100.47.194/Loksabha/Debates/cadebatefiles/ C23081949.html, accessed on 6 October 2022.

49. B. Shiva Rao, 'The Framing of Indian Constitution: A Study', p. 774.

50. Constituent Assembly Debates, Vol. IX, 24 August 1949, http://164.100.47.194/Loksabha/Debates/cadebatefiles/ C24081949.html, accessed on 6 October 2022.

51. Ibid.

52. Ibid.

53. Article 334 of the Constitution, as amended with effect from 25 January 2020, states as follows: 'Notwithstanding anything in the foregoing provisions of this Part, the provisions of this Constitution relating to—(a) the reservation of seats for the Scheduled Castes and the Scheduled Tribes in the House of the People and in the Legislative Assemblies of the States; and (b) the representation of the Anglo-Indian community in the House of the People and in the Legislative Assemblies

of the States by nomination, shall cease to have effect on the expiration of a period of [eighty years in respect of clause (a) and seventy years in respect of clause (b)] from the commencement of this Constitution: Provided that nothing in this article shall affect any representation in the House of the People or in the Legislative Assembly of a State until the dissolution of the then existing House or Assembly, as the case may be.'

54. Ibid.
55. Ibid.
56. Constituent Assembly Debates, Vol. IX, 25 August 1949, http://164.100.47.194/Loksabha/Debates/cadebatefiles/C25081949.html, accessed on 6th October 2022; B. Shiva Rao, 'The Framing of Indian Constitution: A Study', p. 776.
57. Ibid.
58. Ibid.
59. Ibid.
60. Ibid.
61. Ibid.
62. Ibid.
63. Ibid.
64. https://velivada.com/2017/05/17/dr-ambedkars-election-speech-ludhiana-punjab-read/.
65. B.R. Ambedkar, 'Parliamentary Debates', in *Dr. Babasaheb Ambedkar: Writings and Speeches,* ed. Vasant Moon, Ministry of Social Justice and Empowerment 2019, Vol. 15, p. 857.
66. Anurag Bhaskar, 'Reservations, Efficiency, and the Making of Indian Constitution', Vol. 56, No. 19, *Economic and Political Weekly,* 2021, pp. 42–49.
67. Parliamentary Debates, Parliament of India, 1951, pp. 9006–07, https://eparlib.nic.in/bitstream/123456789/760696/1/ppd_18-05-1951.pdf, accessed on 6 October 2022.

68. AIR 1951 SC 226.
69. Ibid.
70. Constituent Assembly Debates, Vol. IX, 25 August 1949, http://164.100.47.194/Loksabha/Debates/cadebatefiles/C25081949.html, accessed on 6 October 2022.
71. Raja Sekhar Vundru, *Ambedkar, Gandhi and Patel: The Making of India's Electoral System*, p. 57.
72. Constituent Assembly Debates, Vol. IX, 25 August 1949, http://164.100.47.194/Loksabha/Debates/cadebatefiles/C25081949.html, accessed on 6 October 2022.

Epilogue

1. Constituent Assembly of India Debates (Proceedings), Volume XII, 25 November 1949, https://eparlib.nic.in/bitstream/123456789/763285/1/cad_25-11-1949.pdf.
2. Ibid.
3. 'Preface to the 1963 Edition', in *A Stake in the Nation: Selected Speeches, B.R. Ambedkar,* ed. Bhagwan Das (Navayana, 2020 Reprint), p. 31.
4. B.R. Ambedkar, 'Ranade, Gandhi and Jinnah', in *Dr. Babasaheb Ambedkar: Writings and Speeches*, ed. Vasant Moon, Ministry of Social Justice and Empowerment 2019, Vol. 1, p. 221.
5. B.R. Ambedkar, 'Role of Dr. B.R. Ambedkar in Bringing the Untouchables on the Political Horizon of India and Laying a Foundation of Indian Democracy', in *Dr. Babasaheb Ambedkar: Writings and Speeches*, ed. Vasant Moon, Ministry of Social Justice and Empowerment 2019, Vol. 17.1, p. 162.
6. Arun Shourie, *Worshipping False Gods: Ambedkar and the Facts That Have Been Erased*' (ASA Publications, 1997).

7. Ibid.

8. For instance, a Brahmin politician said: 'I have no hesitation in saying Ambedkar is a Brahmin. Not wrong to call a learned person a Brahmin.' See 'Constitution Draft Prepared by a Brahmin, Says Gujarat Speaker at Global Brahmin Summit', *India Today*, 4 January 2020, https://www.indiatoday.in/india/story/constitution-draft-prepared-by-a-brahmin-gujarat-speaker-at-brahmin-summit-1633945-2020-01-04.

9. Constitutional historian Granville Austin has responded to such claims: 'At independence, India inherited a well-established system of constitutional law . . . the inclusion of such detail from the 1935 Act and from other constitutions would mean that the existing case law concerning the interpretation of these provisions would be available to aid in interpreting the Constitution. Time has supported all these assumptions.' See Granville Austin, *Indian Constitution: Cornerstone of a Nation* (Oxford University Press, 1966).

10. Sociologist Vivek Kumar notes: ' . . . some self-styled intellectuals could not accept even this little respect and wrote full-length books challenging his integrity and refuting his contribution to the Constitution (Arun Shourie's *Worshipping False Gods* (1997)'. See Vivek Kumar, 'Resurgence of an Icon', *Hindu BusinessLine*, 20 January 2018, available at https://www.thehindubusinessline.com/blink/cover/resurgence-of-an-icon/article64572918.ece.

11. Billy Perrigo, 'As India's Constitution Turns 70, Opposing Sides Fight to Claim Its Author as One of Their Own', *Time*, 24 January 2020, retrieved from https://time.com/5770511/india-protests-br-ambedkar/.

12. Badri Narayan, *The Making of the Dalit Public in North India: Uttar Pradesh, 1950–Present* (New Delhi: Oxford University Press, 2011), p. 78. See also Omar Rashid, 'Prayagraj

Social Institute Draws Ire after It Leaves OBC Teacher Seats Vacant', *The Hindu,* 9 December 2021, https://www.thehindu.com/news/national/other-states/prayagraj-social-institute-draws-ire-after-it-leaves-obc-teacher-seats-vacant/article37907560.ece.

13. Constituent Assembly of India Debates (Proceedings), Volume VII, 4 November 1948, https://eparlib.nic.in/bitstream/123456789/762996/1/cad_04-11-1948.pdf.

14. Melia Belli, 'Monumental Pride: Mayawati's Memorials in Lucknow', *Ars Orientalis,* Vol. 44, 2014, p. 90.

15. 'President Murmu Unveils BR Ambedkar's Statue In Supreme Court on Constitution Day', NDTV, 26 January 2023, https://www.ndtv.com/india-news/president-droupadi-murmu-unveils-br-ambedkars-statue-in-supreme-court-on-constitution-day-4606954.

16. Justice B.R. Gavai, 'Centenary of Dr Ambedkar's Enrollment as Advocate: Reflection on His Ideas of Constitutionalism', https://www.youtube.com/watch?v=qG-8NxUusfA&t=1282s.

17. B.R. Ambedkar, 'Ranade, Gandhi and Jinnah', in *Dr. Babasaheb Ambedkar: Writings and Speeches*, ed. Vasant Moon, Ministry of Social Justice and Empowerment 2019, Vol. 1, p. 222.

18. Constituent Assembly of India Debates (Proceedings), Volume XI, 25 November 1949, https://eparlib.nic.in/bitstream/123456789/763285/1/cad_25-11-1949.pdf.

19. Ibid.

20. Aishwary Kumar, *Radical Equality: Ambedkar, Gandhi and the Risk of Democracy* (Navayana, South Asia, 2019), p. 343.

21. B.R. Ambedkar, 'Revolution and Counter-Revolution in Ancient India', in *Dr. Babasaheb Ambedkar: Writings and Speeches*, ed. Vasant Moon, Ministry of Social Justice and Empowerment 2019, Vol. 3, p. 149.

22. Ibid.
23. Constituent Assembly of India Debates (Proceedings), Volume VII, 4 November 1948, https://eparlib.nic.in/bitstream/123456789/762996/1/cad_04-11-1948.pdf.

Acknowledgements

1. CEDE (Community for the Eradication of Discrimination in Education and Employment) is a network of lawyers, law firms, judges, other organizations and individuals, who are committed towards reforming the Indian legal profession. See https://www.cede.co.in/home.

Index

364	Index

India, 155
competitive examinations,
system of, 102–103
as a means of entry into
the Public Services, 103
confidence in executive,
principle of, 151–152
Congress party, *see*
Indian National
Congress (INC)
Congress Working
Committee, 204
consent for consummation,
age of, 27
Constituent Assembly of
India, 5, 36–37, 111,
113, 167, 173, 175, 210,
214, 226, 227
adoption of
Ambedkar's motion on
reservation of seats for
SCs and STs, 262
Preamble, 175
contemporary
lesson, 190–191
debates over, 256–
262, 310n43
special rights for
minorities, 256
deliberations in political
reservations, 259–260
for framing of the future
Constitution, 176

Fundamental Rights
Sub-Committee
of, 176, 190
issue of equal voting
rights, 50
time limit of ten
years on political
reservations, 266
constitutional advancement,
issue of, 32
constitutional
democracy, 162, 164
Constitutional discourse
during 1915–1950, 32–37
in the nineteenth
century, 22–32
constitutional interpretation,
doctrine of, 190
constitutionalism
idea of, 136–137
social aspects of, 131–133
constitutional law,
principle of, 191
constitutional morality, 163
adoption and
practice of, 162
concept of, 162, 237–238
defined, 163
and history of
Greece, 162–166
maintenance of, 164
by society, 165
constitutional progress,
notion of, 35

Scan QR code to access the
Penguin Random House India website